AN ANALYSIS OF
HEALTH CARE DELIVERY

"If we believe men have any personal rights at all as human beings, they have an absolute right to such a measure of good health as society, and society alone, is able to give them."

ARISTOTLE

AN ANALYSIS OF
HEALTH CARE DELIVERY

James M. Rosser, Vice Chancellor
Department of Higher Education
Trenton, New Jersey

Howard E. Mossberg, Dean
School of Pharmacy
University of Kansas
Lawrence, Kansas

A Wiley-Interscience Publication

JOHN WILEY & SONS, New York • London • Sydney • Toronto

Library of Congress Cataloging in Publication Data:

Rosser, James M
   An analysis of health care delivery.

   "A Wiley-Interscience publication."
Includes bibliographical references and index.
   1. Medical economics—United States. 2. Medical
care—United States. I. Mossberg, Howard E., joint
author. II. Title. [DNLM: 1. Delivery of health
care—United States. W84 AA1 R8a]
RA410.53.R67   362.1'0973   76-30572
ISBN 0-471-73760-7

Printed in the United States of America

10 9 8 7 6 5 4 3 2 1

To
Edward E. Smissman

Late University Distinguished Professor and Friend
The University of Kansas

PREFACE

The concept of good health as a basic human right is still being debated in the United States in academic, political, professional, and economic circles. Unfortunately, while this debate persists, millions of Americans are being denied the full range of benefits of the health and medical sciences. Many of these individuals are not being served because of their socioeconomic and cultural status, be they residents of the large urban centers of this great nation or of isolated rural areas. The needs of these and many other Americans can no longer be ignored. What is at issue today is how to effectively and efficiently respond to the health needs of *all* Americans.

How does one improve the quality of health care? If health truly is a relative state, how then do we measure health or illness and subsequently prescribe proper care or establish appropriate preventive measures? What new and expanded roles are appropriate in the provision of quality health and medical care for the pharmacist, the physician extender, and other health professionals? What changes are needed in health professions education programs? What evolution in the organization and patterns of delivery of services is necessary? What role should the consumer play? What should be the role of public and private agencies in the struggle for change and improvement? Surely no one would dispute the importance of these questions and the need for more debate, research, and experimentation. Their timeliness and urgency spurred our interest in writing this book.

Obviously this book is not intended to offer solutions to all problems confronting the health care industry; rather, it is designed to provide general and specific information, to delineate some of the problems, and to promote discussion which may, we hope, render the resolution of some of the problems somewhat less elusive. Improving the health of Americans is a goal that far exceeds the traditional provision of health services by health workers. Threats to man's health and survival have their determinants in cultural, economic, and social factors that fall outside the traditional and basic intellectual interests of the medical sciences. Therefore, we have attempted to take a fresh look at the health care delivery system and the health industry in the United States, with an orientation toward illuminating the need to expand the useful knowledge base, to change priorities, to correct deficiencies, and to redirect energies. Thus this book, while introductory in nature, should be of assistance to individuals who have general or professional interests in the organization, administration, and delivery of health and medical care.

In preparing this book we have received assistance, advice, and support from numerous individuals: Mrs. Phillipa Chapman, who provided helpful and important research; Dr. Matthew J. Quinn, who assisted with the preparation of the index; Mr. Joseph L. Ravelli, who assisted with the proofreading; Helen Hui-Ying Chen, who prepared many of the illustrations; and Mary Ann Byrne, Mary Anne Pyle, Diane McNicoll, and Janice Demarest, who provided invaluable aid in typing the numerous drafts of the manuscript. Special appreciation is also extended to Chancellor Ralph A. Dungan of the New Jersey Department of Higher Education, without whose support this book could not have been completed.

JAMES M. ROSSER
HOWARD E. MOSSBERG

Trenton, New Jersey
Lawrence, Kansas
January 1977

CONTENTS

CHAPTER ONE

INTRODUCTION

If a health care system can be defined as a group of curative and preventive service components—organized, coordinated, and controlled to achieve certain goals —then it is apparent that there is a national crisis in health care and health care delivery in the United States. The problem is insidious and permeates every level of health care activity, prevention, cure, and rehabilitation. The health care predicament is insidious because it is "individual" in nature, affecting each person and individual groups of people differently. Hence an informed citizenry, as well as an informed cadre of health care professionals, is necessary to combat health conservation problems intelligently and efficiently.

In an era of increasing and justified disenchantment with the current health care delivery system, it is astonishing to observe that so many well-meaning and intelligent reformers propose as a solution the bureaucratization of health promotion and maintenance activities. Moreover the majority of contemporary activities tend to be secondary and tertiary in nature; that is, we are still placing major, and perhaps disproportionate, emphasis on curative services.

The statement "Health is the crown on a well man's head, but the only one who sees it is a sick man" is illustrative of the emphasis on curative services, and perhaps more importantly of the conflict between government and the private sector. The U.S. Government currently places primary emphasis on enhancing the delivery of health care to the *populace,* while the private sector, with its fee-for-service operating system, has always argued that it is concerned with providing quality health care services to the individual. Many hoped that general federal involvement would result in fundamental health reform. However, federal involvement and resources have led to fragmentation of mission and orientation which has resulted in the loss of coordinated management responsibility. Gaps in cooperation and coordination among health and welfare agencies, public and private, have long been considered a major problem by those concerned with the improvement of the human condition. The complexity of the relationship between the public and private sectors becomes more understandable when we add to this, for example, comprehensive health planning activities and the elaborate systems for control over the providers of health services. The battle is being waged by vested interests within the context of the free enterprise concept of economics without adequate, if any, regard for the truism that the services debated and the care needed are critical to the livelihood of our populace and, perhaps, to the survival of the American social order.

Current attention is really being directed toward individuals, their health (or lack of it), and the cost, availability, and accessibility of curative, promotional, and maintenance activities. In other words, consumer rights is the real issue in the current health care reform movement in this country. We can no longer tolerate a health system, dominated by provider interests, that is insensitive to consumer needs. Unfortunately, the consumer in the health marketplace, past and present, is totally dependent and powerless. "While it is the patient who presents himself to the physician, it is the physician who terminates the interview, suggests a further consultation, writes the prescription, orders the diagnostic tests, arranges the hospital admission, recommends the surgery, and authorizes the hospital discharge."[1] The health care delivery system in the United States is, in a sense, a *providers* system, lacking the appropriate highlights on the consumer.

Medical history is replete with examples of provider-oriented efforts to improve health care delivery capability through research and scientific developments, although, as cogently stated by Carlson: "It is axiomatic that introducing change in one part of a system is unwarranted and premature if the ramifications of that change on other parts of the system have not been anticipated and analyzed."[2]

At the risk of focusing too heavily on the hub of any health care delivery system, it is significant to note that there are no public review boards or public participation in the policing of the medical profession. Moreover because of increased specialization and the presence of a highly mobile population, the provision of health services has become more impersonal. This depersonalization of the provision of health services is, perhaps, a major factor in the increase in malpractice suits. Such suits are illustrative of a crisis-oriented consumer approach to obtaining quality health care and some recompense, which, unfortunately for the health of the affected, occurs after the fact. Of course, the preceding remarks have to be tempered by stating that the current unfavorable doctor-patient ratio, in conjunction with the general inability of the average consumer to judge the quality of care or services received, can result in a decrease in quality of service and higher exposure to legal risk. Ironically, perhaps, many health care practitioners now are practicing "defensive" medicine, a circumstance that is unfortunate in a human services profession. Inevitably such a posture is injurious to the consumer in that it drives costs upward, delays treatment, and thus lowers the overall quality of care.

[1]Brian Abel-Smith, "Value for Money in Health Services," *Social Security Bulletin,* **37** (July 1974), p. 17. A perceptive analysis of why the market for health services is not an ordinary market.
[2]Rick J. Carlson, "Health Manpower Licensing and Emerging Institutional Responsibility for the Quality of Care," *Law and Contemporary Problems,* **35** (Autumn 1970), p. 854.

A concept of public accountability that assures maximum responsiveness of the health system to public needs, backed by an adequate data system for monitoring and evaluating performance, obviously is still to be established. An adequate system could forestall malpractice and malpractice suits. Some reformers have suggested (1) the establishment of a national licensing and medical practice law, (2) required continuing education program participation, and (3) local systems of quality control. Effective comprehensive health manpower licensing reforms have yet to occur, although the existence of problems definitely has been acknowledged. State medical societies, in general, have been slow to establish continuing education requirements for maintenance of membership, New Mexico being the only state where continuing education evidence is required for renewal of license for physicians. The third point is covered in the discussion of professional standards review organizations in Part Three.

THE HEALTH DILEMMA AND ECONOMICS: A PRELUDE

As the twentieth century began, the expenditures of local government were by far the dominant agents of aid and support for all civil functions within the United States. Local government at the turn of the century spent more on these services than both the state and federal governments combined.

The decade of the 1930s and the Depression wrought more drastic changes in the financial structure of this country than had been experienced since its founding. The federal government stepped in to provide relief to local governments faced with dwindling property tax receipts and state governments unable to meet their needs from their own resources. By 1940 the local share of total spending had declined.

During World War II, with the ever-climbing rates of military spending, state and local finances were forced into the background. Between 1940 and 1944, federal government expenditures grew from $10 billion to $100 billion, while state and local spending declined slightly from $11.2 billion to $10.5 billion.

State and local governments anticipated that once the war ended tax resources would be available to fund state and local services. But the beginning of the cold war and the concurrent inflation that occurred soon made it apparent that this was not to be the case. State and local government expenditures were increasing, and the need to provide sources of revenue to meet these demands became a continuing and pressing problem of the postwar era.

It was assumed that once the war was over, federal income tax rates would return to their lower prewar levels. But the federal rate remained high in the postwar period, and state governments began to rely on a method of revenue raising that had been rejected by the federal government for its own purposes —the general sales tax.

At the same time, the primary source of local government funds, the property tax, had recovered from its depression slump. Faced with new problems of obtaining money for essential services, local governments responded by pushing property tax rates even higher.

This is where many states in the country find themselves today—with a greater and greater need for revenues, an overtaxed local tax system, and inadeqaate revenue sources at the state level.

Because of the current national fiscal situation, there is a critical need for constructive intervention, voluntary or governmentally imposed, in the provision of human services, including health services. Some current indices are exemplary, for example, national health insurance (pending), and medicare and medicaid expenditure levels (estimated). Unfortunately the taxes levied and relied on at the state, local, and federal level, which help support government, are being paid for disproportionately, with those who can least afford to pay contributing more than their share. In New Jersey, for example, the third richest state in the United States on the basis of per capita income, it is an established fact that the tax structure is very regressive; that is, lower income taxpayers bear a disproportionate share of the tax burden. Moreover, the disadvantaged are the earliest and most vulnerable victims of inflation. Although the United States has experienced double-digit inflation in recent years, there is currently an easing of the problem and economists are predicting that inflation will hover around 7% for the remainder of the seventies.

In the three to four year period following 1972, the cost of living rose 17%; however, for the poor, near poor, and the aged, the increase was approximately 20%. Lower income people generally spend a larger portion of their income on food and health care services, and while food prices have been increasing at a rate of about 14.5% on an annual basis, the rate of price increase in medical care runs approximately one-third ahead of the rest of the economy. On a Consumer Price Index basis, general medical care costs in 1974 were up 19.6%. During the period 1946 to 1971, while general consumer prices rose by 71%, doctors fees and hospital charges climbed approximately 109 and 442% respectively. In view of this, and because the health care system is not organized to make maximum use of the time of health practitioners or the available health facilities, it has been suggested that unless health care providers exercise voluntary restraint, public demands may require drastic, and perhaps unfortunate, federal interventions such as crisis-forced nationalization of the health industry. Paradoxically, the disadvantaged, the poor, the aged, and the sick are among the major beneficiaries of the federal budget and are therefore directly endangered by proposals to control inflation by cutting federal spending. Faced with continuing inflation and a problematic health care delivery system, an unprecedented level of humanitarian concern will be required to make human service programs more efficient, as well as more effective. Whatever level of health care is finally decided on, society will have to pay the price in increased control, taxation, or in the loss of other goods and services. In this regard it is of significance to note that even the Department of Health, Education, and Welfare has no legislative authority to intervene in assuring "effective prices" in the health care field. The health care industry in the United States, currently, is truly a providers' system.

HEALTH AND STATISTICAL INDICES

The purpose of this section is not to offer a solution to the problem of assessing health status, but rather to delineate some of the problems involved and to promote discussion that will assist resolution.

Failure in the past to point out adequately the limitations of contemporary measures has aided specialization and fragmentation in the health field. The variety of meanings assigned to positive health are the result of the lack of an operational definition that reflects the full range of meanings associated with the idea of health levels. Moreover fragmentation and lack of clarification of the meaning of health measures have been augmented by health agencies, research groups, voluntary and professional health associations, and perhaps most of all, by health and life insurance companies. Each has sought to use data related to death, illness, and health in specific ways to further its own, and more often than not, somewhat conflicting interests. Thus agencies concerned with health, or the lack of it, generate data that may not be compatible. There is a conglomeration of different types of indices, each, in many instances, developed within incompatible conceptual constructs, for example, input versus process versus output. The free enterprise structure is also contributory, especially in terms of data generated by agencies that are on the receiving end of third party payments. For example, emphasis in a hospital may be on efficiency, where a full occupancy focus yields data representative of physical and fiscal considerations and therefore leads to data misinterpretation and fragmentation. In this type of situation, the incentive is to reward ill health. Health facilities accreditation agencies further confuse the issue with their concern for intermediate or process information, for example, physician-nurse ratios. The result is an institutional or facility focus rather than a patient focus and a proliferation of considerable data reflective of institutional concerns.

Obviously attempts to understand and promote health and to control disease through modifying behavior, changing expectations, resource deployment, and assessment are data sensitive. Data are the bases for almost all action-oriented programs in the human services area, from planning to evaluation. Current health measures have provided the only available foundation for the assignment of health priorities—prevention, cure, or rehabilitation. Health statistics have become almost an end in themselves and they distort views concerning health, ill health, and appropriate health care delivery mechanisms.

Traditionally health status has been determined by the mortality rate; a decrease in the death rate considered representative of an improvement in health status. The important mortality indexes were crude and age-adjusted death rates, infant mortality rates, and life expectancy rates. Currently changes in the concept of what constitutes a healthy individual or group of people, along with concurrent changes in health problems and programs have impaired the utility of mortality data as a measure of health.[3] These new concerns highlight the imperfections in

[3]National Center for Health Statistics, *Conceptual Problems in Developing an Index of Health* (Washington, D.C.: Public Health Service, 1966).

the validity of contemporary assessment approaches. There is also the present problem of using mortality data as a means of evaluating need and adequacy of health programs. Such data obviously are also improper as criteria for establishing health policies at the national, state, or local levels. Health professionals have yet to approach the rational construction of a single index of health, especially in light of the generally accepted definition of health as "the complete mental, physical, and social well-being of the individual and not just the absence of disease or infirmity." As would be expected, the psychological and socioeconomic consequences of illness as well as chronic diseases are receiving more attention, not only in terms of mortality, but also in terms of prevention of ill health, decreased human productivity, long-term disability, and the need for convalescent services.

From the point of view of the twentieth century concept of good health mortality and morbidity statistics are also inadequate because they measure only the negative aspects of health. Although the notion of health is indeed difficult to define precisely and, therefore, to measure, we must develop an operational definition of health that takes the parameters of good health into consideration, as well as the limitations of the traditional measurable components.

The National Center for Health Statistics has developed a wide variety of health data for the United States. These data appear to be both desirable and necessary to the total health enterprise. Often, however, it is difficult to interpret the assembled statistics. A vast array of problems, conceptual and otherwise, influence and complicate the situation. For example, what are the operational definitions within which index values are to be interpreted? What is needed is an index of health that reduces assessment to a rational and empirical formula that, if nothing else, approximates a "single" index to the full range of meanings associated with good health as well as mortality and morbidity. As noted by White: "One element that is clearly missing (in the health field) is a first-rate medical intelligence service to analyze quantitative information bearing on health-care issues in the light of political, social and economic factors."[4] However, efforts have been and are being made at both the national and international level to develop standards and procedures so that derived data will be more meaningful than in the past as efforts are made to improve the health care system.

The next section should be reviewed against the preceding background.

THE HEALTH CARE PREDICAMENT: A STATUS REPORT

The American people are demanding health care changes of a fundamental nature. There are several reasons for this level of concern: (1) skyrocketing costs; (2) fragmentary services; (3) general inability to obtain care; (4) maldistribution of health care resources; and (5) the fee-for-service system, with primary focus on payment for medical care, versus promotion and maintenance of health. The situation is further complicated by the fact that there are over 30 million "medi-

[4]Kerr L. White, "Life and Death and Medicine," *Scientific American,* **229** (September 1973), p. 33.

cally indigent" Americans. As long ago as 1932, when the Committee on the Costs of Medical Care published its report entitled, "Medical Care for the American People," the first general national assessment of the health care system, problems of fragmentation, unavailability, and inadequacy of health care and services were in evidence.[5] Significantly, two of the five basic recommendations contained in the Committee's Majority Report promoted comprehensive group practice in conjunction with comprehensive prepayment! The prepayment statement did not, however, advocate the elimination of individual fee-for-service arrangements. As has been the case in recent times, the American Medical Association vigorously resisted—when it has not outrightly condemned—the group practice and group payment recommendations, committing the profession to the preservation of solo practice and fee-for-service payment. A schism of national proportions between public interests and organized medicine began in the late 1930s and obviously is still with us today.

Health data are illustrative of a deplorable state of affairs in the United States, as is the case among most industrialized and semiindustrialized countries of the world. The United States is the most advanced country in the world in the area of medical technology and in the general competence of health professionals. Yet with one of the highest levels of income in the world and the expenditure of some 7% of the gross national product for health care, the United States is not even in the top ten countries in terms of the health status of the populace, as measured by traditional parameters. In the 1960s alone, health care costs increased more than twice as fast as the increase in the cost of living. Unfortunately, health benefits have not kept pace with increases in professional competence and higher costs. The United States ranks about thirteenth among the nations of the world in infant mortality and about half of the countries which have lower current rates had higher infant mortality rates in the early 1950s!

The *World Health Statistics Report* for 1970 shows that among the leading twenty-three industrialized or semiindustrialized nations of the world, the United States had the lowest bronchitis death rate. However, among these twenty-three nations, this country's death rate from pneumonia ranks no higher than thirteenth; for ulcer of the stomach and duodenum, no higher than tenth; for cirrhosis of the liver, eighteenth; for infectious and parasitic diseases, eighth; and respiratory tuberculosis, seventh. For deaths from other types of tuberculosis, the United States ranks fourth; and for diabetes-caused deaths, fourteenth.

The United States ranks seventh among industrialized countries in the percentage of mothers who die in childbirth. It ranks no better than eighteenth in the life expectancy of males and eleventh for females. The country is sixteenth among industrialized countries in the death rate of males in their middle years. Fifteen to twenty years ago, in all instances, the United States ranked better. The health of U.S. citizens, in comparison with the health of people of other countries of the

[5] "Medical Care for the American People: The Final Report of the Committee on the Costs of Medical Care," Committee Publication No. 28, University of Chicago Press, 1932. Reprinted by Community Health Service, HSMHA, Public Health Service, U.S. Department of Health, Education, and Welfare, Washington, D. C., 1970.

world, is deteriorating. The inadequacies of the system are further illuminated when we are forced to recognize that there are at least two health care systems in the United States, one for the poor and another for the middle class and the rich.

Figure 1.1 is exemplary of the problems of income and the ability to obtain health services. Out-of-pocket expenditure is the most important payment source for one-third to one-half of the health services for families near and below poverty respectively; whereas, for wealthier families, voluntary health insurance represents a third of the total payment for family health services.

Figure 1.2 contains data that reflect the percent decrease and increase, respectively, of direct payments and insurance payments for health care for the fiscal years 1950 and 1972. Figure 1.2 also contains data that show a significant percentage increase, 17%, in the use of public funds as a source of payment for personal health care from 1950 to 1972 (including medicare and medicaid in the 1972 figure). In 1950, approximately 50% of the American population was covered by some form of private health insurance whereas, in 1972, the figure was more than 80%. The marked increase in the number of individuals covered by health insurance is due to employee benefit plans that include health insurance. Although there have been advances in health insurance coverage, it has been estimated that as many as 40 million people in the United States are without any health insurance protection.[6] "The majority of these are poor and near-poor, nonwhite, unemployed—in general the disadvantaged. . . Also, because of short-comings in many existing plans, millions of other people who *are* covered have inadequate protection from the financial consequences of ill health."[7] Figure 1.3 is

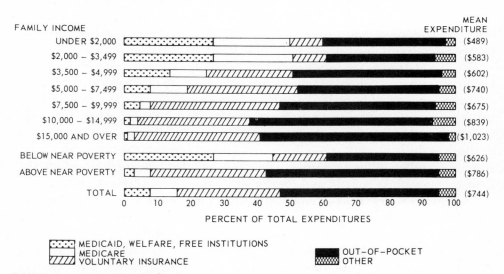

FIGURE 1.1.   Distribution of sources of payment for family health services by income, 1970. Adapted from U. S. Department of Health, Education, and Welfare, *Expenditures for Personal Health Services: National Trends and Variations—1953–1970* (Washington, D.C.: U. S. Department of Health, Education, and Welfare, 1973), p. 10.

[6]*Building a National Health-Care System,* Committee for Economic Development (New York, for Economic Development, April 1973).
[7]*Ibid.,* p. 14.

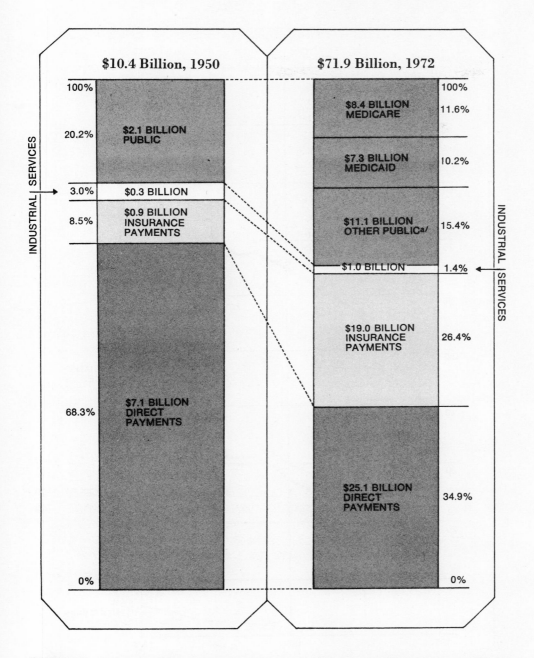

FIGURE 1.2. Personal health care expenditures by source of funds for fiscal years 1950 and 1972. *(a)* Includes workmen's compensation medical benefits, general hospital and medical care (primarily mental and charity hospitals), Defense Department hospitals and medical care, veterans hospitals and medical care, maternal and child health services, school health, Office of Economic Opportunity neighborhood health centers, medical vocational rehabilitation, and temporary disability insurance. Note: Some numbers do not total, due to rounding. Source: *Building a National Health-Care System* Committee for Economic Development (New York: April 1973), p. 13.

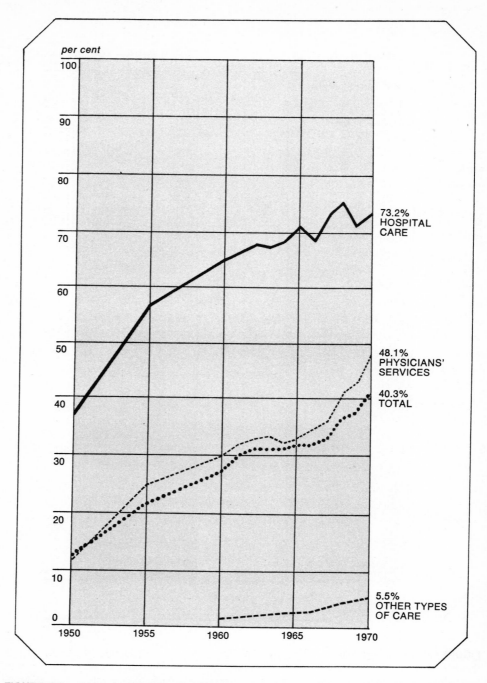

FIGURE 1.3. Proportion of consumer health care expenditures met by private health insurance, 1950–1970. Source: *Building a National Health-Care System* Committee for Economic Development (New York: April 1973), p. 15.

10

a graphic representation of the increase in health care expenditures covered by private health insurance for the years 1950 to 1970.

Although health obviously encompasses social as well as physical and biological science, the health sciences have yet to respond by incorporation of the humanities and social sciences into health professional education programs that current indices require. A health professions education model that attempts to relate the variety of health science education programs to the actual needs of the community has yet to emerge. Even so, the effectiveness of such a model will be validated only when a marked change occurs in the health of individuals and groups in those areas that presently exhibit the lowest health status and receive the poorest health service—the poor, blacks, and other ethnic minorities, both urban and rural. Figures 1.4, 1.5, and 1.6 are exemplary of the dimensions and implications of poverty for the quality of life of the human organism.

In special studies that have been made in urban areas divided geographically into "poverty" and "nonpoverty," the data show a far greater frequency of almost all illnesses in the poorer areas, which have proportionately fewer primary care personnel and health services in general. The poor also have a far higher rate of sickness and death in all of the conditions that are preventable and curable by good medical care. This is not consistent with the fact that the poor spend a greater proportion of their income for health care, despite the enactment of Medicare and Medicaid. In 1970, 14.5% of the income of the lowest income families was spent for medical care, whereas only 3.3% was expended by the highest income families.[8]

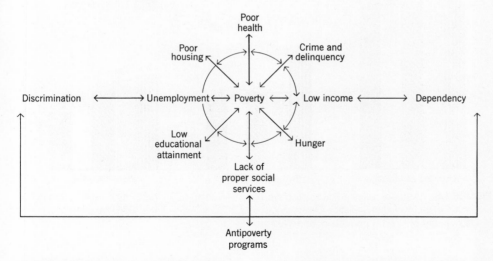

FIGURE 1.4. Poverty: implications for the quality of life. Source: Governor's Office of Human Resources, *Annual Poverty Report: Illinois* (Springfield, Illinois: State Economic Opportunity Office, 1970), p. 6.

[8]U. S. Department of Health, Education, and Welfare, *Expenditures for Personal Health Services: National Trends and Variations 1953*–1970 (Washington, D. C.: U. S. Department of Health, Education, and Welfare, October 1973).

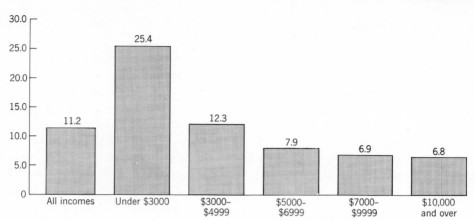

FIGURE 1.5. Percentage distribution of population with activity-limiting, chronic conditions, by family income, July 1965–June 1966. Adapted from National Center for Health Statistics, *Limitations of Activity and Mobility Due to Chronic Conditions, U. S., July, 1965–June, 1966* (Washington, D.C.: U. S. Department of Health, Education, and Welfare, 1968).

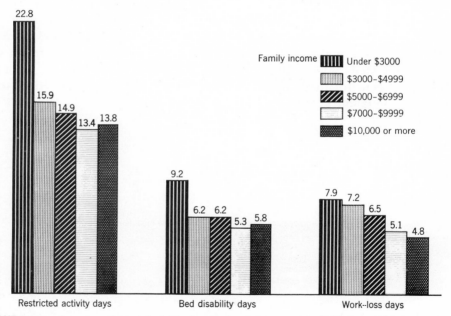

FIGURE 1.6. Age-sex adjusted disability days, by family income, July 1965–June 1966. Adapted from National Center for Health Statistics, *Disability Days, U. S., July, 1965–June, 1966* (Washington, D.C.: U. S. Department of Health, Education, and Welfare, 1968).

An estimated 40 million Americans, black and white, inhabit "the other America"—urban ghettos, migrant worker villages, Appalachia, and Indian reservations. For the most part, urban areas are the most over loaded and depressed centers in the United States with regard to adequate space for living, transportation, recreation, adequate housing, water, waste disposal and education. Attendant to such inadequacies is the decay of physical and social systems necessary for the provision of even a minimum level of the quality of life. Correlatively the influx of people with divergent cultural backgrounds, interests, expectations, concerns, and skills has resulted in the development of environmental stresses that have led to mental breakdowns, suicide attempts, social disorder, increased frequency of crime, drug abuse, and antisocial behavior. The decrease in living space, with its accompanying pollution, contamination, and facilitation of direct contact with pathological agents, has had an adverse effect on the efficacy of human, sanitary, and health care systems, resulting in an increase in the number od deaths and debilitating conditions.

While the city may be regarded as one of man's most impressive creations, it is the site of the most severe environmental problems. Most cities stand as testimonials to a lack of rational planning and design that, if employed, would have resulted in a more favorable balance among man, technology, and environment. Contemporary ecological concerns are the result, in large part, of the stark reality of the decay, human and otherwise, of our urban areas.

That health status differs by race is readily discernible from Figures 1.7 and 1.8.

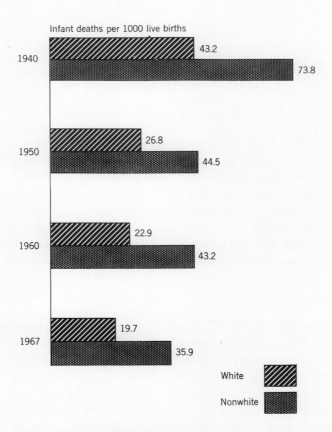

FIGURE 1.7. Infant mortality rate of nonwhites and whites, selected years, 1940–1967. Adapted from National Center for Health Statistics, *Vital Statistics of the U. S., 1967* (Washington, D.C.: U. S. Department of Health, Education, and Welfare, 1969).

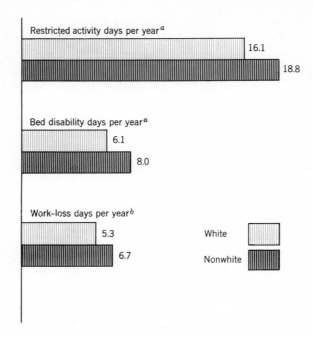

FIGURE 1.8. Nonwhites have more disability days than whites, 1973. *(a)* All family incomes (includes unknown income), all ages. *(b)* All family incomes, all ages seventeen years and over. Adapted from "Profile of American Health, 1973," *Public Health Reports,* **89** (November–December 1974), pp. 504–523.

If it is true that children are a nation's greatest resource, then Figure 1.7 is representative of, perhaps, the most significant challenge to health professionals and the lay public in the United States, white and nonwhite.

Approximately thirty-five years ago, the infant death rate of nonwhites was 70% greater than that of whites. In 1962, it was 90% greater! Moreover, the infant mortality rate among the American Indian population is 60% higher than the national average. Most health professionals are in agreement that different levels of health care and different living conditions are the primary reasons nonwhites, comparatively, are in a poorer state of health. Whites living under conditions of deprivation similar to nonwhites exhibit essentially the same type of health statistics.

As evidenced by Figure 1.7, despite the general decrease in infant deaths from 1940 to 1967, the racial difference has remained. Even though the death rate has dropped over 50% during the twenty-seven year period depicted in Figure 1.7, the nonwhite infant mortality rate in 1967 was approximately 82% greater than the rate for whites (a differential that is 12% above the differential in 1940). The situation is compounded by the gross misallocation of health and medical services, particularly to densely populated, economically poor, urban areas. In such areas, black and other minority and disadvantaged pregnant mothers are themselves subject to higher risk, let alone the higher mortality among their offspring. Even when relative risks of infant death are computed by care received, black infants are subject to a greater risk of infant death than their white counterparts.[9] Where *social risk* is an environment factor ". . . the differences by race [are] great; adequate medical care [does] not have as much impact in reducing mortality for black infants as it [does] for white infants."[10] The data from the study conducted by the Panel on Health Services Research also suggest that educational attainment differences among mothers is closely correlated with infant birth weight and survival. In general, a person will be disadvantaged regarding his or her health status if he or she manifests any or all of the following characteristics: poor, nonwhite, poorly educated, employed in a hazardous occupation, part of a large family, resident of certain geographic regions. The ". . . causes of poverty are also effects, its effects are causes."[11]

PUBLIC HEALTH AND ORGANIZED MEDICINE

At no time in the history of civilized man has there been an approach to the total health of the individual, an effort to conserve and promote a comprehensive devotion to good health rather than to the cure of disease. Since the founding of the American Medical Association (AMA) in 1847, there has been an effective organizational separation of preventive care from curative and restorative care —the former being characterized under the rubric of public health and the latter two under the rubric of organized medicine. The latter's domain focused on the health of the *individual,* whereas the former was perceived as focusing on the health of groups of people usually as a responsibility of government, hence the *sick care* versus *well care* dichotomy that has characterized health care in the United States.

Twenty-five years after the establishment of the AMA, a section on state medicine and hygiene in the Association defined state medicine, or public health, as "the application of medical knowledge and skill to the benefit of communities which is obviously a very different thing from the application of the benefits to individuals in private and curative medicine."[12] Six years later, in 1878, Dr. T. D. Richardson, then president of the AMA, stated that public health was the "prevention or arrest of all diseases which have a tendency to spread through communities and which cannot otherwise be controlled."[13] This professionally conceived cleavage became institutionalized, with few exceptions. By 1910 the AMA had increased its influence to such an extent, through the creation of special committees,

[9]Panel on Health Services Research, *Infant Death: An Analysis by Maternal Risk and Health Care* (Washington, D. C.: Institute of Medicine, 1973).
[10]*Ibid.,* p. 15.
[11]Governor's Office of Human Resources, *Annual Poverty Report: Illinois* (Springfield, Illinois: State Economic Opportunity Office, 1970), p. 6.
[12]Thomas N. Logan, "Report of the Committee on a National Health Council," *Transactions,* American Medical Association, 23 (1872), p. 48.
[13]T. G. Richardson, "Presidential Address, 29th Annual Meeting, "*Transactions,* American Medical Association, 29 (1878), p. 111.

bureaus, and councils, that the association acquired a leadership reputation in the minds of laymen and legislators alike.[14] The medical profession, more than federal and state government agencies, was defined and generally accepted as the primary protector of the health of the individual. Thus fragmentation of responsibility for health has been extant for well over a hundred years.

Fragmentation of the health care system was aggravated further by the development of a rather well-defined three-tier organization of health services based on three major types of health problems[15]:

1.   Primary care—solo practice-based and ambulatory in nature; includes such conditions as respiratory infections, arthritis, asthma, and minor accidents.

2.   Secondary care—reasonably specialized and care-based in modest-sized community hospitals; includes such conditions as burns, accidents requiring hospitalization, and conditions requiring specialized laboratory tests.

3.   Tertiary care—highly specialized and intensive-care-oriented, drawing on best available medical knowledge and medical technology usually available in academic health centers; includes such conditions as cancer, congenital disorders, acute poisonings, and metabolic disorders.

It is worthy to note that there is no well-defined hierarchical relationship among the three levels that, at a minimum, could represent a starting point for restructuring the current health care system.

Figure 1.9 is illustrative of the delivery problems associated with the preceding three-tier system, where the best possible care apparently is available to service the least number of people. Thus the fragmented arrangements that currently exist in the United States result in escalation of cost and maldistribution of medical manpower, as well as problems of accessibility and quality of care. Health and medical care, to be effective and efficient, must exist as a continuum and must be free of differentiation on the basis of sociocultural characteristics, geographic location, and economics.

Since the end of World War I, there has been some erosion of the influence of the AMA, which has been characterized by a slow evolution toward a more governmentally controlled and financed health care system. The following excerpt from a lecture by I. S. Falk is illustrative, albeit implicitly, of this evolution:

The current crisis in medical care has been two generations in the making. In the 1920's the outlook for prospective difficulties was foreseen, and it led to the studies of the Committee on the Costs of Medical Care and to the inaction that followed total reliance on professional leadership and voluntarism. In the 1930's, there were comprehensive proposals for dealing with current difficulties and for anticipating prospective needs, and they failed mainly from political timidity in high places. In the 1940's a patchwork of categorical programs was begun for development of needed personnel and facilities, beginning with the post-war Hill-Burton Act and a miscellany of other specialty commitments. In the 1950's, lulled to torpor by the newer promises of voluntarism and the allegedly constructive forces of the

[14]Carlton B. Chapman and John M. Talmadge, "The Evolution of the Right to Health Concept in the United States, *Pharos*, (January 1971), pp. 30–51.
[15]Kerr L. White, "Life and Death and Medicine," *Scientific American*, **229** (September 1973), pp. 23–33.

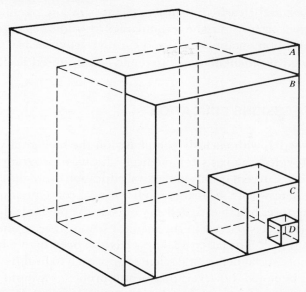

FIGURE 1.9.   Distribution of demand for medical care by a typical population in one year (1970). Note: "Out of a total population at risk of 1000 (Cube *A*), an average of 720 people visited a physician in an ambulatory setting at least once (Cube *B*), 100 people were admitted to a hospital at least once (Cube *C*), and only 10 were admitted to a university hospital at least once (Cube *D*)." Source: Kerr L. White, "Life and Death of Medicine." Copyright © by *Scientific American Inc.,* **229** (September 1973), p. 30. All rights reserved.

marketplace and private insurance, massive developments in the private sector and the bulwarking of the status quo prevailed. In the '60's, with much turmoil and fanfare, fractional provisions for the aged, for mothers and children, and for the poor and the near-poor, were made, but—with the major specifications laid down mainly by the opponents of the enactments—both inadequate programs and newer cost escalations obtained. The result is crisis in the '70's.[16]

William Lyman stated during the Fourth Congress of the United States that, "The right to the preservation of health is inalienable."[17] Yet, there are still barriers that limit promotion of the concept. While acknowledging that there are sociocultural, economic, political, and educational variables that limit the health of individuals and the nation, we must nevertheless begin to challenge existing health policies and organizational and behavioral patterns, derived through tradition and practice, that still mitigate against present health conservation efforts.

With major focus in the 1970s on national health insurance, which will virtually establish the right to good health, policy makers obviously must recognize that a substantial investment in delivery of more health services may not

[16]I. S. Falk, "National Policies and Programs for the Financing of Medical Care," The 1971 Michael M. Davis Lecture, Center for Health Administration Studies (Chicago: University of Chicago Graduate School of Business, 1971), pp. 3–4.
[17]William Lyman, "Comment in House of Representatives," Fourth Congress, First Session, *Annals of Congress,* May 11, 1796, p. 1348.

produce positive and clearly measurable changes in any parameters of health. National health insurance must be accompanied by studied changes in the various aspects of prevention, maintenance, and curative activities and thus may be the harbinger to a governmentally organized and administered health care system.

HEALTH PROFESSIONS EDUCATION

The Flexner model, with exclusive emphasis on the biological sciences and research, has provided the basis for medical education programs in the United States since 1910. Current trends in medical education dramatically illustrate two of the basic weaknesses of the Flexner model vis-a-vis contemporary health needs: "(1) it largely ignores health care delivery outside the medical school and its own hospital, and (2) it sets science in the medical school apart from science on the general campus. . ."[18] The latter weakness has also been highlighted recently by our taking a more social-behavioral sciences approach to health care and promotion. It should be noted, however, that health problems around the turn of the century did not allow for much emphasis on primary prevention, although it is plausible to state that a great majority of health practitioners were sefvicing the "whole" person. Even so, concern for health, as it was subsequently defined, has not been reflected in health professions education programs. Obviously the Flexner model cannot efficiently accommodate current concern with the problems of health care delivery and the socioeconomic environment within which we attempt to provide health care. As noted by Flexner himself, the academic health professional is a teacher who sees himself in the absolute sense of the term, rather than as a responsible component of the health care delivery system.[19]

Because of the influence of the AMA in the field of health care, it is probably safe to state that the Flexner model, in general, has affected the development of most, if not all, health professionals. Illustratively, education in nursing, dentistry, pharmacy, physical therapy, clinical psychology, medical social work, medical technology, and many others commonly utilize medical center resources. "Schools of public health have typically been established in a university medical center setting; in their absence, the medical school and hospital must assume a direct concern with the problems of public health practice, teaching, and research."[20] Because medical education has been a leader in setting standards that justify professional status, "these same educational standards [have been] widely copied in each of the related health professions, and each seeks a degree of professional identity and independence analogous to that of the physician."[21] This has led to a myriad of health practitioners with behavior in a health setting better suited to

[18]The Carnegie Commission on Higher Education, *Higher Education and the Nation's Health* (New York: McGraw-Hill Book Company, 1970), p. 4.
[19]Abraham Flexner, *Universities, American, English, and German* (New York: Oxford University Press, 1930).
[20]William N. Hubbard, Jr., "Health Knowledge," *The Health of Americans*, edited by Boisfeuillet Jones (New Jersey: Prentice-Hall, Inc., 1970), p. 116.
[21]*Ibid.*, p. 117.

traditional applications of knowledge, that is, a disease versus health emphasis. Contemporary health science programs are still reflective of the Renaissance man approach to higher education—they are largely passive, aloof from, and insensitive to the current health needs of society.

The Flexner model has resulted in an increase in the aggregate level of knowledge in the health sciences and specialization, but it has not effectively encouraged problem solving in the social setting. Health problems have been defined and analyzed, but commitments to the solution of such problems are still in an embryonic stage of development. The real product of the Flexner model has been the growth of medical science. The expertise afforded by the new knowledge has not been matched by an equal level of understanding of the significance of man's interactions with his environment as a determinant of health status. It is in this area where the health knowledge and technical proficiency of health practitioners is unable to meet health care delivery needs, let alone expectations. Moreover, health practitioners have not begun to appreciate fully the health challenge presented by the move toward general acceptance of the right to health concept, which means the guaranteeing of adequate health care to all Americans regardless of *means*. Once the financial barriers to health care are lowered, what is now described as a crisis may be merely a preliminary symptom of a terminal disease unless an effective science and system of health care delivery can be developed.

Current health science education activities are indicative of efforts to improve hospital-based, as well as private and community endeavors, in the area of health care delivery. Additional efforts are being made to develop integrated health science curriculum models, to retrain Ph.D.'s in basic science and engineering in abbreviated medical education programs, to develop more flexible health science education programs vis-à-vis professional options, and so forth.[22] Some medical education centers are taking an integrated approach and providing a basic core of education experiences for all students interested in health science education, with multiple track options available regarding final professional differentiation.[23] This approach is receiving considerable attention and has the potential for developing, at the least, a less provincial attitude among its students. However, as noted by Pruitt:

Unless an intimate relationship exists between the trusteeship of the academic health center and responsibility for delivery of all levels of [health] care, the educational programs of the center are less than likely to produce professional personnel in kinds and numbers needed to deliver that care. The measure of their failure will be influenced by the degree to which the academic process is shielded from total responsibility for health care delivery, and freed thereby to indulge the irresponsibility of pursuing purposes in health manpower production not always congruent with those of the society that process is supposed to serve.[24]

[22]The Carnegie Commission on Higher Education, *op. cit.*
[23]D. E. Rogers, "A Dean's List of Proposals," *Medical Opinion and Review,* 5 (October 1969), pp. 24–33.
[24]Raymond D. Pruitt, "Academic Medicine and American Society: Interdependent or Independent?", *Mayo Clinic Proceedings,* 48 (April 1973), p. 289.

Pruitt further contends that academic health professionals "have produced the kinds of [practitioners they] wanted to produce, unconsciously so perhaps, with little concern whether [they] were the kinds most needed by. . . society."[25]

Regardless of how many more individuals enter the health field and how much facilities are improved, a better job of educating health personnel has to be effected if the "system" is to work effectively. Currently there have been no general models proposed that will ensure that a substantial measure of social responsibility will pervade the teaching and practice of every health science discipline and profession. While many new programs are being developed with an emphasis on community health and health-related needs, these approaches to meeting consumer needs through change in professional preparation programs are in specialized form, and marginal at best, for example, community medicine and family practice. Increasing the number of health specialities is more a matter of tradition than it is the solution to health care problems. There does not appear to be a comprehensive effort being made to include content and practice activities in all professional preparation programs that would begin to build a system of providers of health care who are humanely sensitive and have made practice commitments relevant to consumer needs. Within this context, early contact with consumers of health services is essential so that the student will not be unnecessarily delayed in appreciating and experiencing the social and interpersonal aspects of health care delivery service. As Margolis states:

On balance, and despite all the recent federal *caveats* and incursions, it must be said that our medical colleges remain surprisingly indifferent to the urgencies of reform, preferring for the most part to leave that difficult matter to the politicians. There is little evidence that medical schools see themselves as "a public service corporation." Few colleges have responded with any enthusiasm or long-range determination to the nation's health care needs; few have stressed to their students the virtues of rural practice or the sins of excessive surgery; and hardly any have invested sufficient dollars and prestige in promoting the education of family practitioners.[26]

In the future, classroom pedagogy in the health field must involve energetic efforts that facilitate the development of a response sensitive to interpersonal as well as curative issues. There is the need to develop within health professionals the ability to pursue professional objectives that are application-oriented, thereby acknowledging the necessity of coming to terms with the interpersonal realities of health, in a human, social setting, with an orientation toward creativity in responses. A concerted effort must be made to focus on health care as a social science, concerned with prevention, maintenance, curative, and restoration services for people, sometimes singularly but more often than not in combination. Until this is done, health care in the United States will cost more, will provide less satisfaction of health needs, and will yield even poorer services than currently exist.

[25]*Ibid.,* p. 290.
[26]Richard J. Margolis, "Medical Schools at the Crossroads," *Change,* **6** (June 1974), p. 43.

THE CONSUMER, HEALTH, AND THE HEALTH PROFESSIONAL

Good health care as a universal human right and as a societal goal has placed increasingly heavy demands on the providers of health services. So heavy, are the demands that speculation exists concerning whether health professionals, as well as consumers of health services, have been able to keep pace with societal progress, the growth of knowledge in the health sciences, and the expanded capabilities and responsibilities of the health industry. Current health indices are indicative of a gap—one that seems to be widening in some sectors—between the knowledge and skills of the health practitioner on the one hand and the health practices and behavior of the consumer of health services on the other hand. Illustratively, a recent Committee for Economic Development publication contained the following statement:

The nation's health services have retained the organization—or lack of it—that may have been adequate for the health needs of an earlier era. As the major health problems shifted from acute to chronic diseases and toward conditions requiring more extended attention, the system failed to develop a continuous form of care to replace that based on episodic treatment. It also failed to shift from the concept of *sick* care to *well* care.[27]

In the same report, concern for the consumer, of a sociocultural nature, cannot be found among the recommendations of the Committee for Economic Development. Major attention is devoted to a national health insurance program, the restructuring of health care delivery, with an emphasis on physical and fiscal concerns, comprehensive health planning, and manpower development. A traditional concept of consumerism, however, seems to be implicit in the report, that is, consumerism that pertains to representation and participation, control versus partnership, health boards in communities, and consumer input to public agencies. Consumerism in the future should relate to the importance of *the behavior* of the consumer in health care, maintenance, and promotion. The behavior of the consumer is affected by the nature of services and how they are provided, including such factors as availability and proximity, psychological and monetary costs, stigma, social distance, and the like. Thus certain faults of the health care delivery system have their foundations in the sociocultural and socioeconomic structure of the United States, and a constructive response of the health system will, at best, be limited by such extrinsic factors.

Health professionals, in educational and practice settings, should become more sensitive and responsive to the public's (individual's) perception of health needs and priorities, inasmuch as public (individual) attitudes and values are important determinants of change in health status and in the structure and utilization of health services. Surprisingly, perhaps, the knowledge expansion related to the capabilities of medicine has been devoid, in practice, of adequate sensitivity to the knowledge expansion in the social and behavioral sciences—resources of growing *importance* to the long-term improvement of the health of Americans. Health

[27]Committee for Economic Development, *op. cit.,* p. 12.

professionals have to begin to make better use of such knowledge in converting the *right* to access into *actual* access to skills, services, facilities, and systems. Subsequently, health care and promotion activities should be viewed and conceived against the background of economic conditions, educational factors, population problems, family patterns, poverty, and material and human resources. A comprehensive effort demands anticipation and subsequent preparation for all of the social forces to be encountered in providing adequate health care for all. Preventive health services, in particular, are fundamental to the maintenance and improvement of the health of Americans, and the effective delivery of such services is grounded in the interpersonal realities—individual and social (public)—of health. "In actual practice today, there is not much preventive care beyond immunizations, prenatal care, well-baby clinics, and some screening programs."[28] Over ten years ago, Edward Suchman contended that:

Social and cultural factors have always played an important part in determining the way in which health and medical services were organized. The value system of a society helps to shape the public's attitudes, beliefs, and behavior in regard to health and illness. Health institutions, like all social institutions, reflect a society's definition of what constitutes an acceptable and appropriate organization of health activity. The roles assigned to both the practitioner and the recipient [of health care] represent, in large measure, socially prescribed behavior. As an inherently social and cultural activity,. . . health is thus an integral part of the social system, and can be fully understood only in terms of existing social forces.[29]

Thus it should be generally accepted that there are cultural and social variations in the way in which persons define health problems, participate in health maintenance programs, and utilize medical and other health services. Threats to man's health and survival have their determinants in cultural, social, and economic factors that fall far outside the traditional and basic intellectual interests of the health sciences. The tasks of synthesis and redefinition which the health field so badly needs should be augmented through the actualization of a new social sense of mission.

Traditionally the health professional has been trained to make all decisions concerning what, where, how, and why health services are provided. On the other hand, the consumer in the health care marketplace has occupied an insecure and limited position, hence the inability of the consumer to utilize adequately and evaluate the services provided. Consumers should be able to enter into a partnership with the providers of health care, with a significant factor now being consumer education of the provider concerning consumer needs (i.e., "if you want to know about the patient, don't ask the doctor, ask the patient"), and, hopefully, provider education of the consumer concerning health maintenance and promotion. Health practitioners in this mode would be capable of using the consumer's background, as much as possible, as a tool for improving health. Cultural differences, for example, would thus become subordinate to health as a viable value,

---

[28]*Ibid.*, p. 59.
[29]Edward A. Suchman, *Sociology and the Field of Public Health* (New York: Russell Sage Foundation, 1963), p. 15.

with consumer and provider working together toward a common end—the maintenance and promotion of health.

Society is pressuring academic health centers to assume more responsibility for the provision of adequate health care. The potential for the effective acceptance of this challenge exists, if academic health professionals are willing to strike a balance among Flexnerian-type emphases and the sociocultural realities of health care delivery. As previously noted, threats to man's health and survival include social, cultural, behavioral, educational, and economic factors, in myriad combinations and permutations. Therefore the right to health concept, with its implicit humane halo, can be fully realized only through an approach and subsequent system performance that is pragmatic and realistic.

CHAPTER TWO

HEALTH ORGANIZATION

Health care delivery in the United States has been treated historically as a private enterprise industry on the one hand and as a social or public responsibility on the other. These views have determined how health care has been delivered, used, and structured. In the many years since the inception of organized health care in America, these two opposing viewpoints have been intensified by other aspects of American social life. People who see health care as the province of private enterprise also see it as a privilege while social reformers, on the contrary, think that health care is not a privilege but a right. Both groups, however, are beginning to recognize the need for an integrated concept of health that provides coordinated and comprehensive health maintenance, and promotes cost effective services.

The student of health care must be aware of this conflict and of the effect it has had on the structure of health care today. Without recognition of underlying factors and issues, we are unable to develop an effective approach to the alleviation of existing problems. Some of the major problem areas converge around the following:

1. People are generally uninformed of the availability of health care resources and consequently do not use them.

2. Social and cultural variations influence patterns of distribution and the utilization of health care resources. Significantly the notion of health as a positive social value has yet to be institutionalized, although the concept of health maintenance organizations is a step in this direction.

3. A lack exists of clear and comprehensive guidelines for health care delivery, as well as of clear and comprehensive solutions to contemporary problems.

4. There is a lack of consensus regarding priorities for research, including research on delivery systems.

5.   The health care industry is basically a commercial enterprise, and is considered by mnny to represent a monopoly in knowledge and practice.

6.   The financial costs associated with implementing the right to health concept have yet to be fully understood. While acknowledging that there is now no one answer or best definition of how to organize most effectively and administer the health care system, the following components, along with competent administration, have to be considered essential ingredients in any endeavors to provide high quality care: planning and coordination; demography and epidemiology; economy and efficiency; evolution; and consumer involvement.[1]

STRUCTURE, ORGANIZATION, AND RESPONSIBILITIES OF MAJOR HEALTH ORGANIZATIONS

Organizations are deliberately formed in society to perform a specific function or set of functions (although these original functions can and often do become distorted). Health organizations are no different. They have authority and responsibility for creating and implementing systems and programs for the provision of health care. Obviously such agencies vary in size, form, function, autonomy, or locus of authority, and professional composition. The major health organizations of interest are official or public, voluntary or nonprofit, professional and health-related.

Official Agencies

Official agencies are those health units at the local, state, and national levels that depend on tax funds and operate within specific legal limits and regulations. Hence official health agencies, organizationally and functionally—including, of course, services and activities—are authorized and governed by law.[2]

At the federal level, involvement in health care, aside from the general welfare provision of the Constitution, commenced after the yellow fever epidemics of 1793 to 1794, with the enactment of a quarantine regulation by Congress in 1796. The regulation represented a specific, yet limited, level of involvement. It should be noted that only in the twentieth century has the general welfare clause of the Constitution been interpreted in a policy, and not merely philosophical, context.

In 1798 President Adams signed the Marine Hospital Act; in 1906, the Pure Food and Drug Bill was passed by Congress; in 1912, the Marine Hospital Service was incorporated into the more comprehensive U. S. Public Health Service; in 1936, the National Cancer Institute and subsequently the National Institutes of Health were created. After World War II the federal thrust, as exemplified by the

---

[1]Joseph D. Alter, *Narrowing Our Medical Gap* (New York: Exposition Press Inc., 1972).
[2]Frank P. Grad, *Public Health Law Manual* (Washington, D.C.: American Public Health Association, 1973).

1946 Hill-Burton Act, was toward a partnership arrangement with the states. Thus federal involvement in health care appears to have evolved through the general routes of public health (with an emphasis on the prevention of communcable diseases), biomedical research (as illustrated by the establishment and comprehensive activities of the Public Health Service and the National Institutes of Health), and construction of medical facilities (as exemplified by the Hill-Burton Act and the Veterans Administration System). These and many other developments eventually led to the establishment of the Department of Health, Education, and Welfare in 1953.

The 1960s—the years of the great society and the war on poverty saw an increase in federal support for medical care and the inclusion of direct payment for personal medical insurance under Titles XVIII and XIX of the Social Security Act of 1965. Title XVIII, Medicare, established a federal program of health insurance for almost all Americans sixty-five and over whereas Title XIX, Medicaid, represented a corollary program for public assistance recipients. The passage of PL 92-603 in 1972, establishing professional standards review organizations, and the National Health Planning and Resources Development Act of 1974(PL 93-641), represent the latest efforts to foster intergovernmental, voluntary, and professional association collaboration for the promotion of health and optimum quality patient care.

Presently health activities of the federal government, authorized by law and financed by Congressional appropriations, may be categorized as dealing with the general population, special population groups, special problems or programs, and international health. The federal government also has responsibility for maintaining St. Elizabeth's and Freedman's hospitals. There are seven general functions of federal health agencies: (1) direct services (2) regulation, (3) consultation, (4) demonstration, (5) research, (6) education, and (7) grants-in-aid.

Close scrutiny of the years since the establishment of HEW reveals continuation, although to a lesser extent in the latter part of the period, of the professionally conceived and institutionalized artificial dichotomy between public health and private medicine that began in the late 1800s. Currently, increasing government expenditures in the health field, and increasing government recognition of health as a fundamental human right seem to be fostering a sensible approach, with preventive care no longer viewed as separated from curative and restorative care, or the public's health as separate from the individual's health.

In the years since the establishment of HEW, many laws emanating from the exercise of the power to regulate interstate commerce and to tax and spend money for the general welfare have been enacted. These laws have increased the span of authority and responsibility of HEW in the field of health care, including protection, knowledge, and manpower.[3],[4]

The organization and structure of HEW clearly shows the complexity of federal involvement in health, education, and welfare activities. As depicted in Figure 2.1,

[3]Lenor S. Goerke and Ernest L. Stebbins, *Mustard's Introduction to Public Health* (New York: Macmillan Company, 1968), Chapter 2.
[4]John J. Hanlon, *Principles of Public Health Administration* (St. Louis: C. V. Mosby Company, 1969), Chapter 2.

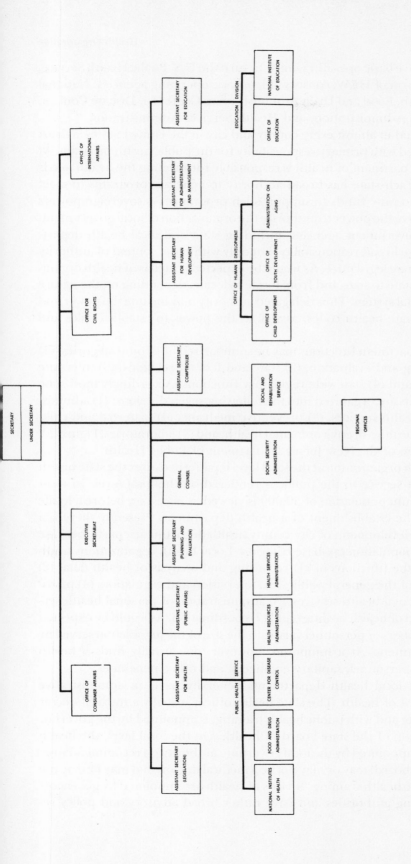

FIGURE 2.1. Department of Health, Education, and Welfare. Source: General Services Administration, *United States Government Manual, 1973–74* (Washington, D.C.: Government Printing Office, 1973), p. 221.

27

HEW comprises five basic operating units. In turn the U.S. Public Health Service, the major health arm of HEW, consists of five basic operating agencies: National Institutes of Health, Food and Drug Administration, Center for Disease Control, Health Resources Administration, and Health Services Administration.

In every state and in almost every county and city in the United States, at least one agency is vested with primary responsibility for the public health program. At the state level a department of health is responsible for meeting the health needs of the citizenry. Each state has broad authority to generate programs to meet social needs and to raise funds to support such programs. As sovereign powers states obviously have the power to authorize the organization of local government. State and local government agencies, including state and local health departments, can exercise broad responsibility, but only within the context of authority delegated by the state legislature. As would be expected patterns of health organization vary from state to state and from locale to locale, depending on the nature of the governmental system. Thus delegated authority may include the power and duty to enforce state health codes, as well as the power to establish rules and regulations.

State health department functions may be summarized into four categories: (1) statewide planning and evaluation, (2) state and federal relations, (3) interstate agency relations, and (4) statewide regulatory functions. Accordingly most state health departments are organized into the following seven divisions: (1) administration (2) local health services, (3) preventive medicine, (4) maternal and child health, (5) dental health, (6) environmental health, and (7) laboratories. Figure 2.2 is a recent diagram of the New Jersey Department of Public Health.

Generally health organization at the local level is patterned after the state health department. Most service to the public is rendered on the local level. In most instances a minimum population of 50,000 is viewed as necessary before a locale should consider the establishment of a health department. Presently there is a trend toward the development of city-county health departments, partly because of the minimum population tax-base criterion. Local health organizations traditionally perform the functions of (1) recording and analysis of health data, (2) health education of the general public, (3) supervision and regulation, (4) provision of environmental health services, (5) administration of personal health services, (6) operation of health facilities, and (7) coordination. As would be expected the types and numbers of personnel vary with the size of the jurisdiction served by the health department. At a minimum, however, one usually finds a health director, nursing personnel, sanitary engineers, and office personnel.

Both state and local health departments generally have an administrative officer and a board of health. The state health officer, usually a medical doctor licensed in the state and with public health training, is appointed by the governor on recommendation of the state board of health. On the local level, the health officer, generally appointed by the local governing authority on recommendation of the local health board, may or may not be a medical doctor, and may or may not have formal public health training. Boards of health are appointed by governors and local governing authorities and have rather broad advisory and policy responsibilities. Although in the past there has been a sizable number of physicians serving on health boards, recently there has been an effort to make boards more broadly representative.

A quasi-official health agency that has occupied a unique and important position in the provision of health care is the American Red Cross. The American Red Cross originated during the Civil War with a particular focus on the health of soldiers. The agency was first recognized in 1882 as the International Red Cross. Subsequently Congress granted a charter to the American Red Cross in 1900. The Red Cross performs diverse peace and wartime functions, including the assumption of active blood donor programs and civil emergency services.

Voluntary Health Agencies

Voluntary or nonprofit health units are organizations supported by private or nontax funds. They are directed by privately employed individuals and are usually governed by self-perpetuating boards of directors representing a wide range of prominent community persons. Voluntary health organizations have no legal powers. They are chartered and licensed by appropriate state and local governing authorities.

The voluntary health agency movement began with the establishment of the Anti-Tuberculosis Society of Philadelphia in 1892, and in 1961 numbered over 100,000 separate agencies at the national, state, and local levels.[5]

Voluntary agencies appeared at a time when governmental health agencies were in an embryonic stage of development and thus "have been in a position to provide needed services, develop and pioneer new methods, and make major contributions to the improvement of the health and welfare of the American people."[6] That such agencies have had a major influence on the health system in the United States and have made invaluable contributions to the health of Americans cannot be challenged.

They . . . provided medical care for the poor before public funds became available; they pioneered diphtheria immunizations and financed the develolment and field trials of Salk Polio vaccine. Through health education, they . . . provided for public acceptance of communicable disease control programs such as tuberculosis and venereal diseases. In addition, these agencies . . . set up research projects to ascertain needs and solutions and . . . sponsored new health services which were not otherwise available through public health channels.[7]

It should also be noted that innumerable civic, fraternal, veterans, church, and other similar organizations sponsor various types of health and welfare activities at the local level, usually with emphasis on health education and direct services.

Voluntary health agencies vary considerably in services and activities. However

[5]*Voluntary Health and Welfare Agencies in the United States: An Exploratory Study by an ad hoc Citizens Committee* (New York: Schoolmaster's Press, 1961).
[6]*Ibid.*, p. 1.
[7]Lloyd E. Burton and Hugh H. Smith, *Public Health and Community Medicine* (Baltimore: The Williams and Wilkins Company, 1970), p. 60.

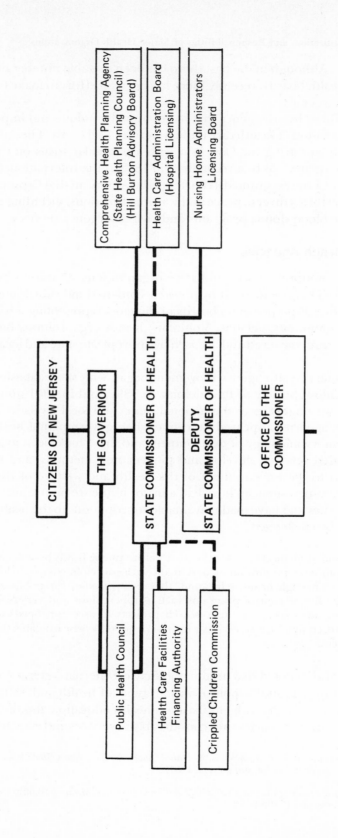

CITIZENS OF NEW JERSEY

THE GOVERNOR

STATE COMMISSIONER OF HEALTH

DEPUTY STATE COMMISSIONER OF HEALTH

OFFICE OF THE COMMISSIONER

Comprehensive Health Planning Agency (State Health Planning Council) (Hill Burton Advisory Board)

Health Care Administration Board (Hospital Licensing)

Nursing Home Administrators Licensing Board

Public Health Council

Health Care Facilities Financing Authority

Crippled Children Commission

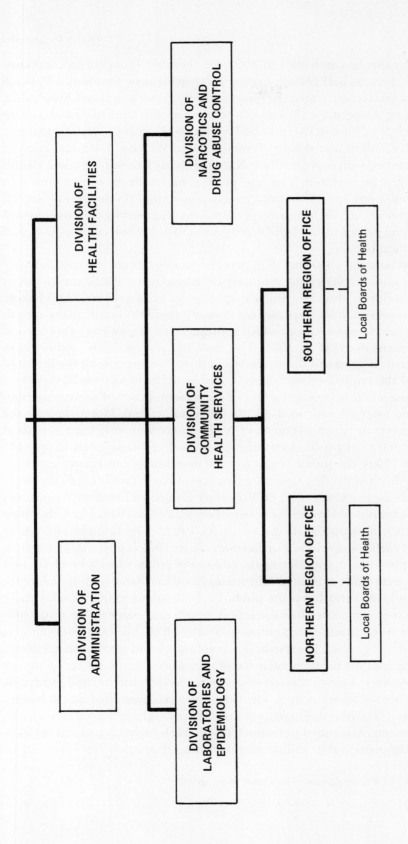

FIGURE 2.2. New Jersey Department of Health. Source: Courtesy of the New Jersey State Department of Health, Fall, 1975.

31

they generally can be condensed into three categories: (1) agencies concerned with specific diseases and certain organs or structures of the body—National Tuberculosis Association, American Cancer Society, American Heart Association, American Lung Association; (2) agencies concerned with the health and welfare of special groups—Planned Parenthood Federation of America, National Society for Crippled Children and Adults, National Social Welfare Assembly; and, (3) agencies concerned with coordination—National Safety Council, National Health Council. As can be deduced from the proceeding, seven basic functions and activities of voluntary health agencies are (1) pioneering, (2) demonstration, (3) supplementation of official health agency activities, (4) guarding citizen interest in health (5) promotion of health legislation, group planning and coordination, and (7) health education.

The period between 1940 and 1958 gave rise to a significant increase, not only in number, but also in variety of voluntary health agencies. Public contributions rose sevenfold during this eighteen-year span, from $188 million to $1.5 billion. This eighteen-year span also represented the latest significant spurt in the growth of voluntary health organizations which continued for at least five years beyond the establishment of HEW in 1953. The establishment of HEW, indirectly as much as directly, heightened the awareness of those concerned with the health of Americans of the unplanned and episodic nature of the expansion of voluntary agencies. Close scrutiny revealed a lack of correlation between agency activities and the broad interests and needs of the public in general. Moreover with the growth of government involvement in health care, and associated tax-based support, the notion of private philanthropy tended to lose some of its appeal.

In the late 1950s, the public began to raise questions about agency activities, purposes, methods of funding, and program operations, culminating in the establishment of the ad hoc Committee on Voluntary Health and Welfare Agencies in the United States funded by the Rockefeller Foundation in 1958. The Committee initiated a study and published the results in 1961.[8] The Committee's report corroborated earlier suspicions. Furthermore, in its 1961 report, the Committee expressed astonishment, considering the amount of public subsidy involved, that essentially "no carefully evaluated information [was] available on how voluntary agencies spend the [funds] that the public . . . [entrusted] to them each year."[9]

Approximately ten years after the report health professionals were still concerned about duplication, fragmentation, and conflict, not only between and among voluntary agencies, but also between voluntary and governmental health agencies.[10] Perhaps the recommendations of the ad hoc Committee on Voluntary Health and Welfare Agencies concerning review, modernization, and burden of responsibility are still worth noting. The Committee recommended that voluntary health agencies: (1) strengthen agency leadership through the recruitment, training, and retention of qualified personnel; (2) establish higher standards for local affiliates; (3) improve public information functions through better reporting of

[8]*Voluntary Health and Welfare Agencies in the United States, op. cit.*
[9]*Ibid.,* p. 13.
[10]Lloyd E9 Burton and Hugh H. Smith, *op. cit.*

finances, programs, and accomplishments; and (4) place greater emphasis on research and the application of new knowledge. Currently it can be argued that the preceding points are also applicable to official health agencies. Hence cooperation between official and voluntary health agencies, with the above as reference points, may represent a reasonable means of analyzing present issues and problems associated with resource utilization and the improvement of health and health care delivery.

Professional Health Associations

Professional health associations such as the American Medical Association (1847), the American Dental Association (1849), and the American Public Health Association (1872) represent distinct types of voluntary health organizations in that they are typified by some form of collective behavior, and are authorized to act as a given health profession's representative. Professional associations also influence the policies related to student admission to health professions education programs and, therefore, ultimately influence the supply of health manpower as well. Virtually all of the health and health-related professions have established their own organizations. Of principal concern to such organizations is the advancement of the standing of their particular profession within the health field, with the general public, and with official or governmental agencies. The latter point is of particular significance inasmuch as professional associations, in some cases, enjoy a quasi-official status in the accreditation and licensure area.

Although they have no statutory authority through government sanction of their accreditation function, professional associations influence health provessions educational establishments; affect their eligibility for governmental aid; and through the withholding of accreditation may, and most often do, influence licensure board decisions to prevent graduates of unaccredited institutions from taking licensure examinations. Not only do the respective accreditation councils consist of practitioners in the profession, but the same is true also of licensure boards. Obviously physician-dominated state licensure boards influence education in related health professions and also professional practice standards.

It is appropriate for the government to assess the entire area of private accreditation as well as its "unofficial sanction" of regional and professional accrediting associations.

Professional associations are usually organized on a national, state, and local level. At every level informational functions are performed through journals, magazines, and newsletters. State, local, and national meetings serve as forums for discussion of current issues and research of general and specific concern to health professionals. The membership, at each level, is usually organized into standing committees and/or sections that deal with spectific issues, problems, and concerns. Meetings are usually devoted to a central theme that has significance for the profession and obviously for the improvement of health care delivery, for example, the 1974 Annual Meeting of the American Public Health Association was devoted to the "Health of Non-White and Poor Americans."

Generally professional associations are organized around a president, governing boards, and councils elected by the general membership. They are supported through membership dues, subscriptions, and contributions, and usually retain an executive director and professional and clerical staff. Many associations are beginning to provide benefits for their memberships in the form of group health and life insurance programs, usually at very competitive prices. Staff, working through committees, also sponsor clinics, short courses, and seminars. Basically these organizations are concerned with the establishment and improvement of standards of membership and performance, the encouragement of innovation, research, and health education, as well as being active in traditional mutual protection activities such as legislative lobbying. As was the case with basic voluntary health agencies, professional associations are also currently characterized by efforts to deal with fragmentation, duplication, and conflicts of interest.

Health-Related Organizations

This category is comprised of philanthropic foundations and commercial or trade associations.

Foundations emerged as significant social institutions in the United States around the turn of the century and increased in number from eighteen in 1900 to 2839 in 1959, followed by a peak period of growth in the 1960s to the present 26,000.[11] These foundations are generally divided into five categories: (1) general purpose, (2) special purpose, (3) company-sponsored, (4) family, and (5) community.

Philanthropic foundations undertake a variety of activities, including the promotion and subsidy of local health programs, particularly in rural areas. They also subsidize basic research, public and professional education, and international health programs. Foundations are particularly noted for providing seed money for projects of potential significance to the improvement of health and health care delivery that have potential for attracting sustained support. Organizationally foundations usually have an executive officer, professional and support staff, and are governed by a board of directors.

Two of the three largest foundations, Ford and Lilly Endowment, have never given much to medicine. The fourth largest, Rockefeller, emphasized public health and medical science only for a thirty-year period after its founding in 1917. Two of the most significant supporters of health institutions are the W. W. Kellogg Foundation (seventh in assets) and the Robert Wood Johnson Foundation (second in assets). The Johnson Foundation is the current leader in medical philanthropy, accounting for one-quarter of foundation grants to medicine. Of a total of $20 million allocated in 1973 by the W. W. Kellogg Foundation, 60 % went to medicine.[12] Both of the latter foundations currently place considerable emphasis on the improvement of primary care.

During the 1960s with increased governmental support for research and medical programs, administered largely through the National Science Foundation and

[11]Edythe Cudlipp, "Private Foundations: How Big a Force in Medicine Today?, *Prism,* **3** (May 1975), pp. 33–36.
[12]*Ibid.*

the National Institutes of Health, foundation support decreased significantly. Moreover, as foundations have been classified as tax-free agencies, governmental probing into their activities has increased in recent years. With the passage of the Tax Reform Act of 1969, government has, in fact, forced foundations into divesting themselves of certain types of their assets, the impact of which, particularly in the health field, has yet to be fully studied.

Included among the health-related organizations are the commercial or trade associations and predominant among these are the several large insurance companies that have carried out extensive and valuable health education and demonstration programs. Trade associations also provide grants-in-aid and technical assistance, publish newsletters, magazines, and journals, lobby for health and safety legislation, and conduct and promote research studies. The Health Institute of America, the American Automobile Association, the National Dairy Council, and the National Livestock and Meat Board fall into this category. As noted by Hanlon, a word of caution is appropriate in dealing with trade associations inasmuch as "their programs are based primarily upon a desire for increased profits and improved public relations."[13]

HEALTH FACILITIES: THE PHYSICAL NATURE OF DELIVERY

The term health facility encompasses various hospitals, nursing homes, health centers, and clinics that serve as centers for the provision of health services and medical care. Each health facility represents the institutionalization of contact between providers and consumers of health services and medical care. The major categories of health facilities to be considered in this section are inpatient facilities, basically comprising short-term and long-term hospitals, which include specialty facilities; and ambulatory facilities, including neighborhood health centers, outpatient clinics, and private practice facilities.

Nonambulatory Medical Care Facilities

Hospitals represent the largest category of inpatient or nonambulatory medical care facilities in the United States. Hospitals are complex institutions, headed by boards of trustees, and medical and administrative staff. Hospitals are generally defined as facilities with at least six beds that are licensed by states as hospitals, or are operated by a state or federal agency as hospitals. In 1971 there were nearly 500 state agencies that licensed and regulated nonambulatory medical care facilities. State health departments generally regulate hospitals and nursing homes; however in the past there has been little policing by state agencies of general compliance with state policy. The primary professional association, the American Hospital Association (1899), annually publishes information describing the nature, organization, and operation of hospitals in the United States. Although the AHA has advisory power over its members, its powers are largely those

---

[13]John J. Hanlon, *op. cit.,* p. 243.

of persuasion. The two principal voluntary accreditation associations are the Joint Commission on Accreditation of Hospitals (1951) and the American Osteopathic Association (1897). Registration with AHA is required prior to an accreditation review by the Joint Commission. In January of 1974, 4900 hospitals in the United States were reported to be accredited by the Joint Commission.[14]

Hospitals, the major medical treatment centers in modern society, have been classified in many ways. The most common forms of classification are based on the type of patients treated and the type of ownership and control of the facility. Generally hospitals are designated as official (governmental), voluntary (nonprofit and taxfree), private (profit-oriented), and specialty. Obviously there are combinations of these four types, for example, official and specialty, voluntary and specialty, along with long-term and short-term combinations. Thus another means of classifying hospitals is by the length of duration of a patient's stay; short-term being thirty days or less, and long-term exceeding thirty days.

General medical and surgical hospitals and metropolitan and community general facilities represented 86% of hospitals of all types, based on the 1971 data. Over 95% of these medical care facilities were classified as short-term. Many of the large hospitals are sponsored by religious organizations. General medical and surgical hospitals are basically secondary care facilities, providing specialized consultant care, including diagnostic and treatment services of a surgical and nonsurgical nature. The health problems encountered are infrequent and specific and although they require hospitalization, the type of care provided can be classified as general and intermittent. Because of rising hospital costs and the many people who can rarely afford hospitalization many metropolitan hospital officials no longer advocate admission to emergency rooms for patients who cannot meet the cost. Figure 2.3 is illustrative of the typical organization of a hospital.

General medical and surgical hospitals receive their funds from four basic sources: (1) federal government (general and specific grants), (2) local governments, (3) direct fees, and (4) third party payment. Usually hospitals plan their budgets in anticipation of what they describe as bad payments and charity. However there does remain a legal uncertainty concerning the issue of a hospital's obligation to treat and care for genuine emergency cases.

A PATIENT'S BILL OF RIGHTS

When medical care is delivered in an institutional structure, the traditional physician-patient relationship takes on a new dimension. Legal precedent has established a hospital's responsibility to the patient. In recognition of these factors, the American Hospital Association's House of Delegates approved a Patient's Bill of Rights in February 1973.

[14]U. S. Department of Health, Education, and Welfare, *Health Resources Statistics: Health Manpower and Health Facilities, 1974* (Washington, D.C.: U. S. Department of Health, Education, and Welfare, 1974).

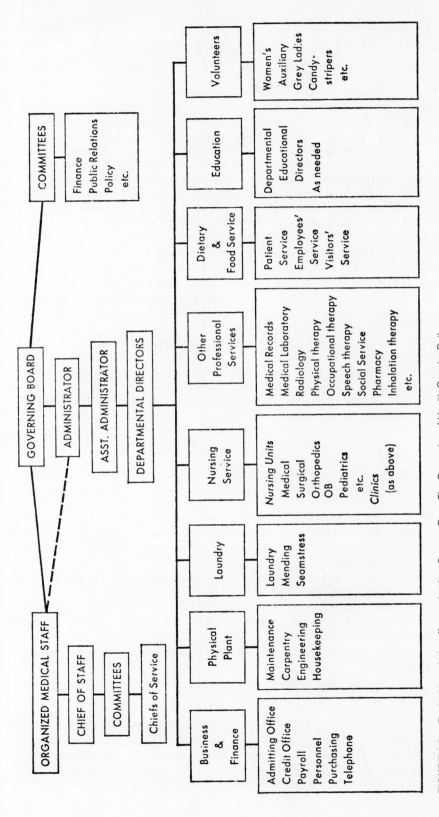

FIGURE 2.3. Typical hospital staff organization. Source: From *The Dynamics of Health Care* by Ruth M. French, 2nd edition, p. 60. Copyright © 1974 by McGraw–Hill Inc. Used with permission of McGraw–Hill Book Co.

1.   The patient has the right to considerate and respectful care.

2.   The patient has the right to obtain from his physician complete current information concerning his diagnosis, treatment, and prognosis in terms the patient can be reasonably expected to understand. When it is not medically advisable to give such information to the patient, the information should be made available to an appropriate person in his behalf. He has the right to know by name, the physician responsible for coordinating his care.

3.   The patient has the right to receive from his physician information necessary to give informed consent prior to the start of any procedure and/or treatment. Except in emergencies, such information for informed consent should include but not necessarily be limited to the specific procedure and/or treatment, the medically significant risks involved, and the probable duration of incapacitation. Where medically significant alternatives for care or treatment exist, or when the patient requests information concerning medical alternatives, the patient has the right to such information. The patient also has the right to know the name of the person responsible for the procedures and/or treatment.

4.   The patient has the right to refuse treatment to the extent permitted by law and to be informed of the medical consequences of his action.

5.   The patient has the right to every consideration of his privacy concerning his own medical care program. Case discussion, consultation, examination, and treatment are confidential and should be conducted discreetly. Those not directly involved in his care must have the permission of the patient to be present.

6.   The patient has the right to expect that all communications and records pertaining to his care should be treated as confidential.

7.   The patient has the right to expect that within its capacity a hospital must make reasonable response to the request of a patient for services. The hospital must provide evaluation, service, and/or referral as indicated by the urgency of the case. When medically permissible a patient may be transferred to another facility only after he has received complete information and explanation concerning the needs for and alternatives to such a transfer. The institution to which the patient is to be transferred must first have accepted the patient for transfer.

8.   The patient has the right to obtain information as to any relationship of his hospital to other health care and educational institutions insofar as his care is concerned. The patient has the right to obtain information as to the existence of any professional relationship among individuals, by name, who are treating him.

9.   The patient has the right to be advised if the hospital proposes to engage in or perform human experimentation affecting his care or treatment. The patient has the right to refuse to participate in such research projects.

10.   The patient has the right to expect reasonable continuity of care. He has the right to know in advance what appointment times and physicians are available and where. The patient has the right to expect that the hospital will provide a mechanism whereby he is informed by his physician or a delegate of the physician of the patient's continuing health care requirements following discharge.

11.   The patient has the right to examine and receive an explanation of his bill regardless of source of payment.

12.   The patient has the right to know what hospital rules and regulations apply to his conduct as a patient.

No catalogue of rights can guarantee for the patient the kind of treatment he has a right to expect. A hospital has many functions to perform, including the prevention and treatment of disease, the education of both health professionals and patients, and the conduct of clinical research. All these activities must be conducted with an overriding concern for the patient, and, above all, the recognition of his dignity as a human being.

Success in achieving this recognition assures success in the defense of the rights of the patient.

Source.   American Hospital Association, *A Patient's Bill of Rights* (Chicago: American Hospital Association, 1972). Reprinted with the permission of the American Hospital Association.

Table 2.1 contains data on inpatient hospital facilities and beds, by type, for the years 1967 to 1972. Table 2.2 lists the number of hospitals by type of ownership for the year 1972. The data in Table 2.1 show a decline in specialty (long-term) hospitals from 1967 to 1972, reflecting a change in the manner of treating certain diseases, obviously with desirable and undesirable consequences. After a peak year in 1969, the data also shown a decline in general medical and surgical hospitals, although the decline is not as significant as in the case of long-term facilities. On the negative side many chronically ill patients are now being treated in higher cost, acute hospital facilities, which, incidentally, increased in number by about 7% from 1961 to 1972. On the positive side there has been a change in the concept of what constitutes the provision of care—a change to a concept that embraces the whole person—with a resultant decrease in the number of high cost specialty hospitals. There has also been a decrease in the total number of hospital

TABLE 2.1.   Hospital Facilities: 1967 through 1972

Type	1967	1969	1971	1972[a]
General Medical and Surgical	6685	6715	6607	6491
Specialty	1462	1130	1071	990
Psychiatric	573	506	533	497
Chronic Disease	333[b]	189[b]	90	78
Tuberculosis	169	116	99	75
Other[c]	387[b]	319	349	340

Beds in Hospital Facilities: 1967 through 1972

General Medical and Surgical	958,729	989,733	1,004,799	1,014,064
Specialty	672,372	576,175	503,189	452,976
Psychiatric	545,913	477,309	418,487	372,603
Chronic Disease	61,211[b]	40,790[b]	24,614	23,962
Tuberculosis	33,335	20,960	17,806	12,351
Other[c]	31,913	37,116	42,282	44,060

[a] Preliminary data.
[b] Includes geriatric hospitals for 1967 and 1969.
[c] Includes eye, ear, nose and throat hospitals; epileptic, alcoholism, narcotic, maternity, orthopedic, physical rehabilitation, and other hospitals.

Source.   Adapted from U. S. Department of Health, Education, and Welfare, *Health Resources Statistics: Health Manpower and Health Facilities, 1974* (Washington, D.C.: U. S. Department of Health, Education, and Welfare, 1974), pp. 345–346.

TABLE 2.2.   Hospitals by Type of Ownership: 1972

Type of Ownership	Total[a]	General Medical and Surgical	Specialty
Government	2770	2248	522
Federal	405	369	36
State–Local	2365	1879	299
Proprietary	986	811	88
Voluntary	3725	3432	81

[a] Preliminary data.
Source. Adapted from U. S. Department of Health, Education, and Welfare, *Health Resources Statistics: Health Manpower and Health Facilities, 1974* (Washington, D.C.: U. S. Department of Health, Education, and Welfare, 1974), p. 365.

beds and admissions. The preceding notwithstanding, hospital costs have risen dramatically in recent years. Per diem costs, for example, have more than tripled in the past ten years. Havighurst attributes the poor market performance of hospitals to the following:

First, health insurance has relieved most consumers of concern about the cost of the health care they consume, allowing costs to rise. Second, most third-party payments are on a liberal, noncompetitive, cost-reimbursement basis, providing hospitals with both a tidy income and assurance that revenues cannot fall below costs at normal occupancy levels. Third, physicians and hospitals have little interest, either directly or as fiduciaries for their insured patients, in holding down either costs or consumption and indeed have both the incentive and the opportunity (in view of consumer ignorance and traditions of professional independence) to increase their income by prescribing or encouraging unnecessary care. Fourth, most hospitals are charitable, non-profit enterprises, meaning that they may attract philanthropic funds irrespective of real need and that these funds and any excess earning (which can be plentiful) cannot be distributed but must somehow be reinvested in projects which are confined to the health industry. These projects are selected by managers and trustees who are effectively responsible to no one but each other, the medical staff, and perhaps some peculiar outside constituency such as a religious or fraternal organization. Fifth, hospitals are forced to engage in non-price competition for doctors, which frequently takes the form of providing expensive but inefficiently used facilities.[15]

The last point suggests that hospitals on the whole are underutilized. Indeed except for some urban areas, occupancy in all hospitals rarely reaches a consistent figure above 80%. Of obvious importance to increased cost is the fact that there has been an increase of almost a full day in the average length of stay in hospitals during the past ten years. As noted by Rogatz, "when occupancy rates are low . . . the consequence can easily be an increase in average length of stay and in . . . occupancy rate."[16] He further notes that the Hill-Burton Act of 1946 undoubtedly "has played a major role in producing our oversupply of beds. While there was merit to the original concept, insufficient attention was paid to the fact that a hospital should be part of a carefully planned health care delivery system,

[15]Clark C. Havighurst, *Public Utility Regulation for Hospitals* (Washington, D.C.: American Enterprise Institute, 1973), p. 2.
[16]Peter Rogatz, "Let's Get Rid of Those Surplus Hospital Beds," *Prism,* **2** (October 1974), p. 13.

assuring coordination among ambulatory, emergency, and inpatient facilities, with careful attention to assigning graded responsibilities to different institutions within a given region, according to the capabilities of each."[17] The recent institution of certificate-of-need as well as rate and utilization review policies and procedures are steps in the right direction.

Although much rhetoric and some trends suggest that hospitals are becoming focal points of the delivery of comprehensive health service, for example, community health centers, Somers argues, albeit on the basis of a crude study:

> . . . the average hospital of the early 1970s remains pretty much what it was a decade ago—a citadel of specialized, technologically-oriented inpatient care. Efforts to broaden the spectrum to include ambulatory care, preventive care, psychiatric care, rehabilitation, social services, and extended care have made some impact, especially in the larger hospitals in the Mid-Atlantic—and to a lesser extent the Pacific—states. In most of the country, however, most conspicuously in the South, such services are few and far between.[18]

The pacesetters, by type of ownership, are the voluntary hospitals, followed by governmental and then proprietary establishments. Of equal significance for urban communities is the observation that "there has been a steady withdrawal of the hospital and its staff from the community needing primary care."[19] In addition the municipal institutions, run primarily for the poor and near poor, have always been under attack for their inefficiency and the impersonal nature of the services provided. When we add to this the fact that the private practice of medicine in the inner city has been declining steadily in recent years we begin to understand better the plight of the urban dweller and the changing pattern of medical care in urban areas. It is true that hospital outpatient departments have expanded and that welfare medical care programs have developed. Unfortunately these efforts are characterized as fragmented, uncoordinated, piecemeal, and stopgap. Obviously there is still a lack of adequate health facilities and health care services in the urban areas of this country.

The existence of proprietary hospitals in urban areas has compounded the problem because they compete with the voluntary hospitals—institutions with responsibilities that are more comprehensive with respect to services rendered and publics served. Proprietary hospitals turn away nonpaying patients, do not usually provide outpatient and emergency services, encourage short-term patients, and avoid expensive and difficult technology. Thus by competing for the marginally sick and more fiscally sound, the proprietary hospitals end up parasitizing the local voluntary hospitals. For these reasons increasing emphasis is being placed on planned regionalization of health facilities.

Although general medical and surgical hospitals have been involved in medical education for some time, beginning with the rotating internship, only recently has the importance of medical education in the community hospital become recog-

[17]*Ibid.*, p. 14.
[18]Anne R. Somers, "The Hospital's Responsibility for Community Health Services," *Twenty Years of Community Medicine,* A Hunterdon Medical Center Symposium (New Jersey: Columbia Publishing Co., Inc., 1974), p. 149.
[19]Lloyd E. Burton and Hugh H. Smith, *op. cit.,* p. 536.

nized by the academic health center and the public. Previously hospitals had only
their own interests at heart—improved quality of care, including continuing
education for staff, and recruitment. No efforts were made to become a focal
point for coordinating and managing the delivery of health and medical care
services to communities. Even at the present time only about 10% of the nation's
hospitals are affiliated with academic health centers although these hospitals
contain about half of all hospital beds.

Teaching hospitals are the most complex of all health facilities because they
serve as classrooms and laboratories for general medical and graduate clinical
education, as centers for medical research, and as patient-care and community-
service facilities. In the fall of 1971 there were 108 medical schools in the United
States. University-based hospitals, while serving as centers for medical education
and research, have generally managed to remain uninvolved with their communities, even though there has been the tendency to locate teaching hospitals in
urban inner city areas. In such facilities there may be a tendency to view teaching
as a means to an end. Knowles states:

The patient population is highly select, representing in the teaching service a gathering of
the aged and medically indigent with acute, advanced, complicated, and frequently rare
somatic diseases. There is little emphasis on the social and economic factors of disease and
hospitalization, save for brief recording of the type of health insurance and the occupational and family histories.[20]

Thus the amount of emphasis placed on patient care can be viewed as a means
of differentiation not only in terms of various levels of hospital care, but even
among hospitals themselves.

University-based teaching hospitals are the principal sites for the provision of
tertiary care or highly specialized and technologically based intensive care. The
health problems usually encountered are rare, complicated, episodic, and require
a biomedical data base along with complex equipment and highly specialized staff.
The development of teaching hospitals, with an emphasis on specialized care,
obviously has influenced the decline in status and absolute numbers of general
practitioners and concern for the provision of primary care.

Affiliation with a medical school has a strong impact on hospital costs. Teaching
hospitals tend to have costs per admission about 11% higher than hospitals not
affiliated with medical schools.[21] As noted by Knowles:

The bill for staying in a teaching hospital is higher than that for staying in a community
hospital because of the added cost of training nurses, physicians and other health workers,
and because of the higher cost of caring for patients with complex illnesses . . . . [22]

Accordingly teaching hospitals provide superb care for the affluent and even the
poor who are fortunate enough to become patients. However the teaching hospi-

[20]John H. Knowles, "The Unseen Ostrich in Our Teaching Hospitals," *Prism* (November 1973), p. 14.
[21]Karen Davis, "Hospital Costs and the Medicare Program," *Social Security Bulletin,* **36** (August 1973),
pp. 18–36.
[22]John H. Knowles, "The Hospital," *Scientific American,* **229** (September 1973), p. 135.

tals are guilty (perhaps more so than others because they are academic health centers) of fragmentation and duplication. Moreover because they usually function independently in the areas where they are located, this lack of coordination adds to the inefficiency and cost of medical care.

Specialty hospitals are health facilities that usually treat specific illnesses or conditions and do not, therefore, provide comprehensive services. Most specialty hospitals are long-term. As can be deduced from Table 2.1, specialty hospitals comprised approximately 13% of all hospitals in 1972, with psychiatric facilities leading this category. Such facilities fall into four specific categories: children's hospitals, mental hospitals, chronic disease hospitals, and tuberculosis hospitals. Children's hospitals can be further subdivided into those affiliated with medical schools, those equivalent to a pediatrics department in a large general hospital, and those designed to treat special problems of children.

Tuberculosis hospitals are organized to provide services for people with related pulmonary ailments as well as tuberculosis itself. They provide restorative and rehabilitative services. Facilities for the mentally ill include short-term diagnostic and treatment centers, as well as long-term rehabilitative and custodial care facilities.

Almost all psychiatric and tuberculosis hospitals are governmentally owned and operated.[23] Of the seventy-five reported in 1972, seventy were operated by state or local government, with the remaining five listed as nonprofit. In the case of mental hospitals 328 (29 federal and 299 state and local) were governmental, 88 proprietary, and 81 nonprofit. There was a gradual decline in these facilities between 1967 and 1972. This is due in large measure to advancements in the prevention and care of tuberculosis since the turn of the century, and in the care of the mentally ill. Additionally short-term general hospitals have begun to provide care formerly given in tuberculosis and mental institutions. The increase in nursing care and other parahospital facilities from 1967 to 1971 has also influenced the decline in these facilities. Nursing care and related facilities increased from 19,141 in 1967 to 22,004 in 1971, representing an increase in beds from 836,554 to 1,201,598.[24]

Chronic disease hospitals place emphasis on the provision of services to patients with a variety of conditions requiring extended rehabilitative and restorative care. Because of the expense involved and the usual age of the hospitalized person, most chronic disease facilities are governmentally owned and operated. Of the seventy-eight facilities identified in 1972, forty-nine were owned and operated by state and local government, eight were proprietary and twenty-one were nonprofit. It appears that private medicine has not shown adequate interest in the chronically ill, particularly individuals in poor financial condition.

As noted in Table 2.1, there has been a significant decline in chronic disease facilities in recent years, during which time the number of persons sixty-five years of age and over increased from 16.6 million in 1960 to 19.9 million in 1970,

[23]*Health Resources Statistics, op. cit.*
[24]*Ibid.*

representing 9.2 and 9.8% of the total population.[25] Because chronic and degenerative diseases are highly correlated with aging the downturn in these facilities is somewhat surprising. Interestingly patients sixty-five years old and over in chronic disease hospitals decreased from 54.5% of all patients in 1960 to 52.4% in 1970.[26] However the total number of patients in chronic disease and related facilities increased over the same time span from 42,476 to 67,120. One would have expected an increase in chronic disease facilities. It may be that modern medicine and the significant increase in nursing care and related facilities (approximatety 8000 from 1963 to 1971) account for the counterbalancing. Medicare, for example, provides support of up to one hundred days of extended care for persons sixty-five years of age or older.

Long-term care facilities, the last category of inpatient facilities to be considered, include county homes, convalescent nursing homes, and homes for the aged. Long-term care facilities represent a relatively new institution in the United States. Two pieces of legislation have catalyzed the development of long-term care facilities: the Social Security Act of 1935, which provided financial support in the form of old-age unemployment insurance to the aged; and the Medicare legislation of 1965, under which over 19.9 million Americans sixty-five years of age and older become eligible for government-insured hospitalization. The Medicare law provides for stays of up to ninety days in a hospital and one hundred days in an extended care facility in any two hundred and fifty day period for persons sixty-five and over. Under Title XVIII an extended care facility is a specific type of long-term care facility. Title XVIII describes an extended care facility as one that provides skilled nursing or rehabilitative and related services as an extension of hospital care. To receive Medicare benefits, a patient must receive at least three days of prior hospital care and must be admitted to the extended care home not more than two weeks after hospital discharge. According to Somers and Somers the objective of extended care facilities is to relieve hospitals of Medicare patients who can be transferred, and therefore to lower program costs.[27] In order to qualify for participation in Medicare, an extended care facility must have a transfer agreement with a certified hospital and must meet minimum medical standards. The indigent or medically indigent are also eligible for skilled nursing home care under Title XIX, Medicaid. Of the five basic services covered under Medicaid, a federal and state cooperative program, one is the provision of skilled nursing home care for eligible individuals twenty-one years of age and older.

In 1966 long-term care facilities came under the accreditation auspices of the Joint Commission on Accreditation of Hospitals. Accreditation standards were established by the Commission in 1968 and, in 1971, the Joint Commission established the Accreditation Council for Long-Term Care Facilities. With the enactment of the Social Security Amendments of 1972, facilities formerly

[25]United States Bureau of the Census, *Statistical Abstract of the United States, 1974* (Washington, D.C.: U.S. Department of Commerce, 1974).
[26]United States Department of Commerce, *Social Indicators, 1973* (Washington, D.C.: Office of Management and Budget, 1973).
[27]Herman M. Somers and Anne R. Somers, *Medicare and the Hospitals: Issues and Prospects* (Washington, D.C.: The Brookings s Institution, 1967).

classified as extended care under Medicare and as skilled nursing homes under Medicaid were consolidated into the category "skilled nursing facilities." Of 2056 accredited facilities in 1973, 1057 were classified as extended care, 824 as nursing care, and 175 as resident or domiciliary care.[28]

Prior to 1965 long-term care facilities were definitely of questionable quality and in many instances an outright disgrace to a civilized society. Although problems of abuse, poor treatment, deliberate physical injury, unsanitary conditions, poor food and preparation, misappropriation and theft, and inadequate control of drugs still persist, the Medicare Act of 1965, as noted above, did facilitate the establishment of standards for long-term care facilities. Unfortunately there is little uniformity and enforcement among the fifty states with respect to minimum standards, terminology, definitions, regulations, or licensure requirements.

Long-term care facilities, which range in size from less than twenty-five to more than five hundred beds, increased by 32% from 1963 to 1971. In actual numbers long-term care facilities and beds increased from 16,701 and 568,560 to 22,004 and 1,201,598 respectively in 1971, with 1,075,724 persons in residence.[29] Additionally nursing care and related homes housed fifty-two persons aged sixty-five and over for every one thousand such persons in the general population of the United States.[30]

In 1971 "78 percent of nursing care and related homes with 67 percent of all beds were proprietary. . . . Voluntary non-profit homes, including those owned and operated by fraternal groups and religious orders, constituted 16 percent of all 'homes.' The 'homes' owned and operated by public agencies (local, state, and federal government) comprise the remaining six percent."[31] The fact that the Social Security Act of 1935 precluded the dependent aged from assistance if they were housed in public facilities spurred the development of proprietary agencies. Although the Act was later amended to include public institutions, it explains the initial advantage and the continuing dominance of the proprietaries and the profit motivation in this area of health care.

Ideally long-term care facilities provide care in an environment as physically and psychologically homelike as possible. The most recent health facilities report of HEW classifies long-term care facilities as follows: nursing care; personal care homes with nursing; personal care homes without nursing; and domiciliary care.[32] Because of wide variations in definition of the term "nursing home," complete understanding of the long-term care industry is obscured. Although the names of the institutions may differ, one or more or all four of the following services will generally be offered:

1. *Residential care* includes room and board, laundry facilities, and personal courtesies such as help with shopping and correspondence.

---

[28]*Health Resources Statistics, op. cit.*
[29]*Ibid.*
[30]*Ibid.*
[31]*Ibid.,* p. 382.
[32]*Ibid.*

2. *Personal care* involves such services as help in walking, getting in and out of bed, bathing, dressing, and preparation of special diets.

3. *Nursing care* requires professional skills and includes administering of medications, catheterizations, and similar procedures ordered by the attending physician.

4. *Therapeutic care* includes physical, occupational, and speech and hearing therapies together with recreational facilities and social work services.

The Joint Commission on Accreditation of Hospitals, specifically influenced by Medicare legislation, accredits two types of institutions which may be called nursing homes. The two types differ primarily in terms of the degree of nursing care provided:

1. Nursing homes that provide twenty-four hour a day nursing service under the supervision of a full-time registered nurse.

2. Nursing homes that provide nursing service under the supervision of a full-time registered nurse, but in which licensed nursing personnel need not be on duty twenty-four hours a day.

Both types of facilities are required to have a planned program of care for each individual patient, written nursing procedures, and a rehabilitation program which helps patients to reach a maximum level of self-care. As would be expected, a licensed physician must regularly care for patients, with visits at least once a month. Usually the homes must retain at least two licensed physicians for advice and consultation. The cost of nursing care, obviously, is tied to the nature of the facility and the range of services provided.

It is generally accepted that some nursing homes are exploiting both their patients and the Medicare and Medicaid programs. The Senate Finance Committee in its 1969 hearings concluded that:

Unnecessary services are being provided on a widespread basis in nursing homes. . . . The majority of the extended care facilities [nursing homes licensed for Medicare] participating in the program do not fully meet the standards set in the law and regulations. . . . Evidence exists that "kick back" arrangements between suppliers—such as pharmacies and physical therapists—and nursing homes may be widespread. . . . There is substantial evidence that many physicians are engaging in the practice known as "gang visits" to nursing home and hospital patients. Under this practice a physician may see as many as 30, 40 and 50 patients in a day in the same facility—regardless of whether the visit is medically necessary or whether any service is actually furnished. . . . Another cause for concern is the alarming growth in chain operations in the nursing home field. Some of these chains actively solicit physician purchase of stock to assure a high occupancy rate. Other chains purchase stock of hospital supply and pharmaceutical supply houses. This leads to arrangements with respect to intercompany sales at what may very well be higher than would otherwise be paid—a form of captive market used to milk the Medicare trust funds. . . . [The Committee] found inflated depreciation allowances and many sales of facilities at inflated prices in order to get maximum payments from Medicare.[33]

[33]Mary A. Mendelson, *Tender Loving Greed* (New York: Alfred A. Knopf, Inc., 1974), pp. 25–26.

According to Mendelson, the General Accounting Office reportedly conducted a study of a sample of nursing care homes in New York in 1972 ". . . and concluded that they were earning a 450% return in five years on their investment."[34]

The American Nursing Home Association and HEW advised the U. S. Senate Committee on Finance in 1967 that as many as 50% of Medicaid recipients in skilled nursing homes were not in need of skilled nursing home care.[35] Nursing homes account for about one-third of all Medicaid funds and the federal government pays 50–80% of Medicaid bills; President Ford's 1976 budget request for HEW included more than 50% of federal health expenditures for Medicaid and Medicare.[36] [37] It is no small wonder that the federal government, as well as many states, including New Jersey, New York, and California, investigates the nursing home industry.

Ambulatory Health Facilities

Currently the bulk of medical care is provided in an ambulatory setting. Ambulatory facilities are the principal sites for the provision of primary care, including health promotion and maintenance, prevention of disease, and early diagnosis, treatment, and rehabilitation. As noted in an earlier section, only 10% of a population at risk is admitted to a hospital and only 2% to academic health center hospitals. In addition it has been estimated that as much as 85% of all ambulatory care is provided outside the academic health centers and affiliated teaching hospitals.[38] Thus the vast majority of individuals in need of health services are obtaining such services in hospital outpatient clinics, neighborhood health clinics, or private practice facilities.

Not many of the different types of ambulatory health facilities are licensed on an independent basis, as most are located in a health facility that is already licensed. A variety of state agencies have licensure authority for outpatient facilities and, as with long-term care facilities, there are varying licensure policies and standards. Although accreditation programs have been established for this type of health facility, participation is on a voluntary basis.

In view of the fact that outpatient health facilities are classified by HEW into sixteen specific categories, ranging from ambulance services to suicide prevention centers, this section is limited in scope and considers only neighborhood health centers, hospital outpatient clinics, and private practice facilities, both solo and group.

Neighborhood health centers originated in the early 1900s to provide ambula-

---

[34]*Ibid.,* p. 30.
[35]U. S. Senate, *Medicare and Medicaid: Problems, Issues, and Alternatives* (Washington, D.C.: U. S. Government Printing Office, 1970).
[36]Mary A. Mendelson, *op. cit.,* p. 39.
[37]"Medicare Takes Most Funds of Federal Health Allotment," *The Nation's Health* (March 1975) pp. 1,5.
[38]Nora Piore, "Discussions" section of "The Evaluation of a Primary Care System," *Primary Care: Where Medicine Fails,* edited by Spyros Andreopoulous (New York: John Wiley & Sons, Inc., 1974), pp. 144–153.

tory services to the poor in the cities.[39] The centers, financed by local taxes, philanthropy, or both, were concerned basically with controlling communicable diseases and preventing infant malnutrition. The early centers were organized by voluntary organizations or local health departments. Although the movement declined during the 1930s, it was revived again during the War on Poverty in the early 1960s. Presently many groups, including community corporations, hospitals, medical schools, and medical societies, are sponsoring neighborhood health centers.[40] While there are few definitive data available on the number and nature of neighborhood health centers, it was estimated that there were 300 to 500 such centers in the United States in 1973.[41]

With the passage of PL 89-749 in 1966, The Public Health Service Act, specifically Section 314(e), federally supported comprehensive neighborhood health centers came off the drawing board with their major focus on the delivery of service to the urban poor and disadvantaged. In mid-1973, 117 federally supported centers were in operation.[42] Approximately 75% of the centers are located in urban areas, with the remaining 25% in rural areas. The federal centers have received their funding through either the Public Health Service Act, the Office of Economic Opportunity, or both. Between 1965 and 1971 a total of $418.7 million had been invested by the federal government. With the demise of the Office of Economic Opportunity the administration of grant programs for federally supported neighborhood health centers was shifted to the Health Services Administration Division of the Public Health Service in the fall of 1973.

In the 1960s neighborhood health centers were established and financed as demonstration programs which encompassed medical (including preventive and therapeutic) and dental care. Figure 2.4 is illustrative of the services provided by a "model" neighborhood health center. Major emphasis is placed on preventive care and early diagnosis. The range of services provided by neighborhood health centers obviously varies according to funding and size. In this regard neighborhood health centers have been hampered by dependency on the demonstration project approach to funding, with federal appropriations varying because of constant budgetary changes—appropriations being closely correlated with the nature of the political climate. The impoundment of federal funds during the Nixon Administration and further cutbacks recommended by President Ford compounded the funding problems of the federally supported centers. In the Ford budget funding for neighborhood health centers was cut by $41 million from the *revised* fiscal year 1975 budget, a reduction of $155 million.[43] Centers have also encountered difficulty in the past in obtaining recognition as providers by Medicare, Medicaid, and other third-party agencies. Another problem has been inability to attract and retain qualified personnel. Yet if properly funded and

[39]J. D. Stoeckle and L. M. Candid, "The Neighborhood Health Center: Reform of Ideas of Yesterday and Today," *The New England Journal of Medicine,* **280,** (June 1969), pp. 1385–1391.
[40]Donald C. McLeod, "Clinical Pharmacy Practice in a Community Health Center," *Journal of the American Pharmaceutical Association,* **60** (February 1971), pp. 56–59.
[41]*Health Resources Statistics, op. cit.*
[42]*Ibid.*
[43]*The Nation's Health, op. cit.*

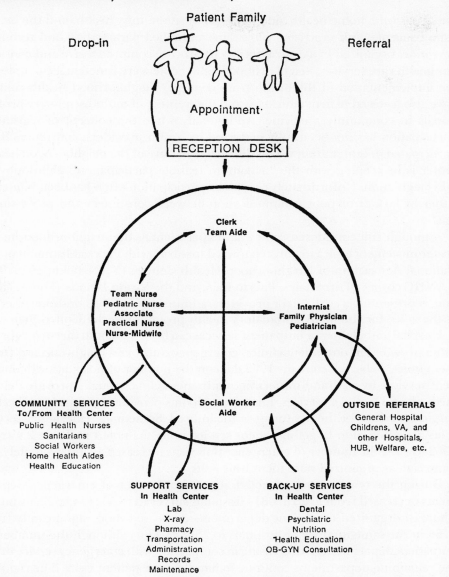

FIGURE 2.4. Family health care team model showing functional relationships with other services in and outside of the health center. From *Narrowing Our Medical Care Gap* by Joseph D. Alter, p. 39. Copyright 1972 by Joseph D. Alter. Reprinted by permission of Exposition Press, Inc., Hicksville, N.Y. 11801.

managed, neighborhood health centers could help to decrease the overall cost of health care.

The impact of federally supported neighborhood health centers has been noticeable, particularly in terms of transfer of demand for primary care services and in the restructuring of health care programs. For example, centers have contributed to the development of new health careers (e.g., nurse practitioner, nurse midwife, home health aide), interest in community health, and the health team concept. With practicing physicians and allied paramedical and technical personnel organized in a central facility to provide comprehensive and continuous health care services, neighborhood health centers are functional examples of the implementation of the health team concept. Neighborhood health centers have also fostered patient education and the training of multidisciplinary professionals in community medicine. Additionally while the concept of consumer participation has not been fully endorsed by health providers, consumers have participated in center affairs. This distinctive feature of the neighborhood health center is in keeping with the "maximum feasible participation" philosophy of OEO legislation. Unfortunately consumer participation often has been hindered either by lack of or poor communication between consumers and professional staff.

Although still considered somewhat experimental, the neighborhood health center movement took a major step toward maturity with the establishment of the National Association of Neighborhood Health Centers (NANHC) in 1970. The NANHC covers all fifty states, Puerto Rico, and the Virgin Islands. The Association, representing a coalition of providers, administrators, and consumers, serves as the voice for the many ambulatory health programs in the United States.

Hospital ambulatory or outpatient services can be divided into three categories: those provided in outpatient clinics, emergency units, and diagnostic and treatment units. Table 2.3 contains 1972 data on the number of hospitals with outpatient services by type and ownership. Outpatient clinics usually provide dental, medical, and surgical services. Emergency rooms provide immediate medical or surgical services for the treatment of the injured. Sometimes, emergency service units are integral to large outpatient service units. As noted in Table 2.4 from 1962 to 1972 the number of emergency unit visits increased at approximately the same rate as organized outpatient unit visits.

During the ten-year period noted above the number of emergency departments decreased from 5725 in 6814 hospitals surveyed to 5023 in 6622 hospitals; whereas, organized outpatient departments decreased more significantly from 3165 in the same number of hospitals to 2038.[44] Thus although the number of outpatient departments is decreasing in comparison with emergency service units, the remaining departments continue to handle more patient visits. The ratios of department to patient visits in emergency units for 1962 and 1972 were 1 : 3493 and 1 : 11,945 respectively; for outpatient departments the ratios were 1 : 10,742 and 1 : 47,596.[45] As would be expected from the sharp rise in outpatient visits, a comparison of inpatient admissions to outpatient visits for the years 1953, 1967, and 1972 reveals that the ratios of outpatient visits to inpatient admissions were approximately 2:1, 4:1, and 7:1 respectively.[44] [46]

The data are convincing evidence that there is a dramatic increase in the

[44]*Health Resources Statistics, op. cit.*
[45]American Hospital Association, *Hospital Statistics, 1972* (Chicago: American Hospital Association, 1973). Also prior annual editions.
[46]American Hospital Association, *Outpatient Health Care: The Role of Hospitals* (Chicago: American Hospital Association, 1969).

TABLE 2.3. Ownership of Hospitals with Outpatient Services by Type of Hospital: 1972

	Hospitals with Outpatient Services[a]	Type of hospital						
		General Medical and Surgical	Specialty					
			Total	Psychiatric	Chronic Disease	Tuberculosis	Other[b]
Ownership							
Government	2605	2239	366	233	26	54	53
Federal	405	369	36	29	—	—	7
State-Local	2200	1870	330	204	26	54	46
Proprietary	861	753	108	55	2	—	51
Nonprofit	3639	3396	243	70	11	3	159
Church	836	792	44	10	2	1	31
Other	2803	2604	199	60	9	2	128
Total	7105	6388	717	358	39	57	263

[a] Preliminary data.
[b] Includes eye, ear, nose, and throat hospitals; epileptic hospitals; alcoholism hospitals; narcotic hospitals; maternity hospitals; orthopedic hospitals; physical rehabilitation hospitals; and other hospitals.
Source. Adapted from U. S. Department of Health, Education, and Welfare, *Health Resources Statistics: Health Manpower and Health Facilities, 1974* (Washington, D.C.: U. S. Department of Health, Education, and Welfare, 1974), p. 481.

TABLE 2.4. Patient Visits to Emergency and Organized Outpatient Units: 1962 through 1972

| | Patient Visits (in millions) | |
Year	Emergency Units	Organized Outpatient Units
1962	20	34
1963	25	48
1964	27	46
1965	30	—
1966	33	58
1967	35	55
1968	36	58
1969	40	53
1970	45	63
1971	51	82
1972	60	97

Source. Adapted from American Hospital Association, *Hospital Statistics* annual editions.

provision of medical care in an ambulatory setting and that organized outpatient clinics continue to be the principal providers of hospital ambulatory care, although emergency units are beginning to provide some nonemergency services. The data in Table 2.3 also show that the majority of hospitals providing outpatient services are nonprofit general medical and surgical facilities, followed by governmental and proprietary facilities in descending order.

Earlier we noted that general medical and surgical hospitals tend to be located in large population centers. In this regard outpatient facilities historically have served the medical needs in the education of physicians and other health professionals. As noted by Nora Piore in *Primary Care: Where Medicine Fails:* "Prior to 1966 outpatient departments were chiefly a charity service for indigent patients, and as late as 1966, clinic charges generally ranged between 50 cents and $5."[47] Piore comments further that:

While little systematic information is available on the true costs of hospital outpatient services, and especially on appropriate allocations of hospital overhead to the cost of these services, it is clear that the costs have risen steeply. House staff, once paid subsistence allowances, now receive quite respectable salaries. Attendants and unskilled hospital employees whose below-minimum wages were once heavily subsidized by supplementary welfare payments, are now largely covered by minimum wage legislation and collectively bargained contracts. At the same time, outpatient service revenue has also increased. . . . In 1968, revenue from services to outpatients accounted for more than seven percent of all voluntary hospital patient revenue. It continued to rise, per visit and as a percent of total hospital income, increasing 70 percent in 1968-1970, compared with a 50 percent rise in revenue from services to inpatients. Average revenue per visit in the United States as a whole rose from $10 to $14, a 42 percent increase in that two-year period, and the outpatient component of total voluntary hospital revenue reached 8 percent by 1970. It is higher today.[48]

Of further significance is a 1969 report published by the National Center for Health Statistics that suggests there are racial differences in the use of outpatient clinics, with nonwhites three times as likely as whites to obtain physician services in a hospital clinic or emergency room (see Figure 2.5).[49] The racial differences did not seem to be income based. Even for persons with family incomes of $7000 and above, nonwhites were still three times more likely to see physicians in hospital outpatient clinics or emergency rooms. Unfortunately the study data pertain to a time frame prior to the full implementation of Medicare and Medicaid, and the study has not been updated.

It should also be noted that the physicians staffing outpatient and emergency rooms are usually interns or residents, one-third of whom are graduates of foreign medical schools. Such staff usually have less training and experience. In this regard there is a real need to continue to move toward upgrading the view of ambulatory services in hospitals. The involvement of active staff, not just interns, residents, and fellows in both inpatient and outpatient services, has to be accomplished if the atmosphere is to be successfully changed. The problem of continuity of care, inherent in the provision of ambulatory services, also has to be accomplished, and within the context of total care.

The last category of hospital ambulatory services, the ancillary or special diagnostic and therapeutic services, includes specialized units such as pathology, x-ray, electrocardiology, inhalation therapy, physical and occupational therapy, and

[47]Nora Piore, *op. cit.,* p. 146.
[48]*Ibid.,* p. 146.
[49]National Center for Health Statistics, *Differentials in Health Characteristics by Color, U. S., July 1965–June 1967* (Washington, D.C.: U. S. Department of Health, Education, and Welfare, 1969).

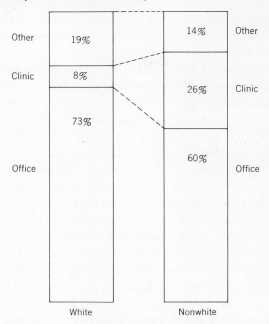

FIGURE 2.5. Percentage distribution of physician visits by place of visit according to color, July 1966 through June 1967. Adapted from National Center for Health Statistics, *Differentials in Health Characteristics by Color, U. S., July, 1965–June, 1967* (Washington, D.C.: U. S. Department of Health, Education, and Welfare, 1969).

clinical laboratories. It has been suggested that there has been dramatic utilization increases of ancillary departments by referral patients in recent years. The increased utilization is indicative of the increasing importance of hospitals in serving the specialized needs of the private practitioner, although creditable utilization data are not available.[50] Even the HEW publication, *Health Resources Statistics, 1974,* does not contain national statistics on this important health resource. As noted by Somers: "Indeed, many hospitals do not distinguish in their records between inpatient and outpatient services of this type and therefore have not noted the extent of . . . change in demand."[51] While it is probably safe to state that ambulatory services are currently recognized as major components of hospital operations, they are "still inadequately recognized in . . . [hospital] organizational, financial, and prestige hierarchies and grossly downgraded in most health insurance programs."[52]

The majority of physicians practicing medicine in the United States are in private practice, either group or solo. During the pre-World War II years the majority of the nation's personal health care expenditures went to the private practitioner whereas during the ensuing thirty years there has been "a steep decline in the role of the [individual] practitioner, both in the delivery of medical

[50] Anne R. Somers, *Health Care in Transition: Directions for the Future* (Chicago: Hospital Research and Educational Trust, 1971).
[51] *Ibid.,* p. 30.
[52] *Ibid.*

care itself, and in the medical power structure."[53] In contrast to the pre-World War II period less than 29% of the nation's health expenditures in 1969 went to the individual practitioner.[54]

The growth of hospital insurance plans, as well as the evolution of hospital and institutionalized medicine (including medical schools and teaching hospitals) to a position of dominance, represent the chief reasons for the shift away from the individual doctor as the center of health care delivery. The three complementary forces that can be identified as being primarily responsible for the shift are: "changes in technology, changes in financing, and changes in the prestige structure of the medical profession."[55] The latter factor is related to increased specialization and associated tangible benefits. An AMA study showed that physicians in small single specialty groups earn substantially higher net incomes than physicians in solo practice. Group physicians in three specialties—internal medicine, pediatrics, and general surgery—have fewer patient visits than solo practitioners, although this is not the case for group practitioners who are specialists in general practice and obstetrics/gynecology. Moreover the revenue per patient visit is higher for the group physician than for the solo practitioner in all five specialties.[56]

Although some general practitioners are now operating in group practices, the majority are still in solo practice. Yet because of the increased complexity of medical practice, the range of services that a solo practitioner can offer is limited. Solo practice has become the least productive means of delivering care.[57] Although the private practitioner is still viewed by some as being vital to continuing patient care management, since 1931 the general practitioner to population ratio has become less than half.[58]

The alternative to solo practice for physicians is group practice which has been increasing in number and diversity in recent years. The Mayo Clinic in Rochester, Minnesota, is considered to be the originator of the group practice movement in the United States.

The American Medical Association has defined group practice as the provision of medical services "by three or more physicians formally organized to provide medical care, consultation, diagnosis, and/or treatment through the joint use of equipment and personnel, and with income from group medical practice distributed in accordance with methods previously determined by members of the group."[59] The group practice movement accelerated after World War II as physicians became more aware of the advantages of shared resources in increasing the efficacy and efficiency of health care delivery. Groups operate either on

[53]Health Policy Advisory Committee, *The American Health Empire: Power, Profits and Politics* (New York: Vintage Books, 1971), p. 30.
[54]*Ibid.*
[55]*Ibid.,* p. 31.
[56]Robert M. Hendrickson, "Solo vs. Group Practice," *Prism,* **2** (November 1974), pp. 28–29.
[57]Alberta W. Parker, "The Dimensions of Primary Care: Blueprints for Change," *Primary Care: Where Medicine Fails, op. cit.,* pp. 15–80.
[58]*Ibid.*
[59]American Medical Association, *Profile of Medical Practice* (Chicago: American Medical Association, 1973), p. 30.

the traditional fee-for-service basis or a prepayment basis. In the latter case recipients benefit through subscription to a broad coverage plan for a predetermined fee. The recent health maintenance organization (HMO) movement developed from this prepaid group practice concept and experience.

There are three basic categories of group practice:

1. Single-specialty groups that provide services in one specialty, except for general practice groups.
2. General practice groups.
3. Multispecialty groups composed of physicians in at least two specialties.

The number of groups has increased from 404 in 1946, to 1546 in 1959, 4289 in 1965, and 6371 in 1969.[60] Unfortunately, the lack of prior definitional standards makes impossible meaningful analysis of the composition of groups. Table 2.5 shows the recent development of an almost equal number of single and multispecialty groups in selected years from 1946 to 1969. The largest number of physicians practicing in groups are in groups with three to four physicians that are predominantly single specialty (see Table 2.6). The variation in size and geographic distribution of groups and group physicians for 1969 is shown in Figure 2.6.[61]

The American Association of Medical Clinics, established in 1968, is a voluntary accreditation association that inspects and certifies group practices. It had accredited eighty-eight group practices by mid-1973.[62] To date only one state, Connecticut, has a specific licensing program for medical practice groups.

Although still in an early stage of development, group practice as a framework for providing health services was criticized by the Committee for Economic Development in 1973:

TABLE 2.5. Medical Groups: 1946 through 1969

		Type of Group	
Year	Total	Single Specialty	Multispecialty and General Practice
1969	6371[a]	3169	3202
1965	4289[b]	2161	2128
1959	1546[c]	392	1154
1946	404[b]	36	368

[a] Three or more physicians.
[b] Three or more full-time physicians.
[c] Three physicians, with two part-time physicians counted as one full-time physician.

Source. Adapted from U. S. Department of Health, Education, and Welfare, *Health Resources Statistics: Health Manpower and Health Facilities, 1974* (Washington, D.C.: U. S. Department of Health, Education, and Welfare, 1974), p. 485.

[60]*Health Resources Statistics, op. cit.*
[61]*Profile of Medical Practice, op. cit.*
[62]*Health Resources Statistics, op. cit.*

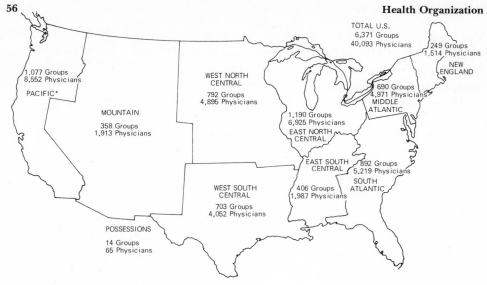

*Includes Alaska and Hawaii

FIGURE 2.6.   Distribution of groups and group physicians by census division, 1969. Source: American Medical Association, *Profile of Medical Practice* (Chicago: American Medical Association, 1973), p. 33. Copyright by the American Medical Association.

TABLE 2.6.   Groups and Group Physicians by Type and Size of Group: 1969

Type of Group	All Sizes	Size of Group					
		3–4	5–7	8–15	16–25	26–49	50 and Over
All groups	6,371	4,139	1315	616	154	97	50
Single specialty	3,169	2,380	640	140	7	2	0
General practice	784	718	61	5	0	0	0
Multispecialty	2,418	1,041	614	471	147	95	50
All physicians	40,093	13,860	7405	6326	3054	3287	6161
Single Specialty	13,053	7,941	3576	1341	128	67	0
General practice	2,691	2,325	320	46	0	0	0
Multispecialty	24,349	3,594	3509	4939	2926	3220	6161

Source.   American Medical Association, *Profile of Medical Practice* (Chicago: American Medical Association, 1973), p. 32. Copyright by the American Medical Association.

The results of group practice for the patient have not been as impressive as the advantages enjoyed by the group; frequently the patients do not receive the benefits of reduced medical costs. Many groups [have] been drawn together by their professional, economic, and intellectual interests rather than by a desire to meet the diversified needs of the clientele.[63]

Later in its report the Committee does state that when group practice is linked to prepayment, full benefits are realized by the subscribing clientele. Within this context, Figure 2.7, although admittedly based on a rather small sample, indicates

[63]Committee for Economic Development, *Building a National Health-Care System* (New York: Committee for Economic Development, April 1973), p. 49.

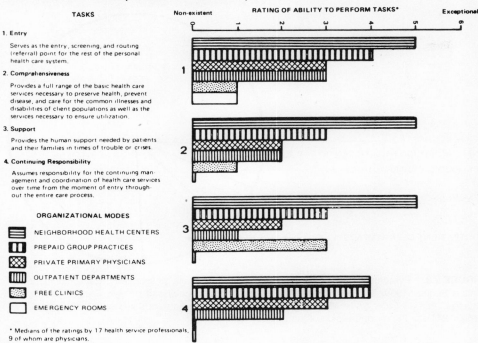

TASKS

1. Entry

Serves as the entry, screening, and routing (referral) point for the rest of the personal health care system.

2. Comprehensiveness

Provides a full range of the basic health care services necessary to preserve health, prevent disease, and care for the common illnesses and disabilities of client populations as well as the services necessary to ensure utilization.

3. Support

Provides the human support needed by patients and their families in times of trouble or crises.

4. Continuing Responsibility

Assumes responsibility for the continuing management and coordination of health care services over time from the moment of entry throughout the entire care process.

ORGANIZATIONAL MODES

NEIGHBORHOOD HEALTH CENTERS
PREPAID GROUP PRACTICES
PRIVATE PRIMARY PHYSICIANS
OUTPATIENT DEPARTMENTS
FREE CLINICS
EMERGENCY ROOMS

* Medians of the ratings by 17 health service professionals, 9 of whom are physicians.

FIGURE 2.7.   Results of provider survey ranking the ability of selected organizational modes in their performance of primary care tasks. Source: Alberta W. Parker, "The Dimensions of Primary Care: Blueprints for Change," *Primary Care: Where Medicine Fails,* edited by Spyros Andreopoulos (New York: John Wiley & Sons, 1974), p. 29, by permission of the publisher.

that providers themselves view neighborhood health centers and prepaid practices as the most satisfactory form of providing primary care. Yet as noted in Figure 2.8, primary care is basically delivered by private practitioners, followed by hospital outpatient departments and emergency rooms, all of which ranked behind neighborhood health centers and prepaid group practices on each of the selected primary care tasks in Figure 2.7.

Patterns of Distribution of Health Facilities: Urban/Rural

As noted previously general medical and surgical hospitals, as well as medical schools and affiliated teaching hospitals, are almost exclusively located in metropolitan areas. More emphasis has also been placed on providing ambulatory care in urban areas through neighborhood health centers, hospital outpatient departments, and emergency rooms. In addition the vast majority of physicians providing patient care, the bulk of which is office or hospital-based primary care, are located in metropolitan areas. A careful review of the literature reveals that the majority of people in need of health care are in need of primary care, basically characterized as ambulatory. Therefore the areas most readily served by the health care system on an access and quality basis are metropolitan. And yet some

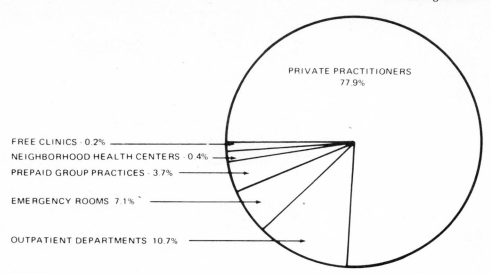

FIGURE 2.8.   Percentage distribution of primary physician visits by selected organizational modes, United States—1969. Source: Alberta W. Parker, "The Dimensions of Primary Care: Blueprints for Change," *Primary Care: Where Medicine Fails,* edited by Spyros Andreopoulos (New York: John Wiley & Sons, 1974), p. 28, by permission of the publisher.

of the most depressed areas in the country in terms of access, availability, and quality of health care services are the urban ghettos. Selig Greenberg reports:

There is a slum neighborhood in Boston where infant mortality exceeds the level of the Biblical plague inflicted on ancient Egypt, when every tenth newborn child died. The infant death rate of 111.1 per 1,000 live births, or one out of every nine, in this section is five times greater than the average for the city of Boston as a whole and more than 15 times the average for a nearby affluent suburban community which has only 7.2 infant deaths for every 1,000 births. In several other Boston ghetto areas, infant mortality rates run from double to more than three times the city-wide average.

This is just one example of how a gap of only a few blocks, but of astronomical social and economic proportions, in one of the nation's foremost medical centers may doom many to untimely deaths and others to lives of suffering and anguish.

In the South End, Boston's worst slum and the site of three outstanding teaching hospitals with a massive pool of medical talent, health conditions are fully as abysmal as in some of the most abject black poverty pockets in Mississippi. . . . In Boston as a whole, the birth rate is 50 percent higher than the death rate. But in one section of the South End, the death rate actually exceeds the birth rate despite the fact that the latter is 45 percent above the average for the city.[64]

The quality of hospital care available to inner city populations has been characterized by Cook as being grossly inadequate in quality and number of beds.[65] Some of the problems associated with the availability and quality of ambulatory care facilities have already been cited. This grim situation becomes even more

[64]Selig Greenberg, *The Quality of Mercy* (New York: Atheneum, 1971), pp. 97–98.
[65]Fred C. Cook, "The Doomed of Watts," *Problems in Political Economy: An Urban Perspective,* edited by David M. Gordon (Lexington: D. C. Health & Co., 1971).

serious when one considers the relationship between poverty and health; the sicker many Americans are the poorer they are, and vice versa.

The plight of the rural population—especially the rural poor—is also very serious. For the past few decades rural America has experienced a large exodus of people to urban areas. The small farmer is being squeezed from his land by big combines; consequently many businesses in rural areas that relied on the farmer are dying, forcing even more people into the city. This leaves the rural areas without an adequate economic base on which to operate most of the public services vital to the well-being of rural people.

Among the vital necessities that are lost as the population moves to urban areas are funds, except those provided by the government, and manpower. Most rural areas, therefore, suffer from varying degrees of the same problems: migration to the city, an aging, medically unserved population, environmental hazards, educational level lower than that of urban residents, and a high poverty level.

As noted by Senator Edward M. Kennedy at the First National Conference on Rural America in April of 1975:

Only 74 percent of the rural non-farm and 61 percent of the farm population have any form of health insurance; and . . . the combination of low income, distance from health care services, and frequently, lack of transportation requires rural people to ask if someone is sick enough for care to be sought.[66]

Among the ethnic groups and areas in the country that are severely affected by the shortage of personnel and facilities in nonmetropolitan areas are the caucasians of Appalachia, the Mexican Americans of the Southwest, the blacks in the Deep South, and Native Americans, wherever they are found. The lack of facilities and personnel is not the only problem these people face, for even when medical facilities are available there are other obstacles which must be overcome: (1) facilities are often isolated and public communication is poor; (2) given their incomes, health services, of necessity, occupy a low priority in their personal budgeting; and (3) the facilities' bureaucracies, which are alien to their culture and values, are often made even more formidable by a language barrier. The AMA explains:

General ill health is accepted as a burden to be borne. This attitude can be changed with health education, outreach case finding, and availability of health services, as demonstrated in the Migrant Health Programs, Medicaid-supported programs, and in rural health center programs such as the King City project in Monterey Country, California.[67]

But the problem of accessibility remains.

Both rural and urban areas are confronted by problems of the accessibility and availability of medical facilities. In the absence of an effective coordinated effort directed at efficiently serving all sectors of the community, resources are fre-

[66] " 'Metropollyana' vs. Rural U. S.: Health Care Needs Still Go Unmet," *The Nation's Health* (May 1975) p. 3.
[67] American Medical Association, Department of Rural Health, Division of Medical Practice, *Health Care Delivery in Rural Areas* (Chicago: American Medical Association, 1972), pp. 6–7.

quently wastefully expended. There has been a movement toward planning for the development and distribution of health facilities since the late fifties, when areawide health planning agencies were established. Although these were private nonprofit agencies, many of them gradually acquired public financing and others obtained some legal powers.

By the mid-1960s, when the problems of access to medical facilities had still not been solved through private efforts, despite rising costs, the federal government moved to stimulate the private sector to implement more positive planning. The dual intent of the legislation for Regional Medical Programs (RMP, PL 89-239) and Comprehensive Health Planning (HP, PL 89-749) was to consolidate the areawide health planning agencies, and to stimulate the planning of health care delivery on a regional basis. Medical resources were to be consolidated in a similar way to educational resources. Both of these legislative goals have met with limited success. The RMP was ended in 1974 and CHP has made little impact in most areas. "The programs were charged with the task of creating an excellent and rational American health system, but they were not given the authority to require a single institution to alter its plans or policies in the smallest detail."[68]

One of the RMP's activities was to stimulate and foster the planning of Health Maintenance Organizations (HMOs). It now seems that the development of rural and inner city HMOs has the potential to provide at least a partial solution to health care delivery problems of these areas.[69] Under the Health Maintenance Act of 1973, the Health Services Administration has been charged with administering technical and financial aid to organizations planning to sponsor HMOs. Organizations from rural and medically underserved areas which qualify for assistance are to receive special attention under the law.[70] It remains to be seen whether the Act provides sufficient incentives to persuade health care providers to establish HMOs in these areas.

Some authors have suggested an indirect solution to the maldistribution of medical facilities. Greenberg discusses the possibility that the distributional difficulties may best be alleviated by improving the transport system:

Most major cities have public transportation systems, and to the extent that the problem is attributable to poor systems, the remedy is to improve them, rather than to increase the number of physicians serving in these areas. In rural areas, the physician shortage might be offset by grouping medical facilities in areas of population density. These might be augmented by establishing local clinics staffed by paramedics and linked to hospital centers by emergency evacuation facilities.[71]

The AMA has underlined the importance of transport to facilities:

The finest health services in the world will do no good in a community unless residents have access to them, and to services and information beyond their area. Many rural areas are

[68]Barbara Ehrenreich and John Ehrenreich, *The American Health Empire: Power, Profits and Politics* (New York: Vintage Books, 1971), p. 196.
[69]For more details on the principles of HMO operation see the section on HMOs in Part Three.
[70]U. S. Department of Health, Education, and Welfare, *Health Maintenance Organization, Program Status Report, October, 1974* (Washington, D.C.: U. S. Department of Health, Education, and Welfare, 1974).
[71]Ira G. Greenberg, et al., "The Role of Prepaid Group Practice in Relieving the Medical Care Crisis," *Harvard Law Review*, **84** (February 1971), p. 895.

plagued by poor transportation, which must be overcome not only for emergency cases but to bring the neediest patients, who are least likely to drive or own cars, to treatment. Many communities organize volunteer emergency services, similar to the VFD, when clinics are established; in some, minibuses link patients and services. Often transportation to more distant medical centers is essential.[72]

The problems of distribution are highly complex, involving both manpower and facilities, organization, and deployment. The concern extends beyond a bipolar urban and rural issue; it goes beyond even the geographically isolated health care or medical organization. Therefore any effort at solving this complex problem must demonstrate a systematic approach to the total community, which, in turn, should remove the artificial dichotomy between urban and rural.

Federal Health Facilities

The federal government provides direct medical services for Native Americans, employees of federal agencies, merchant seamen, and members of the armed services and their dependents, including veterans. The medical services are provided primarily through health facilities maintained by the Public Health Service, the Veterans Administration, the Armed Forces, and the Bureau of Indian Affairs.

The Public Health Service's facilities are managed by the Bureau of Medical Services. Comprehensive medical care for designated federal beneficiaries was provided through a network of eight general hospitals, thirty outpatient clinics, and 248 contract physicians for an estimated 470,500 persons in fiscal 1974.[73] The general hospitals are located in Baltimore, Boston, Galveston, New Orleans, Norfolk, San Francisco, Seattle, and Staten Island. The Service also maintains a hospital for leprosy patients in Carville, Louisiana. The total bed capacity is 2909 for the general hospitals and 450 for the leprosarium. Of a total of 287 facilities operated in fiscal 1974, only the nine hospitals and thirty outpatient clinics were staffed by full-time personnel.

The hospitals and clinics of the Public Health Service, in conjunction with their basic mission of patient care, are the sites of training for a wide variety of health careers, ranging from postgraduate physician education to the training of physician extenders (marine physician assistants) and other medical support personnel. During 1974, seven hospitals provided residency and internship training. The New Orleans hospital, as an example, has a cooperative medical residency program in environmental health with the Tulane University School of Public Health and Tropical Medicine. At the end of 1974 the Bureau maintained over 200 affiliations with health professions education institutions.

Utilization of all of the hospitals, except for the Staten Island Hospital, was down between 1973 and 1974. The decline in average daily patient load was between 0.9 and 40.9% for the eight hospitals.[74] Outpatient services provided by

[72]American Medical Association, *op. cit.,* p. 8.
[73]Public Health Service, *Bureau of Medical Services Annual Statistical Summary, Fiscal Years 1973 and 1974* (Washington, D.C.: U. S. Department of Health, Education, and Welfare, 1974).
[74]*Ibid.*

contract physicians were the only services that showed a significant increase (23.7%) between 1973 and 1974.[75] The increase in total number (up twenty-three since December 1970) and the general accessibility of contract physicians probably accounts for the continued increased utilization of this form of primary care. The thirty outpatient clinics, while showing a 26.3% increase in usage between 1964 and 1974, declined by 11.2% between 1973 and 1974. The per diem costs for the general hospitals rose from $64.09 in 1964 to $86.33 in 1974; at the leprosarium per diem costs, for the same years, were $44.03 and $56.74 respectively.

The Department of Medicine and Surgery of the Veterans Administration, through its present health care system of 171 hospitals, 84 nursing homes, 19 domiciliary facilities and 200 plus clinics, provides medical, dental, and hospital services to eligible veterans and eligible dependents. The hospitals are classified as general medical and surgical or psychiatric. With prior authorization the Administration will cover costs for services provided by the private sector. Per diem costs in V. A. hospitals increased from $18.44 in 1960 to only $57.92 in 1973.[76] In fiscal year 1975 the V. A. budget was $3.1 billion, an increase of $232 million over the 1974 level.

The Veterans Administration is one of the most impressive health care systems in the world. Because of affiliation with academic health centers, over 29 million armed services veterans and an additional several million military dependents have access to a quality of health care that parallels the care provided at teaching hospitals, and all at government expense. In 1974, 91 medical schools had affiliation agreements with V. A. hospitals as did 57 dental schools, 332 nursing schools, 47 schools of pharmacy, 92 psychology doctoral programs, 88 graduate schools of social work, and 749 allied health programs.[77] Thus the Veterans Administration plays a vital role in health professions education programs through direct and indirect means, that is, teaching medical students or making research and clinical facilities available. Veterans Administration facilities also serve as a forum for resident physicians employed by medical schools. On the negative side, current emphasis on primary care and preventive medicine may begin to reduce the educational importance of the V. A. hospital system.

The Department of Defense provides medical care for military personnel and their dependents all over the world through a system of general medical and field hospitals, dispensaries, and medical stations. The military services operate 204 hospitals. Two of the best known military health facilities are the Walter Reed Army Hospital and the Besthesda Naval Medical Hospital. As of December 31, 1972, the Army, Navy, and Air Force employed 6080, 4570, and 4112 physicians respectively. In each instance approximately 90% were in medical specialties, with the remaining physicians in general practice.[78] In all cases the vast majority of physicians are providing patient care in hospital-based practice.

[75]*Ibid.*
[76]Bureau of the Census, *Statistical Abstract of the United States, 1974* (Washington, D.C.: U. S. Department of Commerce, 1974).
[77]Philip M. Boffey, "Medical Schools and the V. A.," *The Chronicle of Higher Education*, **IX** (December 16 1974), p. 5.
[78]Center for Health Services Research and Development, *Distribution of Physicians in the United States, 1972, Volume 1* (Chicago: American Medical Association, 1973).

In 1954 responsibility for the operation and maintenance of hospital and medical facilities for American Indians was transferred from the Department of the Interior to the Public Health Service (PHS) in the Department of Health, Education, and Welfare. The Indian Health Service is presently a major component of the Health Services Administration division of PHS. The Service operates a program of comprehensive health services for over 488,000 eligible American Indians and Alaska Natives. The Indian Health Services' programs encompass preventive, curative, and rehabilitative health services, as well as health professions education training programs that provide support for both Indian and non-Indian personnel. These programs range from master's degrees in public health for physicians, dentists, and nurses, to residencies and internships in general practice, dentistry, pharmacy, and the medical specialties. The educational programs also encompass many of the allied health fields.

The Indian Health Service provides comprehensive services to Native Americans through a network of fifty-one hospitals and their outpatient clinics, eighty-seven health centers, and more than three hundred health stations.[79] In 1973 the Service employed 500 physicians, 180 dentists, and 1100 registered nurses. Additional services can be provided through contracts with community hospitals, state and local health agencies, and private practitioners. The estimated fiscal year 1975 budget was $284 million, 160% above the 1969 funding level of $177 million and $32 million over the fiscal 1974 budget.[80]

[79]Sue Guyon, "The Challenge to the Indian Health Service," *Health Services Reports*, **88** (October 1973), pp. 687–691.
[80]Office of Management and Budget, *The Budget of the United States Government, Fiscal Year 1975* (Washington, D.C.: Government Printing Office, 1974).

CHAPTER THREE

PRIVATE HEALTH INSURANCE AND HEALTH CARE DELIVERY

HISTORICAL DEVELOPMENT

Some of the earliest insurance plans were established by individual hospitals at the end of the nineteenth century to ensure that the hospitals would be paid by their patients. The most successful experiment, which became a model for those that followed, was the Baylor Hospital Plan. The plan was created by Justin Ford Kimball for Dallas schoolteachers, who paid $6 per year for an insurance premium that covered the costs of hospitalization, excluding professional fees. The Baylor Hospital Plan led to the founding of the first multihospital combine in Sacramento in 1932. The hospitals formed a nonprofit insurance company to administer the plan, collected the premiums from subscribers, and generally served as the middleman between the buyer and the provider. After the failure to provide health care benefits under the 1935 Social Security Act, health insurance was left exclusively to the private insurance sector.

Despite the AMA's strong disapproval of prepayment plans, the American Hospital Association and later the American College of Surgeons supported the principle of hospital insurance. The hospital association created a nationwide program for approving plans. After meeting the Association's criteria, individual plans were entitled to use the trademark the hospitals had created, a blue cross.

For many years the AMA actively subverted Blue Cross by expelling doctors hired under group health plans and threatening to stop intern-training programs in associated hospitals, thus pressuring hospitals to turn away patients referred from physicians in group plans. As a result, in 1938, a federal grand jury indicted the District of Columbia Medical Society and the AMA for criminal conspiracy. The medical associations were charged with violating the Sherman Anti-Trust Act prohibiting restraint of trade. The U. S. Supreme Court finally upheld the prosecution, despite numerous appeals from the AMA. However the AMA retaliated by lobbying to gain the passage of legislation which required that no prepaid insurance could be organized unless it was sponsored by 51% of a state's practicing physicians, or had the approval of the state medical society. To date, eighteen states still have legislation that makes prepaid insurance plans illegal, although there are doubts as to the constitutionality of these laws.[1] Thus doctors possessed what Ed Cray calls "the privilege of state-sanctioned monopolies." It has taken many court cases for doctors to gain participation in the first health care programs negotiated as part of collective bargaining agreements in the mass production industries, and some doctors are still subject to retaliation by state medical societies.[2]

Through the war years the private health insurance industry showed phenomenal growth; in 1939, 10 million persons were covered by some form of private health insurance; by 1954, when it became possible to deduct employer expenditures for health insurance as a business operating cost, thereby reducing total tax liability, 32 million persons were insured. It was during the latter part of the preceding fifteen years, 1949 to be exact, that the AMA modified its position on health insurance programs. Confronted with the Truman-supported national health insurance program which was pending in Congress in 1949 (to be tied to Social Security), the Association changed its position and supported the principle of voluntary health insurance programs.

The private health insurance industry is now an integral part of the prevailing medical care system, fitting into this system the fiscal needs of the hospitals, as well as physicians and other providers of medical care.

I. S. Falk writes:

Indeed, private health insurance rapidly became a financial bulwark for that system, even though the underwriting policies invited or required distortions in many practices of the providers to fit the terms of the insurance contracts and the convenience of the insurance carriers.[3]

Organization of Private Health Insurance

Presently there are three major types of private health insurance:

1.   Blue Cross, Blue Shield, and other nonprofit associations.

2.   Commercial carriers; for example, Aetna, Occidental, and Connecticut General.

3.   Independent plans such as community and employer-employee union groups, individual practice plans, private group medical and dental clinics, and dental service corporations.

As can be seen from Figure 3.1 independent plans' percentage of the total

[1]Ira G. Greenberg, et al., *op. cit.*
[2]Ed Cray, *In Failing Health: The Medical Crisis and the AMA* (Indianapolis: The Bobbs-Merrill Company, Inc., 1970), pp. 207–8.
[3]I. S. Falk, "Medical Care in the USA—1932–1972," *The Milbank Memorial Fund Quarterly, Health and Society,* **51,** No. 1., 1973, p. 14.

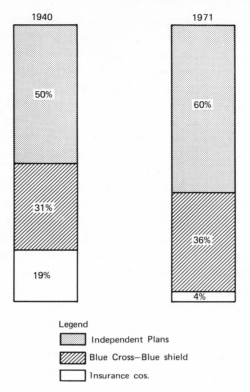

FIGURE 3.1. Percentage distribution of total gross enrollment under private insurance plans, 1940 and 1971. Adapted from Marjorie Smith Mueller, "Private Health Insurance in 1971: Health Care Services, Enrollment, and Finances," *Social Security Bulletin,* **36** (February 1973), pp. 3–22.

enrollment under private insurance plans has declined since 1940, as the "Blues" and the commercial insurance companies have broadened the scope of their coverage and thereby gained a greater share of the market. Blue Cross and Blue Shield plans have a growing share of the market largely due to their competitive cost advantage of having a nonprofit and tax exempt status, They also operate on a "service benefits" basis where they can prearrange a somewhat lower schedule of charges with payments made directly to hospitals and doctors. Commercial carriers that operate indemnity plans reimburse the insured.

Blue Cross and Blue Shield were originally designed to protect the interests of the health care provider rather than the consumer. Even at the present time physicians or hospitals can still control insurance carrier policies. If they are not satisfied with Blue Cross and Blue Shield terms, they can cancel their affiliation. The AHA owns the Blue Cross trademark and hospital representatives are a majority or near majority on the boards of all seventy-four Blue Cross plans across the country. As Blue Cross negotiates and its board approves contracts for payment rates with participating hospitals, there has been, until recently, an obvious conflict of interest. Lately there has been some movement toward including consumers on boards. Similarly the Blue Shield boards are dominated by physicians.

Eighty percent of all Americans are presently covered by some type of health insurance, although coverage for inpatient medical care is more complete than it is for ambulatory care, where only half the population has at least partial coverage. Most of the population over sixty-five is covered by Medicare and a substantial proportion of the lower income population claims Medicaid benefits. Yet health insurance today still fails to provide most families with protection against very large expenses. The industry has only gradually begun to provide health rather than sickness insurance, by broadening coverages to include some preventative medical services and ambulatory care. It has failed completely to make health services available to the poor and the medically indigent. Despite some thirty years of private health insurance operation, an estimated 41 million Americans under age sixty-five have no private insurance against hospital costs; 42 million have no private insurance for surgical care. Moreover, in 1974, only 40% of poor persons who were employed had even limited private insurance against medical expenses; fewer than 10% had insurance against nonhospital services.[4]

In 1974, 64.6% of all personal medical costs were met by third party payments, which means that slightly more than a third of total medical costs had to be covered by direct or out-of-pocket payments.[5] As can be seen in Figures 3.2 and 3.3 there has been a steady drop in direct payments made by American families in the last two decades. Yet the ratio of these out-of-pocket expenses to consumer disposable income dropped only 0.01% from 0.53% in 1960 to 0.52% in 1969 because increased hospital costs in this period cancelled out the consumer's gains from broader insurance coverage.[6] Although private insurance is only increasing its share of the market by 1–1.5% per year, government subsidy through Medicare and Medicaid has risen markedly. Nevertheless Figure 3.4 shows that out-of-pocket payments are not uniform for all personal health care expenditures; the percentage of direct payments is much higher for dentists' services and drugs in particular.

The decreasing proportion of direct payments in total personal health care expenditure also varies substantially depending on the age group of the population. Medicaid and Medicare reduced the proportion of direct payments that those sixty-five and over had to pay to less than one-third, by increasing to nearly two-thirds the government subsidy. Although the impact of third-party payments for those under sixty-five is not as dramatic, it is still significant.[7] Figure 3.5 contrasts the distribution and source of funds for those under and over sixty-five years, before and after the enactment of Medicare and Medicaid.

The present insurance system, in both subtle and direct ways, influences and is influenced by the organization and delivery of medical services. As a case in point, the industry pays out specified sums for services to its subscribers when they prove

[4]Marjorie Smith Mueller, "Private Health Insurance in 1973: A Review of Coverage, Enrollment, and Financial Experience," *Social Security Bulletin*, **38** (February 1975), pp. 21–40.

[5]Nancy C. Worthington, "National Health Expenditures, 1929–74," *Social Security Bulletin*, **38** (February 1975), pp. 3–20.

[6]John Krizay and Andrew Wilson, *The Patient as Consumer: Health Care Financing in the United States* (Lexington, Massachusetts: Lexington Books, 1974).

[7]Barbara S. Cooper and Paula A. Piro, "Age Differences in Medical Care Spending, Fiscal Year, 1973," *Social Security Bulletin*, **37** (May 1974), pp. 3–14.

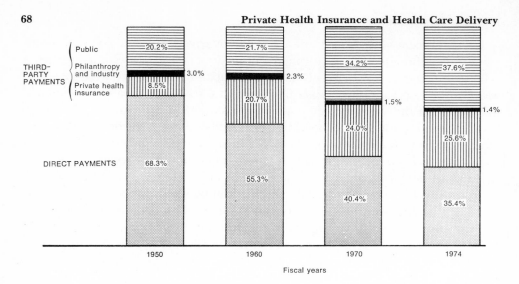

FIGURE 3.2. Distribution of personal health care expenditures by source of funds, selected fiscal years, 1950–1974. Source: Nancy L. Worthington, "National Health Expenditures, 1929–1974," *Social Security Bulletin,* **38** (February 1975), p. 17.

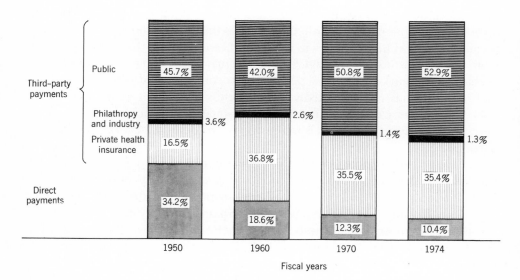

FIGURE 3.3. Distribution of health care expenditures for hospital care, by source of funds, selected fiscal years, 1950–1974. Adapted from Nancy L. Worthington, "National Health Expenditures, 1929–1974," *Social Security Bulletin,* **38** (February 1975), pp. 3–20.

that a certain risk has been "realized," or in the case of Blue Cross–Blue Shield, payments are made to the providers. This system has proved unsatisfactory for the insured for two main reasons.

1.   Rising costs: insurance payments are meant to cover the usual fees and prices

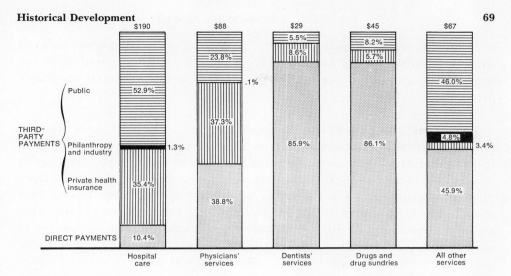

FIGURE 3.4. Percentage distribution of per capita personal health care expenditures, by type of expenditure and source of funds, fiscal year 1974. Source: Nancy L. Worthington, "National Health Expenditures, 1929–1974," *Social Security Bulletin,* **38** (February 1975), p. 15.

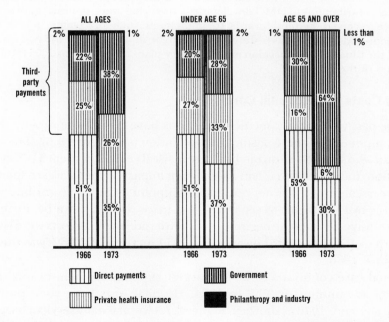

FIGURE 3.5. Percentage distribution of expenditures for personal health care, by source of funds and age group, fiscal years 1966 and 1973. Source: Barbara S. Cooper and Paula A. Piro, "Age Differences in Medical Care Spending, Fiscal Year 1973," *Social Security Bulletin,* **37** (May 1974), p. 11.

over and above the specified deductible. However providers, knowing that most of their patients receive at least a certain reimbursement, tend to increase their fees and prices by about the same amount. This forces carriers to increase their payments in turn, which again leads to a price raising reaction from the providers of care, thus causing the cost spiral to continue.

2.   Limited coverage: under the present system a serious gap has arisen between what the insured person has to pay for care and what is received from the insurance system, with the result that the insured cannot be assured reasonable protection.

The prepaid group health care plans are exceptions to the main forms of health care plans prevalent in America. This type of health care delivery will be discussed in detail later. However it should be noted here that most proposed federal health care legislation points to health maintenance organizations (one of the main types of prepaid group plans) as the preferred delivery system in the future. As a consequence many insurance companies are moving toward the organized delivery of comprehensive health care. Private insurers who are offering this type of coverage frequently offer prepaid group practice or an HMO option as an alternative to the traditional Blue Cross-Blue Shield plans. Marjorie Mueller states:

Private insurers are becoming directly involved with prepaid group-practice plans and HMO's. A number of insurance companies and Blue Cross–Blue Shield plans have made substantial contributions to HMO development, financing and risk-bearing; in some cases they have received Federal grants to implement such programs. Some 30 Blue Cross–sponsored HMO projects were expected to be in operation at the end of 1972. In addition, the Blue Cross Association has long-range plans for as many as 300 HMO projects by the end of the seventies.[8]

Medical Costs and Hospital Care

Over the past two decades medical care costs have risen more rapidly than any other component of the Consumer Price Index (see Figure 3.6). The average American who spent $485 on medical care in fiscal year 1974 spent $198 in 1965.[9]

Inflation undoubtedly has had a significant impact on medical care spending in recent years, although it is not possible to pinpoint its precise contribution. Pure inflation is often difficult to separate from price rises that can be attributed to more extensive care. At the beginning of this decade medical costs were rising at a rate of 15 to 16% per year; however, the 1974 increase of 10.6% was the second lowest since 1966.

Hospital care continued to be the largest expenditure item in total medical spending, accounting for 39% in 1974. Hospital costs have risen particularly dramatically since 1946 as shown in Figure 3.7. Hospital daily service charges have gone up faster than any other medical care item and faster than the average of all items in the Consumer Price Index. For all U.S. hospitals the average cost (to the hospital) per patient day rose from $5 in 1946 to $84 in 1974, and still higher in community hospitals.[10] Yet the net cost to the patient (after third-party payments) of hospital care in constant dollars has scarcely risen since 1950 (see Figure 3.8).

[8]Marjorie Smith Mueller (1973), *op. cit.,* p. 5.
[9]Nancy C. Worthington, *op. cit.,*
[10]American Hospital Association, *Hospital Statistics, 1974 Edition* (Chicago: American Hospital Association, 1974).

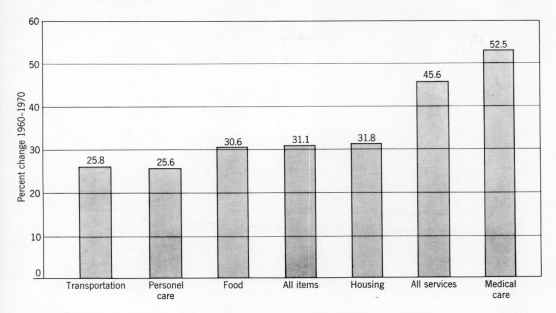

FIGURE 3.6. Comparison of percentage change in selected consumer price index items, 1960 to 1970. Adapted from American Medical Association, *Socioeconomic Issues of Health* (Chicago: American Medical Association, 1974).

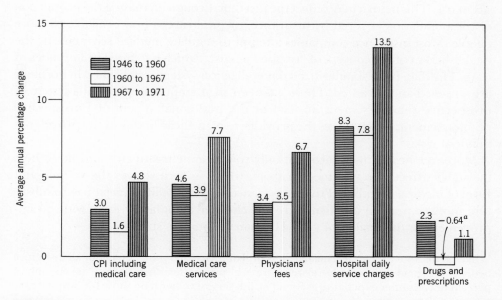

FIGURE 3.7. Consumer price index and percentage change for medical care components, selected fiscal years, 1946 to 1971. *(a)* Data obtained via personal communication with the U. S. Bureau of Labor statistics, April 7, 1976. Adapted from Social Security Administration, *Medical Care Costs and Prices: Background Book* (Washington, D.C.: U. S. Department of Health, Education, and Welfare, 1972), p. 10.

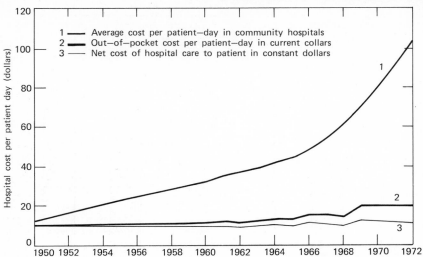

FIGURE 3.8. Hospital cost per patient-day, 1950–1972. Adapted from Martin S. Feldstein, "The Medical Economy." Copyright © by *Scientific American, Inc.*, **229** (September 1973), p. 155. All rights reserved.

It is a very difficult problem to curtail escalating hospital costs and charges when providers and those who subscribe to health insurance plans are insulated from the price increases because of third-party payments. Even regulating hospital charges may not have any effect on patient expenditure because of higher intensity of use. This in turn may reflect the fact that through increasing the proportion of the population covered by insurance, medical care is now available to more people. Most insurance companies attempt to regulate medical payments by the establishment of the concept of "reasonable cost," which is defined in a number of ways. The data from standardized data collection systems established in hospitals are screened and reviewed. There has been an attempt to implement a system of prospective reimbursement, instead of the traditional system of retrospective reimbursement, which forces the provider to plan ahead and puts the provider at financial risk.

Moreover health insurance that only covers some treatments and not others inevitably affects the treatment pattern, which in turn shapes the volume and form of medical spending. Private insurance provides built-in incentives to substitute more expensive inpatient care for cheaper ambulatory care, with no improvement in the quality of care. Herman M. Somers states:

While no definitive data are available, it is probable that about 80 percent of all insurance benefits are paid for hospital-related care .... private health insurance meets only 5 percent of consumer expenditures for all health services other than those for hospital care and physicians' services.[11]

[11]Herman M. Somers, "Economic Issues in Health Services," in *Contemporary Economic Issues,* edited by Neil W. Chamberlain (Homewood, Illinois: Richard D. Irwin, Inc., 1973), p. 129.

In most cases neither office nor home visits are covered.

The patient, or the doctor acting in his interest, attempts to minimize the patient's expenses often resulting in higher medical care costs and overutilization of inpatient hospital services rather than less costly ambulatory services. Thus it is common for insurance to reimburse the charges for certain diagnostic tests only if they are performed while the insured is in the hospital. The patient may, therefore, be hospitalized, with the cost of his stay being borne by his insurance, in order for him to avoid paying for the tests as an outpatient.

A variety of utilization review committees have been implemented that can enforce retrospective disallowance of insurance payments if any treatment has been given excessively. Hospitals participating in Medicaid and Medicare programs have mandatory requirements to establish utilization review committees and certification and recertification of inpatient hospital and nursing home stays. These controls have met with only limited success.[12]

A promising long-range solution to overutilization is the emphasis on a more integrated approach to medical resource allocation. Recent studies have indicated that the rate of hospital utilization under group practice plans is frequently half the rate under Blue Cross–Blue Shield and private insurance policies, and that the rate of inpatient surgical procedures is also lower under group practice plans. This can be accounted for by the fact that group practice plans and HMOs stress comprehensive and preventive health care. As checkups and preventive medical care are often not covered by private insurance, a patient may neglect a condition until it becomes acute and requires expensive hospital care.

Because comprehensive plans have proved to be more efficient and less costly forms of health care delivery, several high level commissions have recommended legislative action, either state or federal, to require a minimum range of benefits in all health insurance sold.[13] There has in fact been a steadily broadening scope of benefits under private health insurance in all areas of ambulatory care. The benefit structure in the nonbasic type of benefits—drugs, dental care, nursing services, x-ray, and laboratory examination—has more than doubled for all ages in the past twelve years in each of these categories, as shown in Table 3.1. Mueller states:

The expansion in the areas of physicians' office and home visits, private-duty nursing, and, to some extent, x-ray and laboratory examination and prescribed drugs comes largely through increased coverage under supplementary major medical and comprehensive insurance policies and extended benefit contracts under Blue Cross–Blue Shield plans. Independent self-insured plans, however, can claim a good deal of the expansion in coverage for drugs. Blue Cross–Blue Shield dental coverage has expanded rapidly in the

[12]For an extensive analysis of the most current form of utilization controls, see: Bruce Stuart, et al., "Control Over The Utilizations of Medical Services," *Milbank Memorial Fund Quarterly, Health and Society,* **51,** No. 3, 1973, pp. 341–394.
[13]U. S. Department of Health, Education, and Welfare, *Secretary's Advisory Committee on Hospital Effectiveness: Report* (Washington, D.C.: U. S. Government Printing Office, 1968); Report Findings and Recommendations of the Subcommittee on Health Care Delivery of the Committee on Medical Economics, *Health Care Delivery in the 1970's,* (Washington, D.C.: Health Insurance Association of America, 1969).

TABLE 3.1. Estimates of the Net Number of Different Persons under Private Health Insurance Plans and Percent of Population Covered, by Age and Specified Type of Care: 1962–73

End of year	Hospital care	Physicians' services				Dental care	Prescribed drugs (out-of-hospital)	Private-duty nursing	Visiting-nurse service	Nursing-home care
		Surgical services	In-hospital visits	X-ray and laboratory examinations	Office and home visits					
All ages										
Number (in thousands):										
1962	129,800	120,528	(1)	65,671	(1)	1,006	47,907	46,143	43,203	4,975
1965	(1)	(1)	(1)	79,500	(1)	3,100	53,200	56,000	60,100	9,900
1966	(1)	(1)	(1)	90,000	(1)	4,227	65,544	68,722	79,004	17,814
1967	145,454	142,082	(1)	92,480	(1)	4,679	71,201	76,080	81,771	18,754
1968	(1)	(1)	128,174	97,703	(1)	5,821	79,280	83,485	90,523	19,046
1969	(1)	(1)	133,914	125,002	(1)	8,510	89,805	91,211	100,343	28,044
1970	154,263	150,001	145,589	142,441	67,832	12,210	100,966	100,235	106,882	32,392
1971	(1)	(1)	148,514	145,207	(1)	15,348	106,985	104,730	110,215	38,636
1972	155,253	152,651	149,734	149,444	67,697	17,904	111,374	108,959	115,904	45,460
1973	158,475	156,913	153,461	152,797	70,038	21,626	124,971	118,805	122,688	69,152
Percent of civilian population:										
1962	70.0	65.0	(1)	35.0	(1)	0.5	26.0	25.0	23.0	3.0
1965	(1)	(1)	(1)	41.2	(1)	1.6	27.6	29.0	31.2	5.1
1966	(1)	(1)	(1)	48.0	(1)	2.2	33.7	35.0	40.6	9.2
1967	73.9	72.2	(1)	47.0	(1)	2.4	36.2	38.7	41.6	9.2
1968	(1)	(1)	64.5	49.2	(1)	2.9	39.9	42.0	45.5	9.6
1969	(1)	(1)	66.6	62.2	(1)	4.2	44.7	45.4	49.9	14.0
1970	75.9	73.9	71.7	70.2	33.4	6.0	49.7	49.4	52.6	16.0
1971	(1)	(1)	72.3	70.7	(1)	7.5	52.1	51.0	53.6	18.8
1972	74.9	73.6	72.2	72.1	32.7	8.6	53.7	52.6	55.9	21.9
1973	75.8	75.1	73.4	73.1	33.5	10.4	59.8	56.9	58.7	33.1

Under age 65

Number (in thousands):

Year										
1967	136,907	133,706	116,656	88,926	(1)	4,596	69,363	73,857	79,302	15,873
1968	141,572	139,061	121,104	93,714	(1)	5,719	76,748	81,309	87,697	16,921
1969	(1)	(1)	126,190	117,472	(1)	8,385	86,880	88,024	96,885	23,962
1970	143,611	140,505	137,229	134,839	64,314	12,079	97,736	97,017	103,064	27,371
1971	(1)	(1)	140,685	137,463	(1)	15,155	103,672	101,450	106,190	33,434
1972	143,309	141,448	141,579	141,694	63,652	17,608	107,855	105,518	111,416	39,987
1973	146,089	145,352	144,592	143,995	65,880	21,392	120,987	115,175	117,872	62,621

Percent of civilian population:

Year										
1967	77.0	75.2	65.6	50.0	(1)	2.6	39.0	41.5	44.6	8.9
1968	78.9	77.5	67.5	52.2	(1)	3.2	42.8	45.3	48.9	9.4
1969	(1)	(1)	69.6	64.8	(1)	4.6	47.9	48.5	53.4	13.2
1970	78.6	76.9	75.1	73.8	35.2	6.6	53.5	53.1	56.4	15.4
1971	(1)	(1)	76.2	74.4	(1)	8.2	56.1	54.9	57.5	18.1
1972	77.0	76.0	76.1	76.1	34.2	9.5	58.0	56.7	59.9	21.5
1973	78.0	77.6	77.2	76.9	35.2	11.4	64.6	61.5	62.9	33.4

Aged 65 and over

Number (in thousands):

Year										
1967	8,547	8,376	5,905	3,554	(1)	83	1,838	2,223	2,470	2,881
1968	(1)	(1)	7,070	3,989	(1)	102	2,532	2,176	2,826	2,125
1969	(1)	(1)	7,724	7,530	(1)	125	2,925	3,187	3,458	4,082
1970	10,452	9,496	8,360	7,602	3,518	131	3,230	3,218	3,818	5,021
1971	11,944	11,203	7,829	7,744	4,045	193	3,313	3,280	4,025	5,202
1972	12,386	11,561	8,155	7,750	4,045	296	3,519	3,441	4,488	5,473
1973			8,869	8,802	4,158	234	3,984	3,630	4,816	6,531

Percent of civilian population:

Year										
1967	45.0	44.1	31.1	18.7	(1)	0.4	9.7	11.7	13.0	15.2
1968	(1)	(1)	36.6	20.6	(1)	.5	13.1	11.3	14.6	11.0
1969	(1)	(1)	39.3	38.3	(1)	.6	14.9	16.2	17.6	20.8
1970	51.4	46.7	41.1	37.4	17.3	.6	15.9	15.8	18.8	24.7
1971	(1)	(1)	37.7	37.3	(1)	.9	15.9	15.8	19.4	25.0
1972	56.4	52.9	38.5	36.6	19.1	1.4	16.6	16.3	21.2	25.8
1973	57.4	53.6	41.1	40.8	19.3	1.1	18.5	16.8	22.3	30.3

1 Data not available.

Source.   Marjorie Smith Mueller, "Private Health Insurance in 1973: A Review of Coverage, Enrollment, and Financial Experience," *Social Security Bulletin*, **38** (February 1975), p. 28.

last few years. A very high proportion of dental care is known to have been union-negotiated.[14]

The conventional form of remuneration for medical care, which private health insurance has helped to sustain, is fee-for-service payment. The physician, however, particularly if he is not affiliated with a specific insurance plan, often charges the patient more than an insurance company will pay for a given service. Therefore it becomes a physician's customary financial incentive to administer as many and as complex services as possible. Generally, as the patient gets well, the physician makes less money, just as he makes less money if the individual never gets sick.

As President Nixon said in an address to the U. S. Congress on February 18, 1971:

Under traditional systems, doctors and hospitals are paid, in effect, on a piece work basis. The more illnesses they treat—and the more service they render—the more their income rises. This does not mean, of course, that they do any less than their very best to *make* people well. But it does mean that there is no economic incentive for them to concentrate on keeping *people* healthy.

The fee-for-service system of payment contrasts with the capitation form of remuneration in prepaid group medical practice, which effectively reverses the illogical, financial incentive of the traditional system. Prepaid insurance is an investment in preventive health care rather than in crisis medical care.

Employment-Based Insurance

Most medical insurance is obtained through the work place, most often by the employee's choice of a high-option plan that is accounted as a cost of labor. Ostensibly most of the payments come from the employer. The Social Security Administration calculated that in 1971 about 80% of the premiums for employer-employee group health insurance were paid for by employers, and that employer contributions represented more than 50% of total private health insurance premiums in the United States.[15] But because rapidly rising costs have hindered labor union efforts to increase take-home pay and fringe benefits, in one sense employees feel that they are paying for their insurance in lieu of wages. Therefore unions, while seeking broader health insurance coverage, are sponsoring a reform—a national health bill—that would eliminate basic health insurance as an issue in collective bargaining.[16]

Group insurance plans far outnumber individual policies. There has been a rapid growth of major medical policies of insurance companies and comprehen-

---

[14]Marjorie Smith Mueller (1973), *op. cit.,* p. 11.
[15]Dorothy P. Rice and Barbara S. Cooper, "National Health Expenditures, 1929–71," *Social Security Bulletin,* **35** (January 1972), pp. 3–18.
[16]For a lucid analysis of this and related developments see, John Krizay and Andrew Wilson, *op. cit.*

sive extended-benefit contracts of Blue Cross–Blue Shield plans as basic health care plans have failed to meet the costs of personal health care needs adequately.[17]

Because insurance contracts are often exceedingly complex, the employee's selection of a policy often depends on his technical knowledge. The major problem of insufficient coverage in employment-based and private insurance is often compounded as a result. However as Krizay and Wilson point out in their excellent analysis of the complexities facing consumers when they evaluate health insurance policies, low-risk coverage under the present voluntary health insurance system is quite costly.[18] "The public's total expenditures for health care would probably be less if each person with an income paid for routine, relatively inexpensive medical services directly out of his own pocket."[19]

Those insured can be unaware of the amount of the deductible in their insurance contract, which can lead to unanticipated direct out-of-pocket payments. Coinsurance, which means that the consumer must pay a percentage of all costs, is another of the methods of payment in many insurance policies. Similarly there may be unrealized exclusion clauses. It has been estimated, for example, that 30% of insurance policies have a 14-day exclusion, the period of greatest risk for a newborn child.[20] In addition most policies have cutoff points for medical bills, or maximum payments provided for in the life of the policy. Thus few Americans are protected against catastrophically high medical bills.

The quality of health insurance an employee has depends on several factors:

1. Whether the employee works for a company that offers a comprehensive group plan; for example, employers in the larger industries, like automobiles and steel, are now paying 100% of premiums.
2. Whether the employee or anyone in the employee's family has a serious chronic disease, in which case they may be ineligible to participate.
3. Whether the employee can afford to participate.

When a person is between jobs, or laid off, or on maternity leave, or encounters other situations that can exclude the person from coverage when sickness strikes, the financial results are frequently disastrous. Medical bills are the prime cause of personal bankruptcy in the United States today. As Senator Edward Kennedy stated:

The fact is that health insurance coverages in America are riddled with holes, and they all add up to the same thing for American families: less protection than they think they have and more expense than they can afford. Every story of financial hardship . . . involves a failure of insurance coverage.[21]

[17]Walter W. Kolodrubetz, "Group Health Insurance Coverage of Full-Time Employees, 1972," *Social Security Bulletin,* **37** (April 1974), pp. 17–35.
Walter W. Kolodrubetz, "Trends in Employee Benefit Plans in the Sixties," *Social Security Bulletin,* **34** (April 1971), pp. 21–34
[18]John Krizay and Andrew Wilson, *op cit.*
[19]*Ibid.,* p. 29
[20]Edward M. Kennedy, *In Critical Condition: The Crisis in America's Health Care* (New York: Simon and Schuster, 1972).
[21]*Ibid.,* p. 55.

Employment-based insurance has a number of inherent problems. Low-paid workers, individuals who are frequently jobless, and those who are self-employed or who work in small firms are likely to have little insurance. They and their families pay a proportionally larger part of their medical bills directly out-of-pocket than those on higher incomes. Moreover because the growth of insurance has raised the price of medical care these bills are larger than they would be otherwise.[22]

Ideally health insurance should help to distribute the costs of medical care across the population so that no one is forced into bankruptcy because of medical bills. The annual distribution of expenditure on medical care is extremely skewed; most families have to spend relatively little, a few families have to spend a great deal. Martin S. Feldstein states:

A study of health spending by Federal Government employees in 1969 showed that slightly more than half of the families with two adults and two children spend less than $260 but that 10 percent of the families spent more than $1,500 and 5 percent spent more than $2,600. These annual amounts include both the families' direct out-of-pocket expenditures and payments by insurance companies.[23]

Those families covered under employment-based comprehensive plans are more fortunate than those forced to buy private insurance, often at twice the expense. It is informative to compare the difference in percentage of insurance premiums paid out in benefits. In 1971 the Blue plans paid out $.90 of the premium dollar in benefits. Insurance companies continue to have the highest operating cost per enrollee, in 1971 more than three times the Blue Cross rate. Individual businesses, as against group businesses, paid out only 54% of premium income in benefits.[24]

Herman M. Somers proposes the following remedies for those whose premiums are not paid by employers:

More effort can be made to convert much of this unfortunate portion of the business into group policies and at the same time enable persons now ineligible for group purchases, and those who hold no policies at all, to join groups at more attractive rates and benefits. For example, it would appear entirely possible to permit the self-employed to enjoy group rates by contriving viable and appropriate groupings by use of associations, geographical, or other bases . . . . Employee-benefit plans could be required to cover employees over lay-off periods, for at least 90 days, as members of the employed group. This would simply be extending a fringe benefit to conform in part with what is already accepted in principle on basic pay through unemployment compensation.[25]

Most indemnity insurance companies "experience rate," which means that different people pay different amounts for a given benefit package. The indi-

[22]For a comparison of some European solutions to the insurance problem, see: Odin W. Anderson, *Health Care: Can There Be Equity? The United States, Sweden, and England* (New York: John Wiley & Sons, 1972).
[23]Martin S. Feldstein, *op. cit.*, p. 154.
[24]Marjorie Smith Mueller (1973), *op. cit.*
[25]Herman M. Somers, *op. cit.*, pp. 130–131.

vidual buyer pays according to the demographic and social class group to which he belongs. If the employee is in a high-risk employment group his rates are correspondingly high. The alternative is "community rating," where, in the fullest sense of health insurance, the healthy are helping to pay for the sick. Health maintenance organizations follow this pattern; basic health service payments are fixed under a community rather than an experience rating system. However only 5% of the population is presently enrolled in HMOs.

CHAPTER FOUR

HEALTH MANPOWER

The health industry has grown enormously since 1950. The number of persons employed in the health industry, for example, more than doubled in the twenty-year span of 1950 to 1970. The health industry is now the third largest industry in the United States, exceeded only by agriculture and construction. In 1971, 4.5 million people were employed in the health field. In other words, one out of twenty civilian workers has a job in the health industry. Figure 4.1 shows the rise in all categories of health care personnel during this century.

Health care personnel are an increasingly diverse group of workers. In contrast to the beginning of this century when two out of every three persons employed in the health field were physicians, today only one out of every twelve health workers is a physician. The great bulk of health workers are now middle level and semiskilled workers. The distribution of health care occupations by years of education is shown in Figure 4.2.

As illustrated in Figure 4.3, half of all health care personnel are involved in the provision of nursing and related services. In fact nursing is the fastest growing medical profession. Figure 4.4 indicates the marked rise in the ratio of active registered nurses per 100,000 population since 1950, in contrast with only a slight rise in the physician/population ratio, and an actual decrease in the ratio for dentists. "The proportion of registered nurses to all active medical professionals (including nurses, physicians and dentists) has increased from 56 percent in 1950 to 62 percent in 1969. In relation to the total population, the ratio of active physicians has increased by 7 percent."[1] According to Public Health Service projections for 1980, the greatest demand for future health manpower will be in the field of medical allied manpower.[2]

The major categories of health manpower we consider here are: physicians,

[1]92nd Congress, 1st Session, Committee Print, *Basic Facts on the Health Industry,* (Washington, D.C.: Government Printing Office, 1971), p. 66.
[2]Public Health Service, *Health Manpower Source Book* (Washington, D.C.: Government Printing Office, 1970).

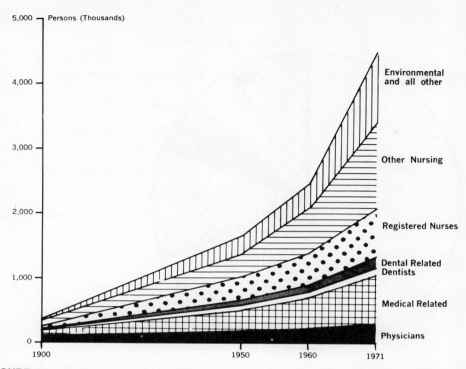

FIGURE 4.1. Increases in health manpower from 1900 to 1971. Source: Committee on Ways and Means, *National Health Insurance Resource Book* (Washington, D.C.: U. S. Government Printing Office, 1974), p. 3.

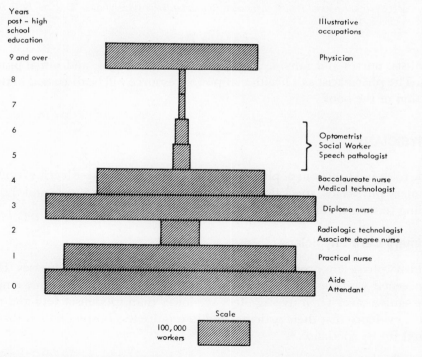

FIGURE 4.2. The medical services pyramid. Source: Bureau of Health Manpower, *Education for the Allied Health Professions and Services* (Washington, D.C.: U. S. Government Printing Office, 1974), p. 3.

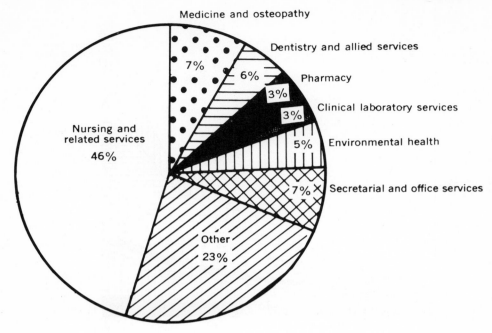

Total: 4.4 million workers

FIGURE 4.3. Percentage distribution of manpower in the health industry, 1973. Source: Committee on Ways and Means, *National Health Insurance Resource Book* (Washington, D.C.: U. S. Government Printing Office, 1974), p. 5.

dentists, nurses and nursing aides, physician's assistants, and nurse practitioners. The pharmacist as a health manpower resource will be discussed in the final section of the book.

PHYSICIANS

The roles and functions of physicians can be divided into three levels of operation: primary physicians, specialists providing secondary medical care and those providing tertiary medical care.

Primary Care Physicians

Primary physicians provide the basic services required for most illnesses. They are concerned with the "whole" patient and often his family, and they emphasize preventive care. Their average fees are lower than specialists' fees and there is some evidence that their patients tend to require less hospitalization than those cared for by specialists.[3]

[3]U. S. Department of Health, Education, and Welfare, *Towards a Comprehensive Health Policy for the 1970's: A White Paper* (Washington, D.C.: Government Printing Office, 1971).

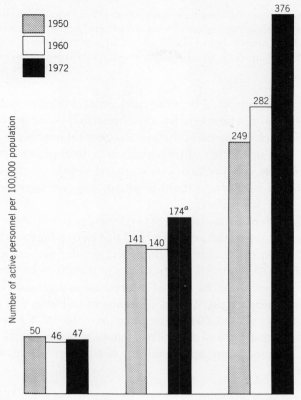

FIGURE 4.4. Comparison of ratio of active dentists, physicians, and registered nurses per 100,000 population, from 1950 to 1972. *(a)* Excludes DOs, data unavailable. Adapted from U. S. Department of Health, Education, and Welfare, *Health Resources Statistics: Health Manpower and Health Facilities, 1974* (Washington, D.C.: U. S. Department of Health, Education, and Welfare, 1974).

Ideally they mobilize and coordinate all the medical services required by their patients. They should play an important role in guiding their patients through secondary and tertiary medical care, should it be required. In this way the patient's continuous treatment is ensured and all the strands constituting health care are pulled together. The National Commission on Community Health Services concluded that a "personal" physician providing primary care is the key to comprehensive health care delivery:

To make it possible for the individual to have easy access to health care, and to facilitate coordinated, continuing health care in a comprehensive services pattern, every individual should have a personal physician who is the central point for integration and continuity of all medical and medically related services to his patient. Such a physician will emphasize the practice of preventive medicine through his own efforts and in partnership with the health and social resources of the community.

The physician should be aware of the many and varied social, emotional, and environmental factors that influence the health of his patient and his patient's family. He will either render, or direct the patient to, whatever services best suit his needs. His concern will be for the patient as a whole and his relationship with the patient must be a continuing one. In order to carry out his coordinating role, it is essential that all pertinent health information be channeled through him regardless of what institution, agency, or individual renders the service. He will have knowledge of the access to all health resources of the community—social, preventive, diagnostic, therapeutic and rehabilitative—and will mobilize them for the patient.[4]

All primary physicians used to be termed general practitioners. Unlike other physicians they could not be specialists although this is no longer the case. In 1969 family practice, which is ostensibly the same as general practice, was recognized as a specialty. Also as the number of physicians in general practice has declined, the number of internists and pediatricians engaged in primary care has grown. In 1971 the combined number of these internists and pediatricians exceeded the number of general practitioners.[5]

In 1963 only 38% of physicians in office-based patient care practice classified themselves as general practitioners. By 1967 this percentage was further reduced to 30%. By 1971 it was 26% although there is now a definite trend in the opposite direction.[6] Since 1970, when 3% of physicians in training were in areas of general practice, there has been a major shift of interest toward primary care training. As of July 1973 there was a total of 1754 residents in training, 755 in the first year, 654 in the second year, and 354 in the third year. In 1973 it was reported that there were one hundred and forty-five family practice training programs in operation, twenty-nine more approved but not yet operating, and twenty with approval pending.[7]

Secondary Care Physicians

Secondary care physicians are almost always specialists who treat a referred patient in a specialty office, or in a general or medical hospital for short-term or uncomplicated illnesses. The specialist normally has a narrow perspective of the patient because he only sees the patient infrequently for a condition needing special attention.

The U. S. Department of Health, Education, and Welfare identifies the following certified or accredited medical and osteopathic specialties:

Allergist	Forensic pathologist
Anesthesiologist	Gastroenterologist
Aviation medicine specialist	General practitioner
Cardiovascular disease specialist	Gynecologist
Colon and rectal surgeon (proctologist)	Internist
Dermatologist	Manipulative therapy specialist

[4]National Commission on Community Health Services, *Health Is A Community Affair* (Cambridge, Massachusetts: Harvard University Press, 1966), p. 21.
[5]American Medical Association, *Socioeconomic Issues of Health* (Chicago: American Medical Association, 1973).
[6]American Medical Association, *Distribution of Physician Series: 1963, 1967, 1971* (Chicago: American Medical Association).
[7]"First F. P. Priority: Filling the Primary Care Gap," *Medical World News,* **14** (September 21, 1973), pp. 72–73.

Neurologic surgeon
Neurologist
Obstetrician
Occupational medicine specialist
Ophthalmologist
Orthopedic surgeon
Otolaryngologist (Otorhinolaryn-
   gologist)
Pathologist
Pediatrician
Physiatrist (physical medicine and re-
   habilitation specialist)

Plastic surgeon
Preventive medicine specialist
Psychiatrist
Public health physician
Pulmonary disease specialist
Radiologist
Surgeon
Thoracic surgeon
Urologist
Intern
Resident
Fellow

The primary care physician can treat his patient at this level, but if he does so, he risks malpractice suits, a particular problem with surgery, for instance, which is a major specialty category. There is no law that prevents those physicians not qualified according to the standards of the American Board of Surgery and the American College of Surgeons from performing operations for which they may not have the expertise. About one-third of the physicians performing operations in the United States are not qualified according to these standards.[8]

Tertiary Care Physicians

Tertiary care is provided by a "superspecialist" usually in medical centers af-filiated with a teaching hospital. The specialist providing tertiary care has an understanding of complex medical technology, is highly skilled in his specialty, and is concerned with rare and complex medical conditions in referred patients.

Figure 4.5 illustrates the important characteristics of the three levels of care in the health care system. It can be seen that this model, which is usually discussed in the context of medical care, can also be used to analyze dental care, mental health care, and optometry.

Preventive Health Care

Part of the reemphasis on primary care has stemmed from the realization that prophylactic health care is a more humane and economical way to maintain health and treat disease. Presently about 92 to 93% of the money spent annually for medical, hospital, and health care is spent for treatment after illness has occurred. Of the remainder, 4 to 5% is spent for biomedical research; only 2 to 2½% is spent for preventive health measures, leaving less than ½% for health education.[9] It is a reflection of the disenchantment with the diminishing returns of this present

[8]Alex Gerber, "Our Outmoded Licensure Laws," *Prism,* **2** (April 1974), pp. 27–29, 67–68. See also, Rosemary A. Stevens, "Are We Ready to Modernize Licensure?," *Prism,* **1** (June 1973), pp. 22–23, 58–61.
[9]Public Health Service, *The Report of the President's Committee on Health Education* (Washington, D.C.: U. S. Department of Health, Education, and Welfare, 1971).

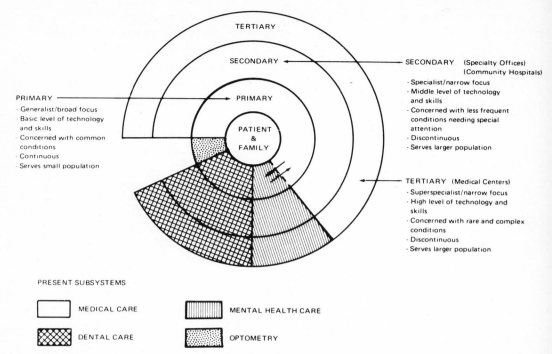

FIGURE 4.5. Personal health care system levels of care. Source: Alberta W. Parker, "The Dimensions of Primary Care: Blueprints for Change," *Primary Care: Where Medicine Fails,* edited by Spyros Andreopoulos (New York: John Wiley & Sons, 1974), p. 19, by permission of the publisher.

orientation of health care that a newer specialty such as Preventive Health Care has aroused increased interest. Although teaching hospitals vary widely in the emphasis they give to preventive and community health care, a number of medical schools now have specialty departments in preventive health. One of the best known is the Department of Preventive and Community Health at New York's Einstein College of Medicine.[10]

Preventive health care can be interpreted and implemented in several ways. It is first a societal measure of public health and safety. Real progress in health in the United States, particularly in reducing mortality rates, has been made because epidemiology has lead to environmental efforts to improve living and working conditions, especially of high risk populations; it has little to do with medical care.

A second aspect of preventive health care, called planned intervention, includes the following aspects:

1.   Immunization programs for children for diphtheria, pertussis, tetanus, poliomyelitis, measles, and rubella are conducted.

2.   Periodic prevention examinations to assure that physical, social, and emo-

[10]Health Policy Advisory Committee, *The American Health Empire: Power, Profits and Politics* (New York: Vintage Books, 1971).

tional development are progressing and that disease or disability is not incipient are held. The physical examinations are increasingly carried out by automated multiphasic equipment.

3.   Specific disease screening for cardiovascular disease, tuberculosis, hearing and eye defects, venereal disease, and so forth, is carried out.

4.   Coordinated community programs to control disease, such as alcoholism and drug addiction, are instituted.

A third aspect of preventive health care is educating the public, designed to increase the individual's understanding of available resources and to stimulate him or her to assume responsibility for maintaining personal health throughout life. Physicians, other members of the health team, health educators, government, schools, and voluntary health agencies all have such responsibility. The government's concern for health education is evidenced by the publication of the report of the President's Commission on Health Education which led to the establishment in 1973 of a Bureau of Health Education in HEW's Center for Disease Control and a HEW contract with the National Health Council to prepare plans for the establishment of a National Center for Health Education.

In spite of the fact that preventive health care is undoubtedly a crucial area of primary care, there has been little definitive research to determine the cost effectiveness of preventive health services. Most health insurance does not cover preventive services although most HMOs do include yearly checkups. Recently some insurance plans have begun to encourage health examinations by including them as benefits. Somewhat contradictory to the federal government's concern for health education and preventive care is the fact that preventive health services are disallowed for Medicare patients or Medicaid inpatients although increasing numbers of states permit health examinations under Medicaid. This broadening of support for preventive health services under private and public health plans is important to offset the clear evidence that patient use of physician services for preventive and routine services increases markedly with income.[11]

QUESTIONS FOR DISCUSSION ON PROBLEMS IN PRIMARY CARE DELIVERY

1.   What is primary care and how does it differ from secondary and tertiary care?

2.   What is the most efficient method of providing primary care?

3.   What are the major problems in primary care delivery? Suggest appropriate remedies.

[11]See E. L. White, "A Graphic Presentation on Age and Income Differentials in Selected Aspects of Morbidity, Disability, and Utilization of Health Services," *Inquiry* (Blue Cross Association), **5** (March 1968); and National Center for Health Statistics, *Characteristics of Patients of Selected Types of Medical Specialists and Practitioners, U. S., July 1963-June 1974* (Washington, D.C.: U. S. Department of Health, Education, and Welfare, 1966).

4.   What are the various roles of members of a health team with regard to primary care?

5.   What incentives would you suggest to increase the supply and improve the distribution of primary care providers?

6.   What role should the community hospital play in primary care?

7.   What should be the level of consumer involvement in primary care?

8.   What effect can Health Maintenance Organizations have on the delivery of primary care?

See Figure 4.6 for a more complete overview of the many problems associated with primary care delivery.

Physician Specialization

Part of the effort to meet the unprecedented growth in demand for medical services during the 1960s was an expansion in the supply of physicians. Despite this increase in total number of physicians, one must also look at the physician's choice of professional activity and specialty to assess the current supply of physicians providing patient care.

There were 366,367 physicians in 1973, of whom 324,367 were active. Ninety-one percent of the active physicians (295,257) were primarily involved in the direct care of patients. The other active physicians were engaged in administration (11,959), research (8332), medical teaching (6183), and other activities (2636). The distribution of all physicians in 1973, active and inactive, is shown diagrammatically in Figure 4.7.

Of the physicians providing patient care, 68% were in office-based practice and 32% were in hospital-based practice. Six specialty areas attracted over 60% of the physicians in patient care. The largest area of practice was general practice (17.9%), followed by internal medicine (15.2%), general surgery (10.0%), psychiatry (6.7%), obstetrics and gynecology (6.7%), and pediatrics (6.6%).[12]

Specialization is a phenomenon of the twentieth century and physicians are no exception. Since 1930 clinical and educational advances have facilitated the establishment of medical specialties. Up until that time only a small percentage of physicians in private practice limited themselves to a single specialty. As can be seen in Table 4.1 the number of medical college graduates limiting themselves to a specialty has grown markedly since 1930. As a matter of fact, about 75% of all active physicians in the United States reported in 1973 that they were specialists. This reaffirms the 1971 statement by Budde that: "Medicine in the United States is no longer experiencing a trend toward specialization. It is specialized."[13]

There are many reasons for the marked increase in physician specialization.

[12]American Medical Association, *Profile of Medical Practice* (Chicago: American Medical Association, 1973).
[13]Norbert W. Budde, "Specialty Distribution of Physicians," *Socioeconomic Issues of Health, op. cit.*, p. 117.

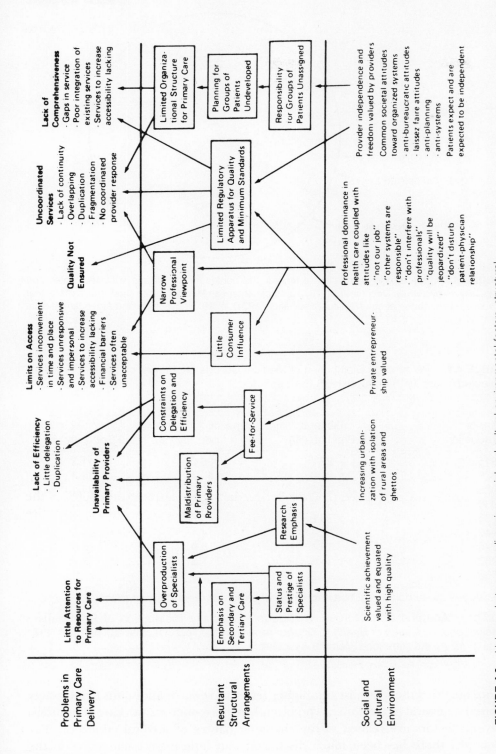

FIGURE 4.6. Linkages between predisposing social and cultural environmental factors, structural arrangements, and primary care delivery problems. Source: Alberta W. Parker, "The Dimensions of Primary Care: Blueprints for Change," *Primary Care: Where Medicine Fails*, edited by Spyros Andreopoulos (New York: John Wiley & Sons, 1974), p. 62, by permission of the publisher.

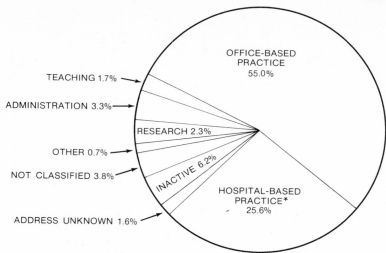

FIGURE 4.7. Percentage distribution of federal and nonfederal physicians in United States and possessions by activity, December 31, 1973. Source: American Medical Association, *Profile of Medical Practice* (Chicago: American Medical Association, 1974), p. 99. Copyright by the American Medical Association.

TABLE 4.1. Percentage Distribution of Medical College Graduates by Type of Practice; Selected Years 1915 through 1955 Classes[a]

Year of Graduation	Type of Practice		
	General Practice (%)	Special Attention to a Specialty (%)	Limited to a Specialty (%)
1915	22.7	36.0	41.3
1920	24.0	40.7	35.3
1925	25.2	40.7	34.1
1930	31.5	38.0	30.4
1935	23.2	20.5	56.3
1940	21.1	14.1	64.8
1945	19.1	5.9	75.0
1950	24.6	7.3	68.1
1955	17.7	5.5	76.8

[a] Excludes those not in practice and those who did not report type of practice.

Source. Adapted from Norbert W. Budde, "Specialty Distribution of Physicians," *Socioeconomic Issues of Health* (Chicago: American Medical Association, 1973), p. 118 Copyright by the American Medical Association

Once qualified the specialist gets higher financial rewards and status from society than the general practitioner, who often has more onerous working conditions. Several factors are related to the changing nature of medical education. For example, there has been much discussion, but little experimentation, on the importance of role models, and the teachers in medical schools are invariably specialists. Some speculate that perhaps existing academic health centers are so committed to specialization that federal support should be diverted to new institutions designed primarily to produce primary care practitioners, although this obviously could lead to the development of a two-class system.[14]

The specialization of American physicians has had marked impact on several important aspects of health care delivery, particularly the productivity, shortage, and distribution of medical manpower.

Utilization of Physician Manpower

The utilization of physician manpower (productivity) as well as the total number of physicians, affects the availability of medical care services.

The physician can have considerable influence on productivity because of his broad powers of decision making. For instance, the physician decides how many and what kinds of auxiliary personnel work with him in his practice. And committees of physicians make many of the critical decisions that affect productivity in the hospitals they are affiliated with. The patient can also affect productivity through his cooperation and general behavior. For instance, a patient who gives a physician a full and reliable medical history and who complies with the latter's instructions regarding drugs and diet can contribute substantially to the efficiency of the care he receives.[15]

It is difficult to compare qualitatively the number of hours primary physicians, as against physicians engaged in secondary and tertiary care, spend in patient care. However it is clear that primary physicians do work longer hours. General practitioners, reportedly, see three times as many patients per week as do specialists such as anesthesiologists and psychiatrists. In 1970 general practitioners and specialists in surgery, internal medicine, obstetrics-gynecology, and pediatrics averaged 45.5 to 49.9 hours per week. Psychiatrists and radiologists and other specialists averaged 34.5 to 37.2 hours per week.[16] While general practitioners represented only 28% of all physicians in office-based practice, in 1969 they were handling 61% of all patient visits.[17] Not unexpectedly, overwork and related physical and emotional strain were listed in a 1969 study as major reasons why physicians leave primary care.[18]

Physician Shortages

The term "shortage" with reference to physicians is used in many different ways. The usual concept is defined as the difference between the supply of physicians

[14]Charles E. Lewis, "Improving Access to Primary Care Through Reforms in Health Education, Orientation, and Practice," *Primary Care: Where Medicine Fails,* edited by Spyros Andreopoulos (New York: John Wiley & Sons, 1974), pp. 81–97.
[15]Victor R. Fuchs, *Who Shall Live? Health, Economics, and Social Choice* (New York: Basic Books, 1974), p. 11.
[16]American Medical Association, *Socioeconomic Issues of Health* (Chicago: American Medical Association, 1972).
[17]American Medical Association, *Distribution of Physicians in the United States, 1969* (Chicago: American Medical Association, 1970).
[18]Ronald L. Crawford and Regina C. McCormack, "Reasons Physicians Leave Primary Practice," *Journal of Medical Education,* **46** (April 1971), pp. 263–268.

and the number needed to meet a minimum standard established by the government or the profession.[19]

As noted earlier, there has been a significant decline in the number of primary care physicians as fewer physicians choose general practice. Despite this trend, however, the present demand is for more primary care physicians. The American Medical Association's placement service in 1969 had 2001 opportunities for primary care physicians, but only 864 sought opportunities, leaving 1137 unfilled positions. On the other hand there was a surplus of specialists in surgery, pathology, obstetrics-gynecology, urology, radiology, and ophthalmology seeking opportunities.[20] The imbalance in the supply of primary care physicians and specialists is one of the main problems of medical manpower in the United States today.

Nonetheless there is considerable controversy in the medical world as to whether there is a shortage of physicians in America or merely a problem of utilization and distribution. As noted by Magraw:

We have, for instance, plenty of professional personnel if only we will increase their productivity in any of the following ways: (1) educate patients to more efficient use of professional service; (2) put an appropriate emphasis on prevention and health maintenance; (3) educate in sufficient numbers an appropriate supporting cast of health workers; (4) develop more efficient organizational patterns for provision of care, such as group practitioners, hospital-based care, neighborhood health centers, and the like; (5) develop a capacity to utilize more fully automation and computers to complement human clinical skills; and, or, (6) augment the numbers of health professionals in specific geographic areas in relation to unmet needs in those areas.[21]

Those with opposing views have long felt that there is an undersupply of physicians. In 1959 the Surgeon General's Consultant Group on Medical Education found the existing ratio of physicians to population "a minimum essential to protect the health of the people of the United States."[22] Although during the 1960s many people felt the undersupply of physicians had reached a *crisis* point, it was not until 1967 that the Board of Trustees of the AMA conceded that the nation's shortage of physicians was reaching "alarming proportions" and called for an "immediate and unprecedented increase" to meet the need.[23]

According to a U. S. Bureau of Labor Statistics projection of manpower needs in 1980, which used 1968 as a baseline year (307,000 physicians), there will have to be a 3.6% yearly increase in order to meet the estimated 469,000 physicians required in 1980. This will enable the physician-population ratio to be improved

[19]The problem of measuring the demand for physicians is expertly dealt with by Rashi Fein, *The Doctor Shortage: An Economic Diagnosis* (Washington, D. C.: The Brookings Institute, 1967).
[20]*Towards a Comprehensive Health Policy for the 1970's, op. cit.*
[21]Richard Magraw, "Priorities and Issues in the Expansion of Existing Medical Schools and the Establishment of New Ones," *Expanding the Supply of Health Services in the 1970's: Report of the National Congress on Health Manpower,* The Council on Health Manpower (Chicago: American Medical Association, 1970), p. 145.
[22]Surgeon General's Consultant Group on Medical Education, *Physicians for a Growing America* (Washington, D.C.: Government Printing Office, 1959).
[23]Donald Janson, "AMA Panel Asks Drive to End Doctor Shortage,"*New York Times,* (June 20, 1967), p.1.

from the 1968 ratio of one physician per 655 people to one physician per 501 people in 1980.[24] As a result of these projections, under the stimulus of the Health Professions Educational Assistance Act of 1963, it is expected that before 1977 thirteen new medical schools and eight new dental schools will begin operation, although this will not meet the total need. With the passage of the Health Manpower Act and the Comprehensive Health Manpower Training Act of 1968 and 1971 respectively, the emphasis has been shifted from the matching grant system to direct subsidization based on a capitation criterion which gives special incentives to medical schools for increasing enrollment and the number of graduates.[25]

Despite the expansion in the number of American medical school graduates from 7264 in 1963 to an estimated 11,732 in 1973, it is only the large scale immigration to the United States of physicians educated in foreign medical schools that appears to have enabled the ratio of physicians to population to remain steady. Since 1970 the annual influx of immigrating physicians educated in foreign medical schools has exceeded the combined graduating classes of U. S. medical schools.[26] Figure 4.8 shows the dramatic increase of foreign physicians admitted to the United States since 1964. Moreover as shown in Figure 4.9, about

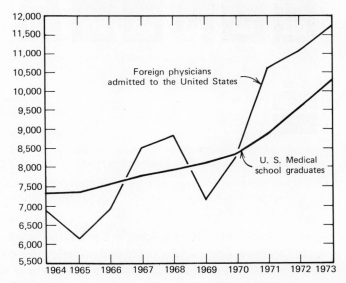

FIGURE 4.8. Comparison of new U. S. medical school graduates and foreign physicians admitted to the United States, 1964–1973. Note: Figures on foreign physicians admitted to the U. S. are from the Immigration and Nationalization Service, U. S. Department of Justice. Figures on U. S. medical school graduates are from *Journal of The American Medical Association*, November 19, 1973. All figures are for the year ending June 30. Source: *Medical Economics*, 51 (June 24, 1974), p. 89. Copyright © 1974 by Litton Industries, Inc. Published by Medical Economics Company, a Litton division, at Oradell, N.J. 07649. Reprinted by permission.

[24]U. S. Bureau of Labor Statistics, *The U. S. Economy in 1980* (Washington, D. C.: Government Printing Office, 1970).
[25]See Abraham Ribicoff, *The American Medical Machine* (New York: Horrow Books, 1972), pp. 160–167.
[26]*Medical Economics*, **51** (June 24, 1974), p. 89.

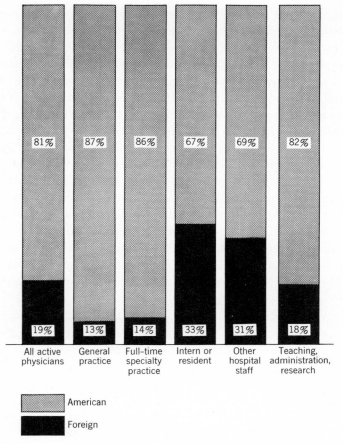

FIGURE 4.9. Proportion of active physicians who are graduates of a foreign medical school, 1973. Adapted from American Medical Association, *Profile of Medical Practice* (Chicago: American Medical Association, 1974).

one-fifth of the physicians currently practicing in the United States earned their medical degrees in foreign medical schools. These data reflect the recent trend of U. S. citizens enrolling in foreign medical schools and returning to the United States to practice medicine.

Physician Distribution

In addition to the shortage of physician graduates we need to understand geographic location in examining the availability of physicians. As can be seen in the data on nonfederal physicians in Table 4.2, the number of physicians per 100,000 population increases with urbanization, although the ratio is higher in nonmetropolitan areas for physicians providing patient care in office-based general practice. While there is general agreement that such maldistribution exists, there is a lack of consensus as to how to correct the situation.

TABLE 4.2.   Nonfederal Physicians per 100,000 Residents by Demographic County Classification: 1970

Demographic County Classification	Physicians Per 100,000 Population		
		Patient Care Physicians Only	
	Total Physicians [a]	Total Patient Care	Patient Care in Office-Based General Practice
Total	152.4	128.6	24.4
Nonmetropolitan			
less than 10,000	47.5	41.9	32.8
10,000 to 24,999	56.6	49.8	32.3
25,000 to 49,999	76.1	67.0	29.3
50,000 or more	103.8	88.3	25.4
Metropolitan			
Potential metropolitan	110.3	95.1	21.7
50,000 to 499,999	140.4	120.3	21.7
500,000 to 999,999	161.2	135.8	20.8
1,000,000 to 4,999,999	194.4	161.5	21.4
5,000,000 or more	232.6	195.0	26.9

[a] The total column represents the total number of physicians (patient care and nonpatient care) per 100,000 population.

Source.   Adapted from American Medical Association, *Socioeconomic Issues of Health* (Chicago: American Medical Association, 1973), p. 120. Copyright by the American Medical Association.

Rural Distribution.   Since it does not necessarily follow that those states best endowed with physicians are also best endowed with primary physicians, thereby providing the easiest access to patient care, it is useful to compare the ratio of primary care physicians to population in different areas of the country; see Figure 4.10. Immediately evident from this figure is the shortage of primary care physicians in certain rural states, particularly in the South and Midwest. In over one-third of the counties in America, the number of doctors per capita is less than one-third of the national ratio; one doctor for every 648 persons. In his February 18, 1971, address to Congress, President Nixon expressed concern about this situation. "In over 130 counties, comprising over 8 percent of our land area, there are no private doctors at all—and the number of such counties is growing."[27]

There is an acute shortage of doctors and other health practitioners in many rural counties because young professionals are reluctant to serve in rural areas. The remoteness, inadequate facilities, and transportation in many rural areas are frequently too disadvantageous when the professional is considering where to work.

The factors that shape a physician's decisions as to where to practice have been

[27]Richard M. Nixon, "National Health Strategy," *Weekly Compilation of Presidential Documents,* **47**:8, (February 22, 1971).

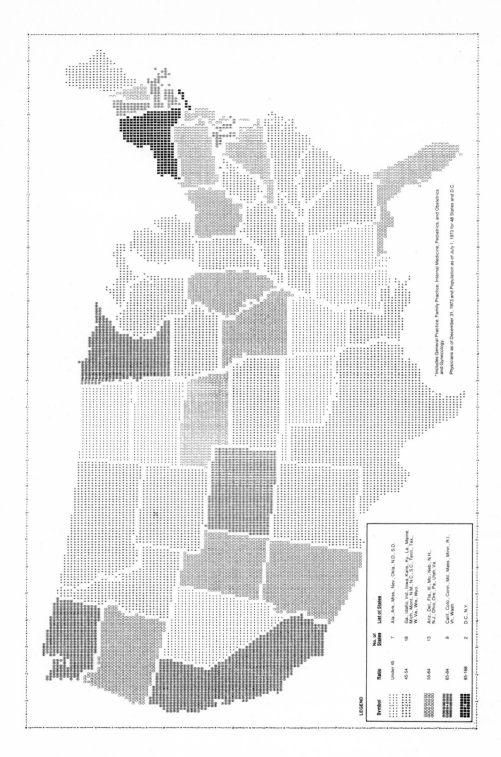

FIGURE 4.10. Number of nonfederal physicians in primary care per 100,000 civilian population within state, December 31, 1973.* Source: Center for Health Services Research and Development, *Distribution of Physicians in the U.S., 1973: Regional, State, County, Metropolitan Areas* (Chicago: American Medical Association, 1974), p. 31. Copyright by the American Medical Association.

LEGEND

Symbol	Ratio	No. of States	List of States
	Under 45	7	Ala., Ark., Miss., Nev., Okla., N.D., S.D.
	45-54	18	Ga., Idaho, Ind., Iowa, Kans., Ky., La., Maine, Mich., Mont., N.M., N.C., S.C., Tenn., Tex., W. Va., Wis., Wyo.
	55-64	13	Ariz., Del., Fla., Ill., Mo., Neb., N.H., N.J., Ohio, Ore., Pa., Utah, Va.
	65-84	9	Calif., Colo., Conn., Md., Mass., Minn., R.I., Vt., Wash.
	85-168	2	D.C., N.Y.

*Includes General Practice, Family Practice, Internal Medicine, Pediatrics, and Obstetrics and Gynecology.

Physicians as of December 31, 1973 and Population as of July 1, 1973 for 48 States and D.C.

96

the subject of many studies.[28] Despite variation in the rating of their importance, several factors in the location decision are well recognized:

1. Nonprofessional attractions of the community, such as climate, recreational facilities, cultural and social opportunities, and the educational system.

2. Professional attractions of the medical environment, including hospitals and the availability of appointments, medical schools, other physicians, and a pool of allied health personnel.

3. Innate preference for urban or rural area, possibly a reflection of other factors like the background of the physician and his or her spouse.[29]

4. Prior attachment to the area, probably related to place of internship and physician's background.

5. Economic factors—both those factors that determine the income of physicians and the per capita income and demographic characteristics of the population.

The physician generally will decide to practice in a community that best satisfies all his or her requirements. Consequently, as shown in Table 4.3, a higher proportion of general practitioners than specialists practice in non-metropolitan areas. The isolation from medical centers and colleagues is not as important to the general practitioner as it is to a medical or surgical specialist. Nevertheless, nonmetropolitan areas that had 26.4% of the total population in 1971 had only 14.5% of all physicians providing patient care.

Urban Distribution. The seemingly positive correlation between population density and total number of physicians in Table 4.3 disguises the critical physician shortage in inner city areas of many of America's largest cities. For example, in some areas of New York there is only one private doctor for every 200 persons but in other areas the ratio may be as high as one to 12,000. Dr. John L. S. Holloman, currently President of the N. Y. Health and Hospital Corporation, emphasizes the inequality in New York City by pointing out that "Two-thirds of the people must get care from one-third of the physicians."[30] Moreover, he contends that there are only 150 physicians serving 223,000 people in central Harlem; whereas, "There are over 4000 physicians on expensive Park Avenue and its side streets."[31]

A similar picture can be drawn for almost all major American cities that have large minority populations, and in many areas the problem is becoming worse. Chicago's inner city neighborhoods have some 1700 fewer physicians today than they had ten years ago.[32] The physicians who are left in these inner city neighbor-

[28]For an overview see either Bruce Steinwald, "Physician Location: Behavior Versus Attitudes," American Medical Association, *Profile of Medical Practice,* 1974 Edition, pp. 34–41; or John McFarland, "The Physician's Location Decision," *Profile of Medical Practice,* 1973 Edition, pp. 89–97.
[29]A Kansas study of 1000 practicing physicians in 1968 leads to the generalization that physicians did not practice in communities smaller than those in which their wives grew up! See Charles E. Lewis in Spyros Andreopoulos, *op. cit.,* pp. 81–97.
[30]Edward M. Kennedy, *In Critical Condition: The Crisis in America's Health Care* (New York: Simon & Schuster, 1972), p. 124.
[31]*Ibid.*
[32]Richard M. Nixon, *op. cit.*

TABLE 4.3. Distribution of Nonfederal Physicians, Hospitals, Beds, Population, and Income by Metropolitan and Nonmetropolitan Areas[a]

	Total (100.0%)	Metropolitan		Nonmetropolitan	
		Number	Percent	Number	Percent
Total physicians (12-31-72)	325,789	280,629	86.1	45,160	13.9
Total patient care	269,095	230,184	85.5	38,911	14.5
Office-based practice					
General practice	49,265	33,203	67.4	16,057	32.6
Medical specialties	47,026	42,046	89.4	4,980	10.6
Surgical specialties	63,055	54,037	85.7	9,018	14.3
Other specialties	39,628	35,390	89.3	4,238	10.7
Hospital-based practice	70,121	65,503	93.4	4,618	6.6
Other professional activity[b]	24,228	22,584	93.2	1,644	6.8
Inactive	20,110	16,345	81.3	3,765	18.7
Not classified	12,356	11,516	93.2	840	6.8
Hospitals (12-1-72)	5,895	2,892	49.1	3,003	50.9
Hospital beds (12-1-72)	883,192	653,842	74.0	229,350	26.0
Resident population (12-31-71)	207,486,300	152,704,100	73.6	54,782,200	26.04
Income (1971)					
Per capita	$ 3,558	$ 3,840		$ 2,796	
Per household	11,330	12,168		8,983	

[a] Note: percentages may not add due to rounding.
[b] Includes medical teaching, administration, research, and other.

Source. Adapted from Center for Health Services Research and Development, *Distribution of Physicians in the U.S., 1972: Volume 2/Metropolitan Areas* (Chicago: American Medical Association, 1973), p. 2. Copyright by the American Medical Association.

hoods are considerably older than the national average and their places are not being filled when they retire.[33]

There have been various policies suggested to relieve the shortage of physicians in rural and inner city areas. Some have suggested the importance of giving consideration to admitting more medical students with a rural or inner city background. Others feel that financial inducements are necessary; either in the form of direct financial incentives for those who will practice in shortage areas, or in the form of loan forgiveness or subsidized loans for medical students who would then be required to provide some years of payback service in designated shortage areas.

The federal government, in 1972, implemented the National Health Services Corps under the auspices of the then HSMHA. The Corps is designed specifically to place doctors and nurses in urban ghettos, rural areas, and other settings where there is often a serious shortage of these and other health professionals. In

[33]For a telling presentation of the dilemma these older physicians face, see: Ruth E. Hardy, "I Don't Want to Leave My Patients, But . . . ," *Prism,* **1** (August 1973), pp. 44–46.

addition there has been an attempt to reorganize manpower in rural areas through regional health planning measures.

In the immediate future, one of the most promising developments is the use of physicians' assistants and nurse practitioners to augment the physicians' services, a development that we discuss later in this chapter.

WOMEN AND MINORITIES IN MEDICINE

In recent years a major effort has been made to increase the enrollment of women and minority group individuals in U. S. medical schools. Since 1970, as shown in Figure 4.11, more progress has been made for women than for minorities. As a matter of fact, in 1973–74, women students were 15.4% of the total enrollment, almost triple the 1959–60 figure of 5.7%; women also were 11.4% of the 1973–74 graduating class. In addition women now account for 8.3% of all physicians. In the last decade their numbers have increased at double the rate of the total physician population.

Since 1969–70, U. S. medical schools have been encouraged to maintain and report minority enrollment statistics. The basic groups for which data are now maintained are: black Americans; American Indians; Mexican Americans; American Orientals; and Puerto Ricans (Mainland). Figure 4.11 is clearly illustrative of proportionate and actual number increases in minority group enrollments in the recent past. In the period 1969–70 to 1973–74 the number of minority group students enrolled in medical schools actually doubled.

As further illustrated by Figure 4.11, black Americans constitute the largest minority medical student group and have experienced the largest increase in percent of total medical school enrollment among the identified minority groups. The enrollment of black Americans increased from 1042 in 1969–70 to 3045 in 1973–74. Yet the 1970 goal of the Executive Council of the Association of American Medical Colleges of 12% black freshmen in medical schools by 1975–76 fell short by 4.5%.[34] The actual increase of black freshman medical students from 1970–71 to 1975–76 was 1.4%. Enrollment statistics for the other minority groups for 1969–70 and 1973–74 are as follows:

	1969–70	1973–74
American Indians	18	97
Mexican Americans	92	496
American Orientals	489	883
Puerto Ricans (Mainland)	26	123

While there are problems of retention among minority group medical students that are far more difficult than those encountered by medical students in general—even allowing for the repetition of academic years—U. S. medical

[34]Davis G. Johnson, et al., "Recruitment and Progress of Minority Medical School Entrants: 1970–72," *Journal of Medical Education,* **50** (July 1975), pp. 713–755.

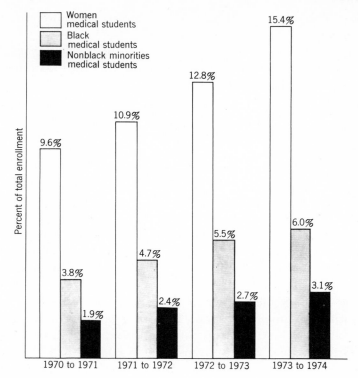

FIGURE 4.11. Comparison of women, black, and nonblack minority medical students, as percentages of total medical student enrollment, 1970–1974. Note: Percentages exclude noncitizens of the United States. Adapted from American Medical Association. *Socioeconomic Issues of Health* (Chicago: American Medical Association, 1974).

schools have and are making concerted efforts to increase the number of minority group individuals who meet acceptable standards of competence for graduation. Illustratively graduation rates for 1972–73 and 1973–74 for minority group medical students were 3.8 and 5.4% of the total number graduating, with black Americans representing 3.3 and 4.5% respectively.

Of obvious importance to enrollment and graduation data for black Americans is the existence of two predominantly black medical schools, one at Howard University in Washington, D. C., and Meharry Medical College in Nashville, Tennessee. Of the 1042 and 3045 black students enrolled in medical schools in 1969–70 and 1973–74, 496 of the 1969–70 enrollees and 667 of the 1973–74 enrollees were matriculating at Howard and Meharry. Until recently both institutions were the major centers for medical and dental education for black Americans. Indeed about half of the black physicians and dentists currently in practice are Meharry graduates.

Since data exist that are indicative of a possible correlation between parental annual income and student educational achievement, as measured by standardized tests, the problem of blacks, as a representative minority groups, becomes more complex. Economics thus becomes a double-edged sword, in terms of both educational achievement and the price of medical education. In this regard it is significant to note that 41% of medical students in 1968 were from families with annual incomes of $15,000 or more, although only 12% of American families were in that income bracket in 1968.[35] In 1970 only 24% of the white students in medical school were from families with annual incomes of $10,000 or less, while 65% of black studente came from such backgrounds. Additionally, from 1968 to 1972, the average difference in median income for white and nonwhite families was approximately $4030, with the peak annual median income for whites and nonwhites being $11,549 and $7106 respectively in 1972.[36]

In order to facilitate access to medical school for low income students the federal government has increased its loan program for medical students. Some states, as well as medical societies and fraternal organizations, also have established loan programs. Moreover the Health Professions Educational Assistance Act of 1976 contains a provision that provides $20 million per year for the three successive years, 1978 to 1980, to increase access to a health professions career for persons from disadvantaged backgrounds.

DENTISTS

More than 70% of dentists are general practitioners in solo practice, although increasingly group dental practices are emerging, a few of which have prepayment plans. The pronounced trend toward specialization that was discussed in detail with regard to physicians has affected all health practitioners, including dentists. There are now eight dental specialties. Half of the specialists engage exclusively in orthodontics and a quarter in oral surgery. About 10% of all dentists are presently in specialty practice.

Both the general population and the number of dentists increased about 15% between 1960 and 1972, so that the dentist-to-population ratio in 1972 was the same as in 1960—47 dentists per 100,000 population. At the end of 1972 there were 119,700 licensed dentists in the United States, approximately 105,400 of whom were active, with 7430 serving in the various branches of the armed forces.[37] The vast majority of active civilian dentists are primarily engaged in direct patient care; 96.6% in 1970.[38] The remaining 3.4% was distributed as follows: administration, 1.1%; teaching, 2.0%; and research and other, 0.3%.

Although there is expected to be no alteration in the ratio of dentists to population in the near future the demand for dental care is expected to almost double by 1980.[39] This rise in demand is projected because of population expan-

[35]American Medical Association, *Socioeconomic Issues of Health* (Chicago: American Medical Association, 1974).
[36]U. S. Bureau of the Census, *Statistical Abstract of the United States, 1974* (Washington, D.C.: U. S. Department of Commerce, 1974).
[37]U. S. Department of Health, Education, and Welfare, *Health Resources Statistics: Health Manpower and Health Facilities, 1974* (Washington, D.C.: U. S. Department of Health, Education, and Welfare, 1974).
[38]U. S. Department of Health, Education, and Welfare, *The Supply of Health Manpower: 1970 Profiles and Projections to 1990* (Washington, D.C.: Government Printing Office, 1974).
[39]*Health Manpower Source Book 21 . . .* , *op. cit.*

sion, anticipated rises in the standard of living and education, and present-day private and public methods of financing dental services. For example, there is increasing pressure from labor unions to include dental care as part of employee fringe benefits; in addition, the Medicaid provision of the Social Security Act provides dental treatment for a wide group of eligible recipients.

In view of the preceding, it is important to note that the number of visits made to dentists varies in direct proportion to a family's income, as shown in Figure 4.12. Families with incomes of less than $3000 make about a third as many visits as families with incomes of $15,000 and over. There is also a significant racial pattern in the use of dental services. White persons made 1.6 visits to the dentist per person per year while persons of other races made 0.7 visits.[40] Research has shown that 45% of all white persons see a dentist once a year, compared to about 23% of nonwhites. Whereas one out of seven whites have never seen a dentist, one out of three minority race members have never seen a dentist.[41] It remains to be seen whether the inclusion of dental services under Medicaid can improve access for the poor and minority group members, despite the vagaries of Medicaid eligibility.

Based on 1970 Census of Population data, approximately three out of every 100 civilian dentists are female.[42] Blacks constituted 2.3% of active civilian dentists

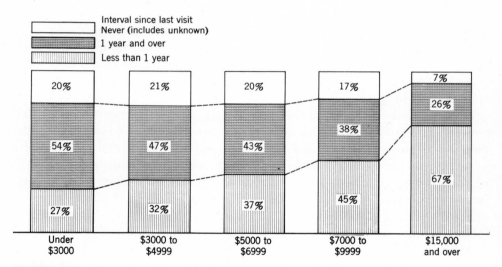

FIGURE 4.12. The poor see dentists far less frequently than persons with higher incomes. Note: Percentages may not add due to rounding. Adapted from National Center for Health Statistics, *Dental Visits: Volume and Interval Since Last Visit, United States–1969* (Washington, D.C.: U. S. Department of Health, Education, and Welfare, 1972).

[40]National Center for Health Statistics, *Dental Visits: Volume and Interval Since Last Visit, United States—1969* (Washington, D.C.: U. S. Department of Health, Education, and Welfare, 1972).
[41]*Basic Facts on the Health Industry, op. cit.*
[42]U. S. Bureau of the Census, *U. S. Census of Population: 1970—Detailed Characteristics* (Washington, D.C.: U. S. Department of Commerce, 1973).

in 1970, about the same as in 1960. Currently blacks comprise 4.6% of first-year enrollments; American Orientals 2.6%; Spanish or Mexican Americans 1.1%; and American Indians about 0.1%.[43] Current information on women is incomplete, although a 1972 American Dental Association publication suggests a future increase in the number of women in the dental profession.[44]

NURSES AND NURSING AIDES

Professional Nurses (RNs)

Professional or graduate nurses are responsible for the nature and quality of all nursing care that patients receive. They are responsible for carrying out the physician's instructions and for supervising licensed practical nurses and other personnel who provide routine care and treatment of patients.

In January 1972 the Interagency Conference on Nursing Statistics estimated about 74% of the active registered nurses were employed in hospitals, nursing homes, and related institutions. Thirteen percent were in public health, school, occupational health, and nursing education, and the remaining 12.7% were in private duty in doctors' offices and other fields (see Table 4.4). These data are further evidence of a significant change in nursing in the past twenty-five years, the relative shift from private duty nursing to salaried employment.

There were 815,000 licensed registered nurses in practice in the the United States as of January 1973, an increase of 35,000 over the previous year, and representing a nurse to population ratio of 1:281.[45] Between 1950 and 1969 the ratio of registered nurses to the total population increased by a third.[46] However

TABLE 4.4. Field of Employment of Registered Nurses: January 1, 1972

Field of Employment	Number of Nurses	Percent of Total
Hospitals and nursing homes	578,000	74.1
Public health and school	54,800	7.0
Nursing education	28,400	3.6
Occupational health	20,000	2.6
Private duty, doctor's office, and other fields	98,800	12.7
Total	780,000 [a]	100.0

[a] Preliminary revised estimate.

Source. Adapted from U. S. Department of Health, Education, and Welfare, *Health Resources Statistics: Health Manpower and Health Facilities, 1974* (Washington, D.C.: U. S. Department of Health, Education, and Welfare, 1974), p. 201.

[43]*The Supply of Health Manpower, op. cit.*
[44]American Dental Association, *Annual Report on Dental Education, 1972–73* (Chicago: American Dental Association, 1973).
[45]*Health Resources Statistics, op. cit.*
[46]*Basic Facts on the Health Industry, op. cit.*

this increase is offset by the large numbers of RNs who have left nursing. In 1972 the American Nurses' Association inventory revealed that 316,611 RNs were not employed in nursing.[47] The high attrition rate and the considerable proportion of registered nurses who are employed on a part-time basis—28% of the total in 1969—are the main factors in the nursing shortage.[48] Repeated efforts have been made, with marginal results, to get these trained individuals who have retired from the labor force back into the nursing field. As long ago as 1967 the National Advisory Commission on Health Manpower recommended that "nursing should be made a more attractive profession by such measures as appropriate utilization of nursing skills, increased levels of professional responsibilities, improved salaries, more flexible hours for married women, and better retirement provisions."[49]

The nursing education pyramid and the qualifications required for licensure are illustrated in Figure 4.13. Graduation from high school is a requirement for admission to all schools of nursing.

In general there are three education routes that prepare individuals for licensure as RNs. Baccalaureate programs usually require four years of study in a college or university, although a few require five years. A graduate degree, which involves one to five years of study beyond the baccalaureate, is ordinarily required for advanced clinical practice, teaching, research, and other advanced positions. Specialty practice is developing rapidly in nursing too. During 1973 interim certification boards were established in community health, psychiatric mental health, geriatric, medical-surgical, maternal and child health nursing.

Associate degree programs, which are approximately two years in length, are usually offered at junior or community colleges. The diploma programs range in length from two and one-half to three years of training and are conducted in hospital schools. Graduates of either of these two programs are not prepared for supervisory or administrative positions in nursing.

Baccalaureate and associate degree programs are presently the major sources of nursing graduates. The output of the hospital based diploma programs has remained at essentially the same level for the past ten years.

Licensed Practical Nurses

Licensed practical nurses, known also as licensed vocational nurses, provide nursing care and treatment to patients under the supervision of a licensed physician or registered nurse. As of January, 1973, there were about 459,000 licensed practical nurses employed in the United States, an increase of 32,000 over the previous year.[50]

Most licensed practical nurses work in hospitals, clinics, homes for the aged,

[47]*Health Resources Statistics, op. cit.*
[48]*Basic Facts on the Health Industry, op. cit.*
[49]*Report of the National Advisory Commission on Health Manpower: Volume 1* (Washington, D.C.: U. S. Government Printing Office, 1967), p. 23.
[50]*Health Resources Statistics, op. cit.*

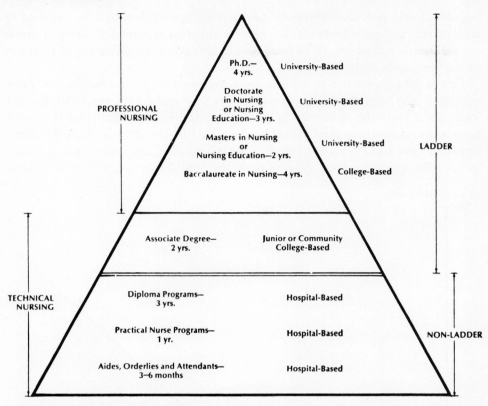

FIGURE 4.13.   The nursing education pyramid. From *The Physician's Assistant: Today and Tomorrow,* p. 49. Copyright 1975 by Alfred M. Sadler, Jr., Blair L. Sadler, and Anne A. Bliss. Reprinted with permission of Ballinger Publishing Company.

and nursing homes. Many others work in private homes, while the remainder work in doctor's offices, schools, and public health agencies.

By law practical nurses must be licensed in all of the fifty states and the District of Columbia (or as a licensed vocational nurse in California and Texas). The requirements for admission into practical nursing school programs vary from two years of high school to a high school diploma. The programs are usually twelve to eighteen months in duration and are offered by: (1) trade, technical, or vocational schools operated by public school systems; (2) proprietary schools controlled by hospitals; (3) health agencies; or (4) colleges. By October 1972, 1310 programs in 1220 schools of practical nursing education had been approved by state agencies. In the academic year 1971–72, there were 61,680 admissions and 44,446 graduates.

Related Nursing Services Personnel

There are various kinds of workers who provide auxiliary nursing services in hospitals, clinics and nursing homes. Nursing aides, traditionally women, help registered and practical nurses by performing less skilled tasks in the care of patients. Orderlies and attendants, traditionally men, perform a variety of duties for male patients and certain heavy duties in the care of the physically ill, mentally ill, and mentally retarded.

Figure 4.14 shows the actual and projected increase in the number of aides, orderlies, and attendants, in comparison to RNs and LPNs, for 1950 through 1980. Data from the American Hospital Association show that related nursing services personnel increased in number from 221,000 in 1950 to 375,000 in 1960. Between 1960 and 1973, the number of aides, orderlies, and attendants increased to 910,000, almost two and one-half times the 1960 figure and 35,000 more than

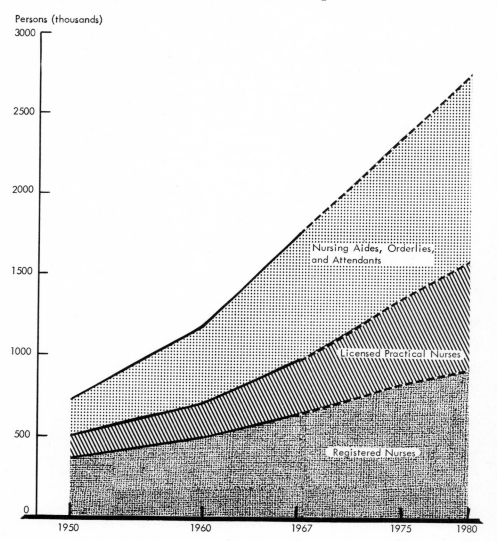

FIGURE 4.14. Employment in nursing and related services, 1950–1980. Source: Maryland Y. Pennell and David B. Hoover, *Health Manpower Source Book 21: Allied Health Manpower, 1950–1980* (Washington, D.C.: U. S. Department of Health, Education, and Welfare, 1970), p. 23.

in 1972.[51] Home health aides are not included in the 1973 figure. Except for psychiatric aides who are licensed in Arkansas, California, and Michigan, licensure is not required for these personnel. Hospitals and clinics usually have their own standards and also provide on-the-job training programs which may last several months.

The last category, home health aides (also called home aides or visiting health aides), is a relative newcomer. These individuals provide supportive nursing services in the home rather than in an institutional setting. Household and personal services are provided to persons who are ill and disabled, with an orientation toward preventing, postponing, or shortening institutionalized care. Homemakers also provide these services, although generally not in situations involving illness. There were 30,700 persons employed in these two fields in 1973.[52]

Most employers, usually public or private agencies, provide on the job training for home health aides, since neither formal education nor health training are employment requirements. Thus home health aides have to work under professional supervision. While some states do have certification programs for home health aides, presently no state requires certification for homemakers.

ALLIED HEALTH MANPOWER

The allied health field "is defined broadly to include the professional, technical, and supportive workers in patient services, administration, teaching and research who engage in activities that support, complement or supplement the functions of physicians, dentists, and registered nurses."[53] Two of the more significant recent developments in the field of allied health have been the introduction of the physician's assistant and the nurse practitioner.

Physician's Assistant (PA)

The development of the physician's assistant is one result of the research for increased access, efficiency, and productivity in the delivery of continuing primary and preventive health care, especially to underserved rural and inner city residents. The Office of Economic Opportunity promoted PAs during the 1960s since it was expected that they would work in isolated rural or poverty areas and also as a way to salvage the skills of 30,000 medics discharged annually during the Vietnam war years. These medics represented a vast potential supply of paraprofessionals, as many of them had extensive health care services experience, occasionally including the direct provision of care.

The concept of a physician's assistant is not new. Types of PAs have been used previously with great success in other countries; for example, the "Feldshers" in

[51]*Ibid.*
[52]*Health Resources Statistics, op. cit.*
[53]*The Supply of Health Manpower, op. cit.*

the Soviet Union and China's "barefoot" doctors.[54] Moreover American physicians have been delegating tasks of all kinds to medical assistants and nurses for many years. What is new is the desire to formalize an educational process to train the PA as an alternative manpower source for extending physician services. The leadership role the AMA has played in the development of the PA concept is both laudable and obvious, especially since PAs are selected, trained, and supervised by physicians. The AMA's Council on Health Manpower continues to play a vital role in the evaluation of the need for and functions of new categories of health manpower. The AMA's Council on Medical Education, in conjunction with the National Board of Medical Examiners, also has an important role in allied medical education, including the accreditation of physician's assistant programs.

The first formal PA program was started at Duke University in 1965, followed by the MEDEX program at the University of Washington in Seattle in 1969. By mid-1974 there were over fifty programs training assistants to primary and physician specialists, excluding nurse practitioners and including programs in the armed forces.[55] Forty-nine of these programs now have full or provisional accreditation status.[56]

Because of the great diversity of programs there is some confusion about the definition of the term PA, or the term physician extender, which is sometimes used to cover nurse practitioners as well. Included under these generic terms are persons being trained to work in a variety of medical specialty areas, at different levels of responsibility and with different specific occupational titles, for example, physician's assistant, physician's associate, clinical associate, and MEDEX. To date the Board of Medicine of the National Academy of Sciences has offered the most definitive job classification of PAs:

The Type A assistant is capable of approaching the patient, collecting historical and physical data, organizing the data, and presenting them in such a way that the physician can visualize the medical problem and determine appropriate diagnostic or therapeutic steps. He is also capable of assisting the physician by performing diagnostic and therapeutic procedures and coordinating the roles of other more technical assistants. While he functions under the general supervision and responsibility of the physician, he might under special circumstances and under defined rules, perform without the immediate surveillance of the physician. He is thus distinguished by his ability to integrate and interpret findings on the basis of general medical knowledge to exercise a degree of independent judgment.

The Type B assistant, while not equipped with general knowledge and skills relative to the whole range of medical care, possesses exceptional skill in one clinical specialty or, more commonly, in certain procedures within such a specialty. In his area of specialty, he has a degree of skill beyond that normally possessed by physicians who are not engaged in the specialty. Because his knowledge and skill are limited to a particular specialty, he is less qualified for independent action. An example of this type of assistant might be one who is

[54]Tsung O. Cheng, "China's 'Barefoot Doctors'," Prism 1 (April 1973), pp. 16–19; and Joseph Kadish and James W. Long, "The Training of Physician Assistants: Status and Issues," Journal of the American Medical Association, 212 (May 1970), pp. 1047–1051.
[55]U. S. Department of Health, Education, and Welfare, A Directory of Programs Training Physician Support Personnel, 1973–74 (Washington, D.C.: Government Printing Office, 1974).
[56]Donald W. Fisher, "Physician Assistant: A Profile of the Profession" (paper presented at the Conference on Health Manpower, Tarrytown, New York, April 16–18, 1975).

highly skilled in the physician's functions associated with a renal dialysis unit and who is capable of performing these functions as required.

The Type C assistant is capable of performing a variety of tasks over the whole range of medical care under the supervision of a physician, although he does not possess the level of medical knowledge necessary to integrate and interpret findings. He is similar to a Type A assistant in the number of areas in which he can perform, but he cannot exercise the degree of independent synthesis and judgment of which Type A is capable. This type of assistant would be to medicine what the practical nurse is to nursing.[57]

The PA obviously can serve in all types of settings: physician's office, clinic or hospital, the patient's home, an extended care facility, or a nursing home.

Educational training for PAs varies from twelve months to five years, and ends with the award of a degree or certificate. The prerequisites for admission to these programs, depending on the degree of education and experience of the applicant, also vary. The training usually consists of a combination of academic instruction and clinical experience, and the total cost of training a PA is estimated to be from one-third to one-fifth the cost of training a primary care physician, which in view of increased concern with medical costs is an important consideration.

Not surprisingly, considering the brief history of the PA concept, there are still a number of unresolved questions with regard to PAs. These concern their supervision and legal standing; their relationship with other members of the health team, in particular the nursing profession; their acceptance by patients; and their future career prospects. There is little consensus on the limits of the PA's responsibilities, or what constitutes "reasonable supervision." It seems likely that judicial interpretation will be required here. As yet the limited number of PAs practicing has meant that the full scope of the legal implications of the PA movement has not been revealed. Insurance carriers are, however, writing malpractice coverage for both the employing physician and the individual PA.

The specific details of the legal position of the PA vary from state to state. However by the end of 1974 thirty-seven states had enacted legislation establishing two basic types of regulatory mechanisms. On the one hand, eight states amended their medical practice acts to give the physician authority to utilize a PA under his supervision and direction, with the supervising physician given considerable flexibility in the selection and utilization of the PA.[58] On the other hand, twenty-nine states have enacted legislation which grants authority to a state agency, usually the state board of medical examiners, to establish regulations concerning education and practice for PA's. Nationally the question of certification remains unresolved, although certification rather than licensure is the preferred mechanism. Opposition to licensure is widespread although the alternatives vary: codification of tasks the physician can delegate; enforcement of

[57]Board of Medicine, National Academy of Sciences, *Physician's Assistants: Report of a Study* (Washington, D.C.: Board of Medicine, National Academy of Sciences, May 1970), pp. 3–4.
[58]See William J. Curran, "The California Physician's Assistants' Law," *New England Journal of Medicine*, **283** (December 1970), pp. 1274–1275; Winston J. Dean, "State Legislation for Physician's Assistant: A Review and Analysis," *Health Service Reports*, **88** (January 1973), pp. 3–12; and Roger M. Borkin, "Need for Statutory Legitimation of the Role of Physician's Assistant," *Health Service Reports*, **89** (January–February 1974), pp. 31–36.

prior approval of training programs; or the establishment of detailed PA job descriptions.[59] Interestingly certification standards are generally higher than those for licensure. Nevertheless the prerequisites for the National Board of Medical Examiners (NBME) certification examination are sufficiently flexible to allow for individual differences in education and experience. As an added note, a National Commission on Certification of Physicians' Assistants was established in August of 1974, which, in conjunction with the NBME, supervises the administration and distribution of results of the certification examination.

Various studies have indicated that the physician's productivity is increased by physician extenders. For example the experience to date with MEDEX graduates shows that there is an increase in patient volume, new patients seen, and the number of new conditions treated, although there is not yet a clear understanding of these results.[60] There is also a decrease in appointment and office waiting time, as well as a decrease in physician hours worked per week. Patients rate MEDEX graduates quite high in terms of technical competence and quality of care provided subsequent to their employment.[61] Of comparable importance is the fact that about 75% of active MEDEX graduates are employed in ambulatory, fee-for-service, and general/family practice settings.[62] Similar results have been reported for all graduate physician's assistants, for example, 77% are employed in the primary care field.[63] Although the evidence on the effect of PAs on the cost of medical care is inconclusive, by freeing the physician from more routine care the PA can maintain and possibly improve the quality of medical care by providing the physician with more time with the patients he needs to see and also by enabling him to have time available for continuing medical education. PAs also fill a very important and often neglected role of patient education and counselling. Moreover available data suggest that patient acceptance of PAs is good, with the possible exception of patients having considerable affluence and those at the lower end of the socioeconomic spectrum.[64] [65]

A critical question with regard to the further development of the role of PAs pertains to reimbursement. Part B of Medicare presently pays for services usually rendered in a physician's office by paramedical personnel, but under current law will not pay when a physician submits a charge for a professional service performed by a paramedical person in cases when the service is traditionally performed by a physician. Government reimbursement policy has undoubtedly influenced the reluctance of private nonprofit health insurance plans to make physician extenders eligible for third-party reimbursement.[66]

[59]Alfred M. Sadler, et al., *The Physician's Assistant: Today and Tomorrow* (New Haven: Yale University Press, 1972).

[60]National Council of MEDEX Programs, *A Progress Report on MEDEX Programs in the United States* (Seattle: National Council of MEDEX Programs, 1974).

[61]Eugene C. Nelson, et al., "Patients' Acceptance of Physician's Assistant," *Journal of the American Medical Association,* **228** (April, 1974), pp. 63–67.

[62]National Council of MEDEX Programs, *op. cit.*

[63]Donald W. Fisher, *op. cit.*

[64]E. Harvey Estes and D. Robert Howard, "The Physician's Assistant in the University Center," *Annals of the New York Academy of Sciences,* **166,** 1969, pp. 903–910.

[65]Eugene C. Nelson, *op. cit.*

[66]Judith R. Lave, et al., "The Physician's Assistant: Exploration of the Concept," *Hospitals,* **45** (June 1971), pp. 42–51.

There is a certain conflict in the federal government's attitude toward PAs. While Medicare payments have been withheld from PAs since 1971, the federal government has provided more than $12 million annually to train PAs! Prior to 1971 several private foundations provided the initial financial support for these programs. The Social Security Administration is now conducting a study of the reimbursement patterns for PAs and other physician extenders not currently covered by Medicare and Medicaid.

As of April 1975 it was estimated that there was a combined total of 2500 PA graduates and students in training, the vast majority of whom are white males.[67] Because PAs were supposed to provide primary care services in areas where there is a shortage of physicians, early data do suggest that "physician assistants are concentrating in primary care medicine in the more underserved areas."[68] Obviously the long-term concentration preference and distribution of PAs will be the most important indication of the success of the concept. If, in the future, PAs become predominantly specialists, or if they are legally required to be supervised very closely by physicians, the same patterns of overspecialization and maldistribution that presently characterize the physician population may develop.

Leaving aside the crucial but unresolved question as to whether, in the long run, PAs will substantially improve patient access to quality primary care, particularly in rural areas and in the inner city, the PA's demonstrated ability to improve the physician's productivity has meant there is a considerable demand for PAs. There is no problem for PAs to gain employment, and it seems anticipated problems about interstate transfer are being worked out. It remains to be seen how satisfactory a PA's role and remuneration will be in the long run and what career ladders can be developed.

Nurse Practitioners (NPs)

The opportunity for registered nurses to take specialty courses to extend their nursing roles was extant long before the first formal nurse practitioner program was established at the University of Colorado in 1965. The Colorado program was viewed by its developers as one solution to the health manpower shortage and as a means of improving health care delivery. The establishment of this program also had the effect of further illuminating the need for a new perspective of the nurse in terms of professional independence and role identity, especially in light of the continuing interdependent relationship among physicians, nurses, and other members of the health team, including PAs. In this regard, and because of a large degree of overlap in the practice area between nurse practitioners and PAs, the nursing profession has questions concerning the need for the PA, the "lack of universally accepted guidelines for use of PAs in the health care system, comparable salaries, and the carrying out of physician's assistant orders by the nurse."[69] On the salary issue, Mahoney has reported that PAs, as a group, are earning higher annual salaries than nurse practitioners.[70]

[67]Donald W. Fisher, *op. cit.*
[68]*Ibid.*, p. 8.
[69]Alfred M. Sadler, et al., *op. cit.*, pp. 46–47.
[70]Margaret E. Mahoney, "The Future Role of Physician's Assistants and Nurse Practitioners," *National*

The relationship of nurse practitioners to PAs is a controversial subject. Each profession has its territorial perspective, although NPs and PAs are often defined similarly under the rubric of the term "physician extender." Yet there is considerable variance in the requirements for admission into training programs for NPs and PAs. In general NP programs train licensed registered nurses with (master's programs) or without (certificate programs) a baccalaureate degree, whereas prerequisites for entry into PA programs vary from high school graduation or experience as a medical corpsman to a baccalaureate degree.

Nurse practitioner programs include didactic and clinical components and vary in length from one month to two years. Educational costs associated with NP programs are estimated to be lower than those for PA programs since the programs generally are of shorter duration; however, valid costs per graduate for PAs and NPs cannot be obtained because adequate and comparable cost data are not presently available. In 1973–74, there were eighty three nurse practitioner certificate programs in existence and 54 master's degree programs.[71] The major focus of the programs is primary care, with three areas of concentration: family planning, family practice, and pediatrics.

Nurses are licensed in every state and have the responsibility and authority under the legal framework of nursing practice acts to delineate the scope of nursing practice. Licensure and certification being terms that are of significance to the current controversy surrounding the NP-PA issue, it is important to note the legal difference between licensure and certification:

Licensure—The process by which an agency of government grants permission to persons to engage in a given profession or occupation by certifying that those licensed have attained the minimal degree of competency necessary to ensure that the public health, safety, and welfare will be reasonably well protected.

Certification or Registration—The process by which a nongovernmental agency or association grants recognition to an individual who has met certain predetermined qualifications specified by that agency or association.[72]

Certification is not a legal sanction to practice. Registration is currently being defined as something less than licensure but under the control of state boards of medical examiners which establish legal practice parameters. While current procedures (certification or registration) require physician supervision of PAs, nursing practice acts provide registered nurses with the flexibility to perform a wide range of activities only physicians performed in the past; however, Colorado and Washington did amend their nursing practice acts in 1973 explicitly to cover the NPs expanded role. As stated by the American Nurses' Association:

Health Services: Their Impact on Medical Education and Their Role in Prevention, edited by John Z . Bowers and Elizabeth Purcell (New York: Josiah Macy, Jr. Foundation, 1973).
[71]American Nurses' Association and U. S. Department of Health, Education, and Welfare, *Preparing Registered Nurses for Expanded Roles, 1973–74: A Directory of Programs* (Washington, D.C.: U. S. Department of Health, Education, and Welfare, 1974).
[72]U. S. Department of Health, Education, and Welfare, *Report on Licensure and Related Health Personnel Credentialing* (Washington, D.C.: U. S. Department of Health, Education, and Welfare, 1971), p. 7.

The nurse practitioner engages in independent decision-making about the nursing care needs of clients and collaborates with other health professionals, such as the physician, social worker, and nutritionist in making decisions about other health care needs. The nurse working in an expanding role practices in primary, acute and chronic health care settings. As a member of the health care team, the nurse practitioner plans and institutes health care programs.[73]

The only prohibitions under nursing practice acts pertain to diagnosing and prescribing. However legal problems still are a source of major concern regarding the acceptance and full utilization of NPs and PAs.[74] Because of the present malpractice furor physicians and physician extenders may have to contend with civil suits filed under the doctrine of *respondent superior* or *negligence per se*. In the case of the former the employer is responsible for all negligent acts of employed persons where such acts occur within the scope of employment, regardless of whether or not the employee is licensed.[75] However licensure "is relevant in some jurisdictions to the procedural matter of the burden-of-proof regarding negligence."[76]

In the case of the latter a physician extender and an employer could be accused of violating their state's medical and nursing practice acts. For the NP (and employer) it could mean the performance of tasks going beyond the scope of a state's nursing practice act, including the difficulty which would be associated with determining competence within the context of "custom and usage; and, violation of the state's medical practice act by performing (or, in the case of a physician employer, delegating) 'medical' tasks which are not officially exempt under the act, regardless of the quality of care provided."[77]

Much like PAs, nurse practitioners represent a means of increasing the availability and quality of health care. To date evaluations similar to those for PAs have been reported for NPs concerning professional competence, improvement in quality of care provided, reductions in physician workload, and patient acceptance.[78-80] Unfortunately, as was the case with PAs, no conclusions have been reached regarding the effect of the NP on the cost of medical care. With regard to distribution, NPs are reportedly practicing successfully in urban and rural areas, in solo and group practices, and in a wide variety of health facilities and agencies, from hospitals and health departments to collegiate student health services and Indian Reservations.[81]

[73]American Nurses' Association and U. S. Department of Health, Education, and Welfare, *op. cit.,* p. v.
[74]An excellent review based on a 1973 survey of some of the major issues surrounding the PA-NP debate can be found in Chapter 5 of A. S. Ford's *The Physician's Assistant—A National and Local Analysis* (New York: Praeger Publishers, 1975).
[75]*Report on Licensure and Related Health Personnel Credentialing, op. cit.*
[76]*Ibid.,* p. 4.
[77]A. S. Ford, *op. cit.*
[78]Henry K. Silver and James A. Hecker, "The Pediatric Nurse Practitioner and the Child Health Associate: New Types of Health Professionals," *Journal of Medical Education,* **45** (March 1970), pp. 171–176.
[79]Charles E. Lewis, et al., "Activities, Events and Outcomes in Ambulatory Patient Care," *New England Journal of Medicine,* **280** (May 1969), pp. 645–649.
[80]George E. Wakerlin, et al., "Physician's Assistants–Nurse Associates: An Overview," *Missouri Medicine,* **69** (October 1972), pp. 779–836.
[81]A. S. Ford, *op. cit.*

Although current literature still reflects major differences of opinion among the principal professional associations concerning PAs and NPs, it is reasonable to speculate that there may never have been separate programs if the AMA had conferred with the ANA prior to releasing its plan in 1970 to develop programs for training nurses as physician assistants. The proposition was rejected quite strongly by the ANA because it considered nurses independent from physicians and felt, moreover, that one profession should not dictate curriculum to another.[82] The National League for Nursing also deplored the behavior of the AMA.

The real issue at the present time should not be "turfsmanship" or professionalism. Rather, the issue should center on means by which the providers of health care can work collaboratively to determine who, in various combinations and permutations, is best qualified to assume responsibility for the provision of timely, cost effective, and quality health care. Emphasis in the future must be on maximizing the capability of the interdependent professionals in the health care field to work together toward this end.

---

[82]See Alfred M. Sadler et al., *The Physician's Assistant—Today and Tomorrow* (New Haven: Yale University Press, 1972), for an interesting discussion of this dispute.

CHAPTER FIVE

CONTEMPORARY HEALTH
CARE DEVELOPMENTS

Of recent developments in the health care field, none are more significant than health maintenance organizations (HMOs) and professional standards review organizations (PSROs). Both of these developments represent congressional efforts to restructure health care delivery, with a definite intent to contain or reduce the cost of providing medical care. An additional congressional action, the National Health Planning and Resources Development Act of 1974 (PL 93-641), may be viewed as providing the conceptual and organizational framework within which a National Health Insurance plan may be operated, and may be the harbinger of a national health care delivery system. Each of these recent developments, along with the Newark Comprehensive Health Services Plan, a Medicaid Waiver type of HMO, is the focus for discussion in this chapter.

HEALTH MAINTENANCE ORGANIZATIONS

The most frequently discussed innovation in the present health care delivery system is the Health Maintenance Organization (HMO). This term has nevertheless been criticized by many as a misleading conception (see Figure 5.1):

The expression "health maintenance organization" probably promises too much. Medical care is primarily a remedial service, and, while there are some preventive measures (such as prenatal care and some immunizations) that are worthwhile, preventive medicine practiced by providers cannot achieve health benefits even remotely approaching those obtainable from public health measures, over which HMOs will have no direct influence.[1]

[1]Clark C. Havighurst, "Health Maintenance Organizations and the Market for Health Services," *Law and Contemporary Problems,* **35** (Autumn 1970), p. 719. See also, David Mechanic, "A Note on the Concept of 'Health Maintenance Organizations,' " *Public Expectations and Health Care: Essays on the Changing Organization of Health Services* (New York: John Wiley & Sons, 1972), pp. 102–111; and Sanders T. Frank, "HMO's and the Great Semantic Hoax or How Does One Consume Health, Anyway?," *Prism,* **2** (April 1974), p. 60.

FIGURE 5.1. Health maintenance organizations. Source: *Medical Economics*, **51** (September 16, 1974), p. 197. By permission of the artist.

A HMO is a system of organizing, financing, and delivering medical and health care services to a defined and voluntarily enrolled population. *The concept of a HMO is not synonymous with the prepaid group practice model, although most current HMOs are based on this model.*

Although group health plans sprang up in the 1930s, their development, as depicted in Figure 5.2, has been slow compared with the private carriers and the Blue Plans. Table 5.1 shows that enrollments in group practice prepayment plans, for most types of care, have more than doubled since 1953 whereas enrollment in conventional comprehensive plans in the private sector tripled. Growth has been slow for a number of reasons: (1) organized medicine has opposed vigorously the spread of prepaid group plans; and (2) the issue of medical ethics has been used to prevent plans from advertising, thus hindering recruitment and restricting public awareness of the plans.

Millions

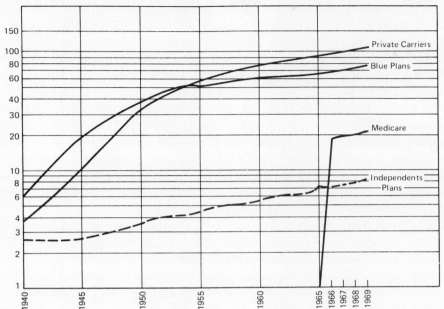

FIGURE 5.2.   Gross enrollment in all health insurance plans that include hospital coverage, by type of carrier, 1940–1969. Source: John Krizay and Andrew Wilson, *The Patient As Consumer: Health Care Financing in the United States* (Lexington, Massachusetts: Lexington Books, 1974), p. 3. Reprinted by permission of the publisher.

TABLE 5.1.   Private Health Insurance Enrollment under Independent Group Practice Prepayment Plans, by Specified Type of Care: 1953–1973

| | | Physicians' Services | | | | |
Year	Hospital Care	Surgical Services	In-hospital Visits	Office, Clinic, or Health Center	Dental Care	Drugs
1953	1802	2410	2507	2853	452	*a*
1956	2428	3177	3399	3395	248	*a*
1959	2526	3280	3400	3694	318	*a*
1961	2586	3484	3643	3643	398	518
1964	2695	3504	3176	3844	438	889
1966	2771	3763	3430	4158	*a*	*a*
1967	3060	4130	3760	4480	*a*	*a*
1968	3043	4051	3730	4404	518	1382
1969	3730	4750	4210	5050	800	1720
1970	4131	5032	4532	5432	910	2121
1971	4415	5230	4880	5630	965	2321
1972	4679	5473	5123	5865	977	2543
1973	4905	5671	5288	6066	1001	1741*b*

a Data not available.

b Excludes those enrolled under plans that sell drugs to members at reduced rates.

Note: Numbers are in thousands.

Source.   Adapted from Marjorie Mueller Smith, "Private Health Insurance in 1973: A Review of Coverage, Enrollment, and Financial Experience," *Social Security Bulletin,* **38** (February 1975), p. 31.

There are about 142 HMOs now in operation as government backing has enabled them to increase fourfold between 1970 and 1974.[2] HMOs presently provide services to an estimated 5,300,000 people. However a number of very large HMOs account for most of these services. The two major prototype HMOs with the largest number of enrollees are the Kaiser Permanente Medical Care Program and the Health Insurance Plan of Greater New York (HIP).

The Kaiser Program services 2.3 million members in California, Oregon, Washington, Ohio, Colorado, and Hawaii. It was started in 1938 to provide medical care to Kaiser workers and their families in remote districts; in 1945 the plan was opened to the public.[3] Unlike HIP the Kaiser Program maintains its own hospital system. For every 100,000 members, Kaiser estimates that facility planning requires 180 hospital beds, 90 physicians in medical groups, 800 ancillary personnel and approximately $12 million in capital investment.[4]

The administrative heart of the Kaiser Plan is the Kaiser Foundation Health Plan, Inc. It is a nonprofit organization that does not provide health care services, but is responsible for enrolling health plan members, collecting their dues, providing health care facilities, and contracting with medical groups and hospitals to provide services. The Permanente Medical Groups, the Kaiser Foundation Hospitals, and the Permanente Services are all legally separate, but they are closely associated with the plan. The interrelationship among them is shown in Figure 5.3.

In 1967 the National Advisory Commission on Health Manpower conducted a detailed study of the Kaiser Plans. The Commissioner reported that the Kaiser Plans provided high quality care and were innovative in many ways, but commented negatively on the lack of substitution of auxiliary personnel for physicians and on the delivery system's overly traditional manner of organization.[5]

The Health Insurance Plan of Greater New York (HIP), a nonprofit membership corporation, was established in 1947 as an indemnity corporation, or prepayment agency, under New York insurance laws. An unpaid Board of Directors is responsible for policy and operations.

In 1974 HIP had approximately 770,000 members, most of whom were union members whose coverage was fully paid by their employers, public and private. The plan contracts with about thirty independent partnership multispecialty medical groups to provide a broad range of health services to subscribers. Under the plan members do have the flexibility to change medical groups and family physicians within a group. The medical groups affiliated with the plan operate under the auspices of a medical director and an administrator. Accountability to subscribers is provided through the following: (1) Medical Control Board; (2)

[2]U. S. Department of Health, Education, and Welfare, *Health Maintenance Organizations: Program Status Report, October 1974* (Rockville, Maryland: Department of Health, Education, and Welfare, 1974).
[3]See Anne R. Somers, editor, *The Kaiser Permanente Medical Care Program: A Symposium* (New York: The Commonwealth Fund, 1971), for comprehensive coverage of the program's history and present organization.
[4]David Mechanic, *op. cit.*
[5]*Report of the National Commission on Health Manpower, Volume 11* (Washington, D.C.: U. S. Government Printing Office, 1967).

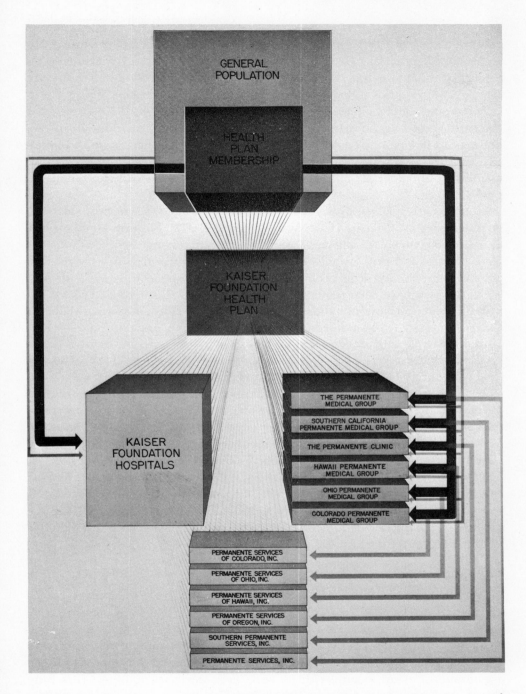

FIGURE 5.3. The organization of the Kaiser Permanente medical care program. Source: Anne R. Somers, editor, *The Kaiser Permanente Medical Care Program: A Symposium* (New York: The Commonwealth Fund, 1971), p. 31. Copyright 1971, Kaiser Foundation Hospitals.

Subscribers Service Department; (3) Claims Division; (4) Joint Committee for Improved Medical Care; (5) consumer councils; (6) the Medical Department. It is through these entities that HIP ensures professional standards, monitors levels of service, and responds to inquiries and complaints from enrollees.

In keeping with its pioneering tradition, HIP established in 1973, as a further means of increasing subscriber satisfaction with the plan, the position of ombudsman, a first among health insurance carriers in the United States. Additionally, in 1973, HIP established a Peer Review program, using the regulations established under PL 92-603 (Professional Standards Review Organizations) as guidelines.

Until recently HIP was prevented by New York law from owning hospitals (HIP operated only La Guardia Hospital in Queens in 1973) and thus could assume only limited control over and responsibility for health services provided under the plan. Control and responsibility has rested, in large measure, with the medical groups. Because of the legal prohibition concerning hospital ownership, subscribers to the plan have been required to carry their own Blue Cross or equivalent insurance to cover hospitalization costs. Even with the restrictions removed, HIP has encountered considerable difficulty in its efforts to provide hospital services. Since Blue Cross provides direct reimbursement to hospitals, and because of the hospitals' concern for loss of some autonomy, HIP has been unable to convince local community hospitals to enter into contractual arrangements.

Whether or not plans own their own hospital facilities is the most important difference among plans. Plans without hospitals are at a severe financial disadvantage and, therefore, usually have higher premium rates.[6]

Based on a 1969 AMA survey of medical groups in the United States, there were 396 groups operating on a prepaid basis, but only 85 were providing prepaid health services that totaled more than 50% of the gross dollar volume of business.[7] It is also interesting to note that the average size of prepaid group practices is sixteen and one-half physicians; however, if Kaiser-Permanente and HIP are excluded from the calculation, the average number of physicians is less than five in prepaid group practices.[8]

General Characteristics of HMOs

While there is no set formula for the establishment of HMOs, they may be distinguished as follows.

Nonprofit/Profit.   Generally HMOs are public or nonprofit private health care organizations that are financially selfsustaining. In the case of nonprofit private organizations, as an example, there were over thirty-seven Blue Cross–Blue Shield programs in operation in 1974.[9] Through 1974 private insurance com-

[6]See Ira G. Greenberg et al., "The Role of Prepaid Group Practice in Relieving the Medical Care Crisis," *Harvard Law Review*, **84** (1971), pp. 907, 913–919.
[7]American Medical Association, *Profile of Medical Practice* (Chicago: American Medical Association, 1974).
[8]David Mechanic, *op. cit.*
[9]*Health Maintenance Organizations: Program Status Report, October 1974, op. cit.*

panies had invested about $40 million through loans, grants, and mortgage financing of thirty-two HMOs. There were also about fifty-five private insurance companies involved or interested in the development of seventy-six HMO-type organizations.

Comprehensive.   A HMO has a contractual responsibility to members to provide total, high quality care; the HMO must assume legal responsibility for the quality of care. The health care provided includes disease prevention, treatment, and rehabilitation. A HMO delivers to its members physician services in the home, office and hospital; inpatient and outpatient hospital services; extended care services; diagnostic and laboratory services; x-rays and therapy in hospital and office; and in some cases, pharmaceutical, mental health, optometric, and dental services. Ideally a single medical record is kept for each patient. A HMO also provides emergency medical services in or out of the HMO area.

Voluntary Enrollment.   Members enroll voluntarily in HMOs, and there is always another type of health insurance available. Therefore HMOs need to be particularly responsive to consumer requirements because the individual has the choice, usually once a year, to withdraw from membership. HMOs usually have at least an annual period of open enrollment.

Prepayment.   HMOs are reimbursed through a prenegotiated and fixed periodic prepayment. Each HMO member, or an employer, or Medicaid and Medicare on behalf of the member, pays the community-rated premium. Therefore the risk of high cost catastrophic illness is spread across a broad base.

Capitation.   Physicians are paid on a capitation basis rather than on the traditional fee-for-service method payment. This form of remuneration effectively reverses the physician's traditional financial incentive, inasmuch as the physician ideally has a vested interest in keeping the patient well under this system. Because the physicians share the risk of overutilization and reap the rewards of lower utilization, patients are cured as expeditiously as possible. The capitation form of payment develops the physician's interest in the activities of the entire group of physicians, thereby facilitating peer review.

Medical Group.   The physicians and other professionals on the health team must constitute an autonomous, self-governing unit, with complete discretion in professional matters. These autonomous medical practice groups can either contract with the central HMO or the groups themselves can bear a portion of the underwriting risk responsibility for their subscribers—a type of Foundation for Medical Care (FMC).[10] [11]

Commencing with the San Joaquin County Foundation for Medical Care in 1954, "organizations of physicians have undertaken to review utilization of care,

[10] A number of organizations and institutions are now sponsoring HMOs—medical schools; city and county hospital systems; the Blue Cross–Blue Shield Plans; private insurance companies; several large corporations; a few consumer groups; existing fee-for-service multispecialty group practices; and local medical societies.
[11] For a range of responses to FMCs, see *American Medical News,* August 10, 1970; Greenberg et al., *op. cit.;* and Havighurst, *op. cit.*

to monitor insurance claims, and to set criteria for benefits and fees."[12] In 1973 there were eighteen statewide and forty-three county FMCs in operation in twenty-seven states.[13]

Foundations for Medical Care are formed, generally in nonmetropolitan areas, when solo practitioners who are members of a local medical society work with insurers to provide a package of health insurance benefits for a defined population. The premiums can be prepaid with physician reimbursement on a fee-for-service basis—a distinctive feature of FMCs. Participating physicians operate out of their own offices and maintain individual medical records. The fees charged are usually lower than the average prevailing rate, with hospital coverage to FMC subscribers usually provided by Blue Cross or some commercial insurance company. An additional distinct feature of FMCs is the fact that individual physician claims are reviewed to make sure they meet certain criteria of quality, appropriateness, coverage, and amount.

Foundations, as implied above, fall into two categories: (1) comprehensive, and (2) claims review. The former design and implement prepaid health insurance programs and thus have the capability of assuming some prepaid benefits package risk sharing.[14] They also perform peer review functions as noted above. The latter are limited exclusively to peer review and as such may represent ideal PSRO (Professional Standard Review Organization) models.

In order to qualify as a HMO, FMCs must provide comprehensive health care to a defined population on a prepaid basis, which some FMCs are now doing.[15] Moreover comprehensive FMCs are included in the 1973 HMO legislation (PL 93-222), where definitions were purposely made flexible enough to leave room for experimentation in the delivery of health services.

While conflicting reports have been published concerning the impact of FMCs on the cost of health care, there is some agreement that FMCs have facilitated improvements in the quality of care provided.[16] [17] However as noted by Roemer in 1974, "hard evidence on the advantages of either economies or health gains . . . is slim."[18]

HMOs: Advantages and Disadvantages

There is no necessity, as with most private insurance plans, for HMO members to be hospitalized to obtain premium coverage and to get medical attention. As shown in Table 5.2, HMO plans have lower hospitalization rates and use relatively fewer hospital days than the Blue plans or other indemnity insurance company

[12]Committee for Economic Development, *Building a National Health Care System* (New York: Committee for Economic Development, 1973), p. 49.

[13]"Medical Foundations," *Boston Globe* (September 10, 1973), p. A–3.

[14]Richard H. Egdahl, "Foundations for Medical Care," *New England Journal of Medicine,* **288** (March 1973), pp. 491–498.

[15]*Ibid.*

[16]*Ibid.*

[17]Milton I. Roemer and William Shonick, "HMO Performance: The Recent Evidence," *Milbank Memorial Fund Quarterly,* **51** (Summer 1973), pp. 271–317.

[18]Milton I. Roemer, "Can Prepaid Care Succeed: A Vote of Confidence," *Prism,* **2** (April 1974), p. 58.

TABLE 5.2. Hospital Use Under Different Types of Plans

Hospital Days, not Including Maternity Days, per Thousand Persons Covered by the Federal Employees Health Benefits Program

	1962	1964	1968
1. Blue Cross–Blue Shield	882	919	924
2. Insurance	760	949	987
3. Group practice plans	460	453	422
Selected Plans			
Group Health Association, District of Columbia	462	484	363
Health Insurance Plan of Greater New York	483	612	459
Group Health Cooperative of Puget Sound, Seattle, Washington	372	467	364
Kaiser Foundation Health Plan, Oregon Region	350	475	254
Kaiser Foundation Health Plan, Northern California Region	500	474	468
Kaiser Foundation Health Plan, Southern California Region	378	381	428
Kaiser Foundation Health Plan, Hawaii Region	705	522	357
4. Individual practice plans	538	530	471
Selected plans			
Foundation for Medical Care of San Joaquin County, California	458	578	390
Group Health Insurance, New York	547	673	652
Hawaii Medical Service Association	535	483	433
Seguros de Servicio de Salud de Puerto Rico	658	644	553
Washington Physicians Service, District of Columbia	531	523	438

Source. Adapted from Committee for Economic Development, *Building a National Health-Care System* (New York: Committee for Economic Development, April 1973), p. 57.

plans. HMOs also perform fewer elective surgical operations, including tonsillectomies, hysterectomies, and appendectomies.[19]

The reasons for the lower utilization of inpatient hospital services are in dispute. The reasons usually advanced are: (1) an emphasis on ambulatory service and good preventive care, (2) the removal of incentives for unnecessary work by substituting salaries for fees, (3) peer influence, (4) group controls, and (5) the lower ratio of beds to population, which affects their availability. Debate on the explanatory causes continues.[20]

Although comparative evaluations are difficult, the quality of medical care provided by HMOs appears at least as good as other delivery systems. Different studies have shown variations in patient attitudes to HMO care, but satisfaction is generally high and the various negative responses to the "clinic atmosphere" are similar to responses from patients receiving health care in private office settings.[21]

[19]*Ibid.*
[20]Avedis Donabedian, "An Evaluation of Prepaid Group Practice," *Inquiry,* **6** (September 1969), pp. 3–27; see also Roemer and Shonick, *op. cit.*
[21]Roemer, *op. cit.*

Table 5.3 is a summary of the most frequently stated advantages of the prepaid group practice type of HMO for the employer, consumer, and physician.

The most often mentioned possible disadvantages associated with HMOs are: (1) the financial incentive may be to cut services in order to make a profit, (2) the elimination of freedom of choice in the selection of physician and health facility, (3) lack of provision of out-of-area coverage, and (4) the impersonal nature of care. Obviously amelioration and/or alleviation of these disadvantages are within the capability of the providers and members.

Further despite the widespread support for the HMO concept, the procedure for setting up a HMO is not simple, as can be seen from the flowchart in Figure 5.4. Even the Kaiser Foundation Health Plan experienced difficulties in making extensions of the plan in other states financially viable within the period anticipated.[22] Prepaid group practices generally do not break even for the first one to five years.[23] Havighurst explains:

HMO formation is costly and risky business, often involving major construction, extensive delays in reaching break-even operation, difficulty in employing medical staff and experienced managers, and problems in attracting sufficient numbers of consumers. Thus, although the potential for profitably delivering low-cost health care of acceptable quality would seem to be considerable, the risk attending any particular initiative in the formation of a HMO would also be substantial.[24]

A continuing problem is that, in practice, there are few incentives or pressures for enrollees to join recently established HMOs.[25]

The implementation of a National Health Insurance Program has been proposed as one way to further increase legislative pressure for HMOs. Perhaps this would entail financial incentives to the consumer to enroll in a HMO and for current providers of medical care to reassess the desirability of participating in such delivery modes.[26] Without further incentives there are severe inpediments to the rapid growth of HMOs, despite their record in eliminating overutilization, introducing substantial efficiencies in the use of existing resources, and providing competitively priced comprehensive health care without sacrificing quality.

HMOs and Federal Involvement

On February 18, 1971, President Nixon drew national attention to HMOs by endorsing them as one means by which the federal government could assert its leadership in initiating structural and organizational changes in health care delivery while fostering self-regulation. As stated by President Nixon:

HMO's simultaneously attack many of the problems comprising the health care crisis. They emphasize prevention and early care; they provide incentives for holding down costs and

[22]Somers, *op. cit.,* pp. 155–177.
[23]Greenberg et al., *op. cit.,* pp. 917, 949.
[24]Havighurst, *op. cit.,* p. 749.
[25]Harry Schwartz, "Modern Hospital Boasts Everything But Patients," *The New York Times,* Sunday, March 23, 1975, p. 43.
[26]Greenberg, *op. cit.*

TABLE 5.3. Summary of the Advantages of Prepaid Group Practice Medical Care to Various Groups

Facilities
- Allows for the most effective and rational use of facilities in serving the public.
- Creates a rational system in which needs can be accurately predicted and a budget and growth plan based thereon developed.

Employer
- Lower hospitalization rates help keep employees out of the hospital and on the job.
- Allows the employer to offer an alternative to his employees, without added cost to himself, which provides more benefits to his employees and which is not forced upon them.
- Has built-in cost containment mechanism.

Consumer
- Provides high quality, comprehensive medical and health care services with most effective use of the health care dollar.
- Has built-in quality controls.
- Has built-in cost containment mechanisms.
- Guarantees availability of necessary medical and health care services.
- The Consumer has free choice of physicians within the group and is encouraged to choose a family physician within the group.
- Accepts responsibility for actually providing services so there is a receptive focal point to which the consumer can direct discussion of his medical and health care needs.
- There is continuity care.
- Preventive services are covered.
- Allows the consumer to budget his medical and health care costs and removes the lingering fear of financial ruin from a serious or catastrophic illness.
- Physicians work as a team, in consultation with each other, to provide high quality, medical and health care services.

Physicians
- Allows the physician to work reasonable hours without having to worry about the availability of top quality medical care services to his patients during his off hours.
- Allows the physician to take his vacations with pay and without fear of having his patients stolen from him.
- Pay is competitive with what physicians make in a fee-for-service practice.
- There are tax advantages.
- There are good fringe benefits including life insurance, health and medical coverage, and retirement plans.
- Allows the physician to budget his income.
  Allows the physician time off for continuing education, teaching, and research activities.
- There are no financial barriers to practicing good medicine.
- There is a medical center type of setting in which there are usually interesting cases to discuss and in which consultations with specialists are immediately available.
- All the most modern equipment is immediately available.

Source. Jeffrey A. Prussin, "This is Prepaid Group Practice Medical Care," *Health Maintenance Organizations–Proceedings of a Conference, 1972* (Denver: Medical Group Management Association, 1972), Appendix I, reprinted by permission of the publisher.

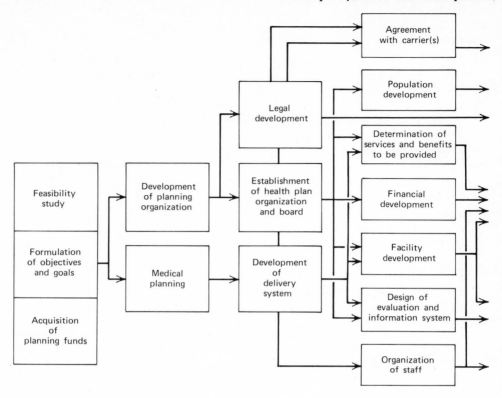

for increasing the productivity of resources; they offer opportunities for improving the quality of care; they provide a means of improving the geographic distribution of care; and, by mobilizing private capital and managerial talent, they reduce the need for federal funds and direct controls . . . .

Because HMO revenues are fixed, their incentives are to keep patients well, for they benefit from patient well-days, not sickness. Their entire cost structure is geared to preventing illness and, failing that, to promoting prompt recovery through the least costly services consistent with maintaining quality. In contrast with prevailing cost-plus insurance plans, the HMO's financial incentives encourage the least utilization of high cost forms of care, and also tend to limit unnecessary procedures.

HMO's provide settings for innovative teaching programs (using the entire team of health professionals and supporting personnel), as well as for continuing education programs for practitioners. They also provide a setting in which new technologies and management tools can be most effectively employed, in which the delegation of tasks from physicians to supporting personnel is encouraged, and in which close and constant professional review of performance will provide quality controls among colleagues.[27]

Spurred by Congressional and administration support HMOs have emerged rapidly in the past two years as an alternative to traditional fee-for-service health care. Actually HEW has been encouraging the development of HMOs since 1971, primarily through a modest planning and development grant program, the

[27]U. S. Department of Health, Education, and Welfare, *Towards a Comprehensive Health Policy for the 1970's: A White Paper* (Washington, D.C.: U. S. Government Printing Office, May 1971), pp. 31–32.

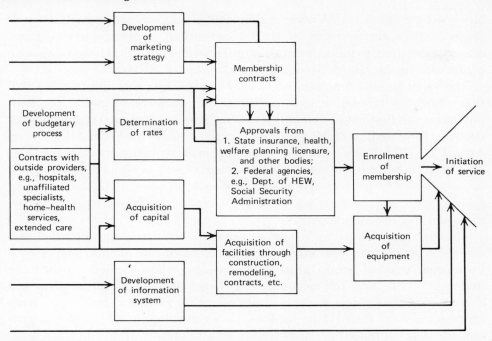

FIGURE 5.4. What must be done to start a successful health maintenance organization? Source: *Building a National Health-Care System*, Committee for Economic Development, (New York: April 1973), pp. 54–55.

initiation of interagency liaison support activities, and the provision of technical assistance to interested parties. With the enactment of the Health Maintenance Act of 1973, Congress authorized the expenditure of $375 million over a five-year period for loans and grants to support planning, development, and initial operation of HMOs. By July 1976, it is expected that 1700 HMOs serving 40 million enrollees will be in operation. The Health Maintenance Act of 1973 defines an extensive and comprehensive benefit package that must be provided to each member. Of equal importance, the law has a certification provision that allows for the override of state laws restricting the right to establish prepaid group practices which offer comprehensive benefits. The legal barriers to prepaid group practices are due to state incorporation laws and insurance regulations, both of which are the result of successful lobbying by organized medicine.[28]

Federal law specifies that every employer in the United States with twenty-five or more people on the payroll who are covered by the federal minimum wage law and who offer health benefits to their employees must offer the option of an equivalently priced coverage under a HMO plan if there is an approved HMO in the area. In addition fourteen states and the District of Columbia have prepaid Medicaid contracts with HMO-type organizations. "There are currently 74 contracts in operation which cover HMO-type care for over 340,000 Medicaid eligi-

[28]For a more comprehensive discussion of the legal barriers issue, see Greenberg, *op. cit.*

bles who have enrolled."[29] Under Section 1902 (R) of the Social Security Amendments of 1972, the Secretary of HEW is authorized to provide technical and actuarial assistance to states desiring to contract with HMOs. Technical assistance is provided by the Health Services Administration of HEW.

The Social Security Amendments of 1972 also contain a provision (Section 226) that allows for reimbursement to HMOs for Medicare recipients for both physicians and hospital and other institutional services. Proposed regulations for eligibility for a Medicare HMO contract were published in the Federal Register on August 27, 1974. It is significant to note that group practice prepayment plans have been authorized to receive reimbursement of 80% of either reasonable cost or reasonable charges for services since the establishment of the Medicare program in 1965. Approximately 335,000 Medicare beneficiaries are presently covered, at a cost of $50 million.[30]

Although one of the basic incentives for HMO legislation was the belief that care could be provided more economically, a recent study of Medicare experience with seven selected group practice prepayment plans yielded inconclusive findings.[31] While total reimbursement per beneficiary in five of the plans was lower than in the fee-for-service controls, two of the plans had higher payments for plan members than did the fee-for-service control groups. However, in general, the data supported previous studies which indicated "lower hospital inpatient costs and higher physician costs for plan members than nonmembers."[32] Apparently the complexity of the problem of evaluation of prepaid group practice types of health care organizations has not changed much since Donabedian made the following statement in 1965: "It is perhaps naive even to have attempted to answer the question, 'How does prepaid group practice perform?' One must further ask, 'What kind of group practice, how organized, operating, in what kinds of settings?' and so on."[33]

PROFESSIONAL STANDARDS REVIEW ORGANIZATIONS

While federal involvement and expenditure for the provision of health services have increased significantly in the past decade, the federal government generally has been reluctant to assert itself in matters concerning organization, cost, and quality of care. However as a result of amendments to the Medicare Act in the last three to four years, the federal government has begun to move with some diligence to influence organization and quality of care, and to control costs. Congress began to experiment with the restructuring of the health care industry through the Health Maintenance Organization Act of 1973, a topic covered in the

[29]*Health Maintenance Organization: Program Status Report, October 1974, op. cit.,* p. 5.
[30]*Ibid.*
[31]Mildred Corbin and Aaron Krute, "Some Aspects of Medicare Experience with Group-Practice Prepayment Plans," *Social Security Bulletin,* **38** (March 1975), pp. 3–11.
[32]*Ibid.,* p. 3.
[33]Avedis Donabedian, *A Review of Some Experiences with Prepaid Group Practice* (Ann Arbor: University of Michigan Bureau of Public Health Economics, Research Series No. 12, 1965), p. 41.

preceding section. Major focus here is on initial efforts to control medical costs and improve the quality of care through the establishment of a nationwide system of doctor-dominated professional standards review organizations (PSROs).

A national peer review system to monitor medical care was established with the passage of PL 92–603 (amendments to the Social Security Act) in 1972. Under the law HEW delineates geographical areas, encompassing a minimum of 300 physicians, each of which must form a PSRO. However only a nonprofit professional association, representing at least 25% of all physicians practicing in one of these areas, can qualify as a PSRO. Membership is voluntary and any licensed physician is eligible to join the PSRO in his or her area. If, however, an appropriate physicians' professional association in each area has not applied to be designated as a PSRO by January 1, 1976, the Secretary of HEW does have the authority to designate another medically competent organization, such as a health department or medical school, to be the PSRO.

Through a new Office of Professional Standards Review, HEW awards three sequential types of PSRO contracts.

1.   Planning—an organization has to submit a formal plan for the assumption of the duties and functioning of a PSRO in the designated area; only one organization per PSRO area can be conditionally designated as the PSRO, although more than one organization can apply.

2.   Conditional designation—these contracts require the implementation of a peer review system and allow provisional operation of the PSRO for a period of two years.

3.   Annual—upon satisfactory completion of the conditional period, HEW enters into one-year renewable contracts with the PSRO. Contracts can be terminated upon ninety days notice by either party.

Prior to January 1, 1976, the Secretary of HEW had to inform the doctors of medicine or osteopathy in a designated area of the Secretary's intention to enter into an agreement with an organization. This provision allowed for due process in case there were physicians in the designated area who objected to the proposed agreement designation.

The Secretary of HEW is expected to give priority in the designation of PSROs to qualified existing organizations, for example, Foundations for Medical Care, with demonstrated competence in review. An important fact, with implications for HMO-type organizations, is that PSROs must utilize already existing review systems which they deem adequate. Remuneration, equal to expenses reasonably incurred in carrying out duties and functions, is made to PSROs by the Secretary of HEW.

Under PL 92-603, PSROs are expected to "promote the effective, efficient, and economical delivery of health care services of proper quality for which payment may be made (in whole or in part) under the Social Security Act." PSROs thus have the responsibility of establishing norms and standards for reviewing the necessity, quality, and appropriateness of institutional care covered by Medicare, Medicaid, and Maternal and Child Health Programs. If the care provided does not meet these criteria, payment will be withheld. However the law does provide for the establishment of an appeals process at the local, state, and HEW level.

Because the law restricts PSRO activities to the review of patient care financed under the Social Security Act, it has become necessary for health providers to extend the concern for controlling cost and improving quality beyond the protected population. Accordingly the AMA Task Force on Guidelines of Care, a subcommittee of the AMA Advisory Committee on PSRO, has agreed that PSRO review should apply to *all* patients including those in government hospitals.[34] Inasmuch as PSROs embody the long-accepted notion of peer review, peer pressure, not government pressure, will be the primary means of upgrading physician performance, changing patterns of utilization of health facilities, and controlling cost. Indeed the House of Delegates of the AMA formally adopted *Guidelines for the Establishment of Medical Society Review Committees* in 1966, although it is important to note that the AMA did not support the PSRO bill because the Association believed the concepts it detailed were too structured, too regulatory, and in need of more study. Nevertheless, because only physicians can be members of PSROs the law places them in a commanding position; neither other health professionals nor consumers are included in PSROs. Just as importantly, perhaps, Section 1167 of the law contains a provision protecting providers from civil liability when the care provided is in compliance with professionally developed norms of care, diagnosis, and treatment. Only time will demonstrate the impact of this provision on the medical malpractice problem.

Although the law does not apply specifically to ambulatory care, doctors in a PSRO can petition HEW for its inclusion. Professional Review Standards Organizations could also serve as control mechanisms were Congress to enact a national health insurance program. In this regard the manner in which PSROs evolve and their subsequent comprehensiveness and effectiveness may dictate whether or not self-regulation is feasible in the health professions. In a more definitive sense, perhaps, PSROs may represent the last chance for physicians to exercise a leadership role in the regulation of their profession. Of obvious importance to the long-term health of PSROs is the development and implementation of rigorous field testing and evaluation designs.

As a means of facilitating the establishment and use of professionally developed norms and standards of care (diagnosis and treatment), technical assistance is provided by statewide Professional Standards Review Councils and a National Professional Standards Review Council. Statewide PSROs are established when there are three or more PSROs operating in a state. The statewide councils will be comprised of one representative from each PSRO; four physicians, two of whom may be designated by the state medical society and two of whom may be designated by the state hospital association; and four persons knowledgeable in health care selected by the Secretary of HEW to represent the public (at least two recommended by the Governor). The principal duties of the statewide councils

---

[34]"PSRO's and Norms of Care," *Journal of the American Medical Association,* **220** (July 1974), pp. 166–171.

are to coordinate the activities of and disseminate information among PSROs in the state; assist in evaluating the performance of each PSRO; and, when necessary, assist the Secretary of HEW in developing and arranging for the replacement of a PSRO.

The National Professional Standards Review Council, consisting of eleven nonfederal physicians appointed by the Secretary of HEW to three-year terms, is required by law to perform the following duties:

1.   Advise the Secretary on matters pertaining to PSROs.

2.   Assist statewide councils in the performance of their duties and functions.

3.   Review the operations of statewide councils and PSRO organizations.

4.   Facilitate or conduct studies with a view to maintaining or improving the effectiveness of the Council. The Council is also expected to aid in the development of regional norms, which it shall approve, for diagnosis, care, and treatment.

In the case of both national and statewide councils, the Secretary of HEW is authorized to reimburse the councils for expenses "reasonably and necessarily incurred."

As an additional means of fostering PSRO development, the Office of Professional Standards Review of HEW is establishing statewide PSRO Support Centers. The Centers are being developed "to stimulate and support the development and operation of the PSRO program and local PSROs in a manner consistent with . . . legislative intent and the policies of the Secretary."[35] The support centers will be established through competitive bidding. As with the other PSRO organizational entities, support center organizations, to qualify, must be composed primarily of physicians licensed to practice in the state where the center will operate.

"If the state of the art in assessing medical care quality is not sufficiently dismal, then the state of the art of examining ways to change the behavior of physicians or institutions certainly is."[36] Indeed the problems of assessment, change, and quality assurance are complex and difficult. However the preceding quote notwithstanding, through the evaluation of patterns of utilization of health facilities based on diagnosis, location, procedures, services provided, types of coverage, and so on, PSROs should facilitate the development of a data base and information system that will underlie constructive changes in the health care delivery system.

THE NATIONAL HEALTH PLANNING AND RESOURCES DEVELOPMENT ACT OF 1974[37]

When President Gerald Ford signed the National Health Planning and Resources Development legislation into law (PL 93-641) on January 4, 1975, he authorized

[35]Office of Professional Standards Review, *OPSR Memo No. 3* (Rockville, Maryland: Department of Health, Education, and Welfare, March 1974), p. 3.
[36]Robert H. Brooks, "A Skeptic Looks at Peer Review," *Prism*, **2** (October 1974), p. 32.
[37]National Health Planning and Resources Development Act of 1974, 42 USC 300K.

the implementation of one of the most potentially profound pieces of health legislation in this century. Public Law 93-641, an amendment (Titles XV and XVI) to the Public Health Service Act, may represent the first serious effort by the federal government to establish a nationalized health care delivery system.

No doubt, as indicated by its authors, the Act is viewed by many as the means through which a national health insurance program can be established. The lines of control, as exemplified in Figure 5.5, should be clear. Moreover, if one couples this law with the recent HMO Act and the PSRO legislation, it becomes evident

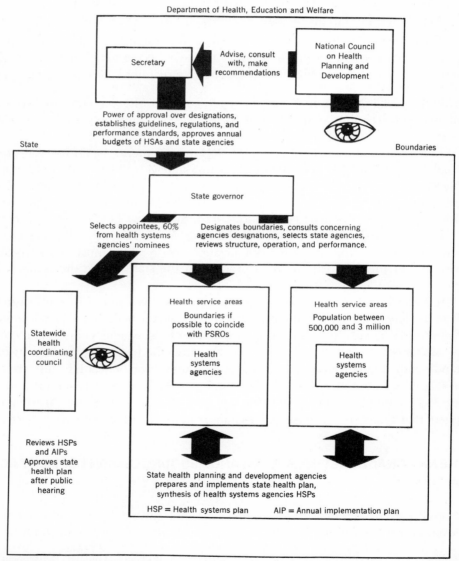

FIGURE 5.5. (Eye-Oversight function) Organization of health planning agencies established under the National Health Planning and Resources Development Act of 1974.

that three elements critical to reform and change in the health care delivery system are now extant. While these laws contain considerable promise for the cost-effective, high quality, and equitable delivery of health care to all Americans, they also represent the acceleration of federal efforts to regulate the health care industry. The pump has been primed. Health providers, consumers, state, local, and federal government officials are now in the position of facilitating the development and subsequent implementation of regulations for the Act which may determine how health care needs will be met in the United States in the future. Can decentralization and community involvement, along with professional self-regulation work, or is centralization and strong federal regulatory involvement through the Secretary of the Department of Health, Education, and Welfare the only way?

Presently the source of considerable controversy are issues that pertain to federal and state relations under the Act, and HEW's orientation toward nonprofit private areawide health systems agencies. In the latter case there is a difference of opinion between state governors who favor public accountability in the health care system, which integrates planning and regulatory functions, and HEW, which supports planning as the responsibility of the nonprofit private sector. The debate will continue until such time as the federal regulations are written and the Act operationalized. A July 1976 deadline for promulgation of the regulations was included in the law.

The Act authorizes a multimillion dollar program that combines CHP, RMP, Experimental Health Services Delivery Systems, and Hill-Burton into a single program. Legislative authority for the existing programs expired on June 30, 1974. Since that time the programs have been funded with released impounded monies or through continuing resolutions. Title XV of the law revises health care planning and development programs and Title XVI is a restricted version of the Hill-Burton program for construction and renovation of health facilities, now linked to the planning process. The law also envisages the linking of planning and implementation, a very difficult task in view of the fact that none of the entities established under the Act have the powers of initiation or implementation, unless, of course, a designated agency is a unit of government and has statutory powers. Aside from the ability to influence change via health systems plans, the agencies created under the Act have only *negative* powers, for example, certificate of need and authority, the disbursement of grant funds, and the approval of contracts. Whether or not these powers can be utilized in a creative manner to bring about the desired end is questionable at best.

In order to achieve the basic purposes of the Act—equal access to quality health care at reasonable cost; inflation and cost control; alleviation of problems of maldistribution of personnel and facilities; increasing the utilization of ambulatory and intermediate care facilities; improving the technical quality of care; increasing provider involvement in the development of health policy; and improving consumer health education—the Secretary of HEW is authorized to establish a permanent, fifteen member, National Advisory Council on Health Planning and Development. The Council will be advisory to the Secretary on all matters pertaining to the implementation of the Act. As depicted in Figure 5.5, the law also provides for: (1) designation of Health Service Area boundaries; (2) designation of Health Systems Agencies; (3) selection of State Health Planning and Development Agencies; and (4) appointment of Statewide Health Coordinating Councils. For Fiscal Year 1976, Congress authorized $338 million for the implementation of the Act.

Health Service Areas

In designating Health Service Areas the law gives responsibility to the governors of the several states, within the context, of course, of HEW guidelines. The Act also requires that governors consult with "the chief executive officer or agency of the political subdivisions within the State . . . ."

A Health Service Area must include a minimum population of 500,000 and must not divide a standard metropolitan statistical area (SMSA) without due justification. The designation of Health Service Areas is also expected to be guided by considerations such as:

1.   The appropriateness of the area for the effective planning and development of health services.
2.   The existence of a comprehensive health planning agency currently funded under Section 314(b).
3.   The availability of at least one center for the delivery of highly specialized health services.

The Secretary of HEW, after consultation with a governor, can make boundary revisions. Publication of final designations was scheduled for August 1, 1975.

Health Systems Agencies

Subsequent to the designation of Health Service Areas, the Secretary of HEW, after consultation with a governor and other public officials as deemed appropriate, is authorized to designate a nonprofit private or public entity as the Health Systems Agency (HSA) for an area. Among other things, under the law Health Systems Agencies are responsible for preparing health systems plans (HSPs) and annual implementation plans (AIPs), approving grants and contracts for approved projects, reviewing and approving all proposed federally supported projects under the Public Health Service Act, and assisting in the planning and development of new facilities, health services, or organizations such as HMOs. The Agencies are funded on a $0.50 per capita basis to a maximum of $3.75 million. If matched with nonfederal funds, an additional $0.25 per capita can be authorized within specific limits.

Any designated agency must have a governing board comprised of a majority, but not more than 60%, of consumers. The remaining members are to represent health care providers and elected public officials. Although the law appears to be unclear concerning the autonomy of the governing boards, legislative intent, elicited by local governmental officials and associations during floor debates, makes it clear that such boards are subject to the rules and regulations of an agency that is a unit of local government. This is an important issue, since Health Systems Agencies may have considerable authority on an areawide basis. In this regard it is important to note that Agencies are required to coordinate their activities with PSROs "and other appropriate general purpose or special purpose regional planning or administrative agencies . . . ."

Due to fundamental policy differences between HEW and state governors, and also due to floor debates concerning further federalization, controversy exists among state, local and federal officials over the designation of Health Systems Agencies. Aside from the public/nonprofit private issue, debate also focuses on the fact that the Agencies contract with and are accountable to the Secretary of HEW. There may be an additional problem with RMPs seeking to become Agencies, especially in light of the fact that they were never viewed as being accountable to local or state public officials.

Since the law mandates that designations be made within eighteen months after enactment, July 1976 was the deadline specified for agency designations.

State Health Planning and Development Agencies

One of the entities required at the state level under the law is a state agency. The law authorizes the Secretary to enter into and renew agreements for the designation of state agencies. The agreements may be terminated by either the governor of a state or the Secretary upon ninety days notice.

The State Health Planning and Development Agency, selected by the governor, is charged with the responsibility for developing, reviewing, and revising (at least annually) a state plan composed of the plans of the Health Systems Agencies. The State Agency will also be responsible for: (1) administering "certificate of need" programs for new services and delivery modes, including HMOs, and for new health facilities; (2) periodic review of institutional health services; and (3) review of the state medical facilities plan, in cooperation with the Statewide Health Coordinating Council.

Section 1522 of the law authorizes the establishment of an appeals process to handle disputes between Health Systems Agencies and State Health Planning and Development Agencies. The process must be consistent with state law governing the practices and procedures of administrative agencies, and must take place under the auspices of a state agency (other than the Health Planning and Development Agency) designated by the governor.

In general the State Agency performs a coordinating function with enforcement authority only if it also happens to be a department of state government with specific statutory powers.

Statewide Health Coordinating Councils

The Statewide Health Coordinating Council (SHCC), appointed by the governor of each state, is intended to be advisory to the State Agencies, but with significant policy authority over the agencies. The Act mandates that at least 60% of the members of the Councils shall be from nominees submitted to the governor by each of the Health Systems Agencies within a state. The other appointments are made by the governor as he deems appropriate. Each HSA shall have at least two representatives on the SHCC. In addition, of the providers of health care who are members of the SHCC, at least one-third must be direct providers of health care. Each SHCC will perform the following functions:

1.   Coordinate and review annually each Health Systems Agency's HSP and AIP and report to the Secretary of HEW.

2.   Prepare, review, and revise, at least once a year, state health plans, with adoption only after due notice and a public hearing. The state health plan being the synthesis of HSPs of the HSAs within a state, the SHCC thus can revise HSA plans in order to achieve better coordination or to more effectively meet statewide health needs.

3.   Review annually the budget of HSAs and provide comments to the Secretary of HEW.

4.   Advise the State Agency on the performance of its functions.

5.   Review annually and approve or disapprove state plans and applications under the Public Health Service Act, the Community Mental Health Centers Act, and the Comprehensive Alcohol Abuse and Alcoholism Prevention, Treatment, and Rehabilitation Act of 1970.

NATIONAL HEALTH INSURANCE

Lobbies have been pressing for national health insurance in America since the Progressive Era at the beginning of the century. There was a particularly strong, though divided, movement for compulsory health insurance at the time of World War I. Since that time several efforts have been made to institute some form of compulsory health insurance: the Capper Bill in 1933; the "National Health Bill of 1939"; the Wagner-Murray-Dingell bills of 1943 and 1945; and several national health insurance bills introduced between 1945 and 1950.

A renewed drive began around 1960. It focused on the poor and elderly, as these were two groups frequently not covered by private health insurance. Most low-income people cannot afford insurance and many companies will not insure the elderly because of their high rate of illness. Despite strong opposition from organized medicine, in 1965 Congress passed two amendments to the Social Security Act, Title XVIII (Medicare) and Title XIX (Medicaid).

Medicare is a federally financed and administered program that provides hospital and medical insurance protection for over 23 million people, primarily those 65 years of age and older. Policy and administrative control of the program resides within the Bureau of Health Insurance of the Social Security Administration in HEW. The Bureau contracts with 132 commercial health insurance companies and Blue Cross–Blue Shield plans.[38] These companies perform claims review and make payments for benefits provided. In 1973 Medicare benefits totaled over $9 billion, about 12% of the total health care bill in the United States.

The Medicare program is limited, however, and pays on the average only about half of the elderly's medical bills. This is because the program does not cover a sizable portion of bills for services provided in doctors' officies, certain routine medical services, nonsurgical dental services, and also because of limitations on payments for hospital, chronic nursing home, and other long-term institutional care.

Medicaid, which was designed to meet the medical needs of 40 million Americans whose incomes are defined by the federal government as below the poverty line, covered only 23.5 million in 1973.[39] Estimates for 1974 and 1975 were 27.2 and 28.6 million respectively. Total Medicaid program cost for 1973 was $9.1 billion.

All states except Arizona are participating in this federal matching-grant program; however, there is great variation in eligibility rules, coverage, and quality. Because of this great variation, and because of increased cost of the program, "most states have tightened eligibility requirements, reduced coverage, and failed to improve the quality of their programs."[40] This situation certainly has been affected adversely by congressional inactivity. Since the beginning of this decade, for example, Congress has been dilatory in establishing comprehensive eligibility standards. Most recently Congress postponed the deadline by which states were to implement comprehensive eligibility standards from 1975 to 1977.[41]

Unfortunately the major problem with both Medicare and Medicaid is that they have been principal factors in the continued rise in the cost of medical care. The reasons range from improper certification and billing procedures to outright chicanery—all coupled with what has to be described as a no monitoring and enforcement system at best. Everyday the nation's major newspapers are filled with stories about the difficulties encountered in attempting to manage these two very substantial governmental programs. Hence the widespread concern that national health insurance, which will make access to health care possible for a wider segment of the population, will be instituted without altering the structure, organization, modes of delivery, and mechanisms of cost and quality control that characterize the present health care system. For example, Krass contends that:

The proposals for National Health Insurance take for granted the wisdom of our current approaches to the pursuit of health, and thereby insure that in the future we will get more of the same. These proposals will simply make available to the non-insured what the privately insured now get: a hospital-centered, highly technological, disease-oriented, therapy-centered medical care. The proposals have entirely ignored the question of whether what we now do in health is what we should be doing. They not only endorse the

---

[38]Committee on Ways and Means, *National Health Insurance Resource Book* (Washington, D.C.: U. S. Government Printing Office, 1974).
[39]*Ibid.*
[40]John Krizay and Andrew Wilson, *op. cit.,* p. 82.
[41]*Ibid.*

status quo, but fail to take advantage of the rare opportunity which financial crises provide to re-examine basic questions and directions. The real irony is that real economizing in health care is probably possible only by radically re-orienting the pursuit of health.[42]

Further, and in an even more pointed fashion, Krass criticizes the unqualified embracing of the no-fault principle in all of the proposals for national health insurance. He contends that the proposals and their authors "choose to ignore, or to treat as irrelevant, the importance of personal responsibility for the state of one's health. As a result they pass up an opportunity to build both positive and negative inducements into the insurance payment plan, by measures such as refusing or reducing benefits for chronic respiratory disease care to persons who continue to smoke."[43] Truly a radical, yet enlightening proposal!

The preceding notwithstanding, and despite the many problems associated with Medicare and Medicaid, there is definitely a renewed interest in some form of national health insurance as the means by which reform in the current health insurance industry, and perhaps in the health care delivery system itself, can take place. Support for the current movement is based on the reality that the poor still have very inadequate coverage and the fact that few American families, even those with some form of health insurance, are protected against the high costs of rare catastrophic illness. Moreover, the present mix of public and private health insurance still evidences a bias toward high-cost curative care, and does not emphasize preventive medicine or efficiency.

In a more positive vein Congress has embarked on a seemingly integrated and progressive program of reform involving HMOs and PSROs, and culminating with the recently passed National Health Resources and Development Act of 1974. This latter piece of legislation may provide the conceptual framework within which the type of synthesis and synergism postulated by Krass can take place, although early implementation efforts have been marked by controversy.

Table 5.4 is a summary of the principal features of major national health insurance bills that were introduced in the 93rd Congress.[44]

During the early months of the 94th Congress revised versions of four of the six major national health insurance proposals were reintroduced. Extensive changes were made in the Health Care Insurance (Medicredit) proposal whereas limited changes were made in the Health Security, National Health Care, and National Health Care Services Reorganization and Financing proposals. The Medicredit proposal now would require employers to pay 65% of the premium of a standard benefit plan, with employees not required to participate in the plan. Previously the proposal's chief sponsor, the AMA, was opposed to requiring employers to offer a standard health insurance plan. The new bill also increases covered hospital care

[42]Leon R. Krass, "Regarding the End of Medicine and the Pursuit of Health," *The Public Interest*, No. 40 (Summer 1975), p. 41.
[43]*Ibid.*
[44]See also United States Senate Committee on Finance, *National Health Insurance: Brief Outline of Pending Bills* (Washington, D.C.: Government Printing Office, 1974); Committee on Ways and Means, *op. cit.;* and U. S. Library of Congress, Congressional Research Service, Education and Public Welfare Division, *National Health Insurance: A Summary of Major Legislative Proposals Introduced into the 93rd Congress,* by Kay Cavalier and Richard Price (Washington, D.C.: Government Printing Office, 1974).

TABLE 5.4. A Comparative Summary of Selected Major National Health Insurance Proposals Introduced in the 93rd Congress

A COMPARATIVE SUMMARY OF SELECTED MAJOR NATIONAL HEALTH INSURANCE PROPOSALS
INTRODUCED IN THE 93rd CONGRESS

TITLE	SPONSOR(S)	GENERAL APPROACH	SCOPE OF BENEFITS	COST ESTIMATES	FINANCING	ADMINISTRATION	PAYMENTS TO PROVIDERS	EFFECTS ON HEALTH CARE DELIVERY SYSTEM
Health Security Act-S.3/H.R. 22 Introduced: 1-4-73 Earlier versions: 91st Congress-S.4297 (8-27-70) 92nd Congress-S.3 National Health Insurance, United Automobile Workers, and AFL/CIO.	Senator Edward M. Kennedy/Representatives James C. Corman and Martha Griffiths. Organizational support for bill: Committee for (1-25-71)/H.R. 22 (1-22-71)	National health insurance plan administered by the Federal government. Financial mechanism combined with a restructuring of health care delivery system. No private health insurance would be used under the plan.	Comprehensive health benefits, with no payment required of patients for covered services. Full coverage for physicians services inpatient and outpatient hospital care, home health services, supporting services such as optometry, podiatry devices and appliances; limited benefits for dental, psychiatric and nursing care and prescription drugs. Otherwise, no deductibles, co-insurance, waiting periods, maximum, or cutoffs.	Program would cost $73 billion in FY76, $21 billion of which represents money which would have been spent on Medicare and Medicaid.	Health Security Trust Fund created with income derived as follows: 50%-federal grant revenues 36%-3.5% tax on employers' payrolls 12%-1.0% tax on employees' wages and on unearned income up to $15,000 a year 2%-2.5% tax on self-employment income up to $15,000 a year. Persons over 60 would be able to exempt the first $3,000 in unearned income from the 1% Health Security tax. Employers could agree to pay all or part of their employees' contribution, without altering their present obligations to purchase health benefits. If employer's current obligation exceeds 3.5% of payroll, the excess would be applied toward the 1% which otherwise would be withheld from wages.	Administered by a five-member Health Security Board in HEW. Board appointed by President with consent of the Senate. National Health Security Advisory Council representing consumers (who would constitute a majority) and providers, would assist Board by advising on policy and evaluating program operation.	National budget established for each year. Funds allocated to each region on a per capita basis. Providers paid on the basis of negotiated budget designed to pay reasonable costs. Eligible independent practitioners paid by various methods, including fee-for-service, capitation, salary, and on a supplemental basis for those locating in underserved or remote areas. Health maintenance organizations or professional foundations would be paid on a basic capitation rate multiplied by the number of eligible enrollees and could share in up to 75% of any savings within specified limits. The Health Security Board establishes payment schedules and procedures.	Medicare terminated. Federal aid to states for Medicaid and other Federal programs would be terminated, except where broader benefits are provided under such programs. Financial, professional, and other incentives provided in order to stimulate:HMO and professional foundation development; training and efficient utilization of health practitioners; and the development of community-based home health care programs for the chronically ill or disabled. Resources Development Fund ($200 million in first year and $400 million in second year) created to reinforce and supplement these incentives. Establishes a Federal Commission on the Quality of Care to assess standards and regulations safeguarding the quality of service provided under the program. National participation standards established for practitioners and institutions. Encourages preventive health care.

139

TITLE	SPONSOR(S)	GENERAL APPROACH	COST ESTIMATES	SCOPE OF BENEFITS	FINANCING	ADMINISTRATION	PAYMENTS TO PROVIDERS	EFFECTS ON HEALTH CARE DELIVERY SYSTEM
National Health Care Services Reorganization and Financing Act-H.R.1 Introduced:1-9-73 Earlier version: 92nd Congress-H.R.14140 (3-28-72)	Representative Al Ullman. Organizational support for bill: American Hospital Association.	Mixed public and private health insurance plan. Comprehensive health care benefits program for entire population, phased in over a five-year period. The plan would couple employer required private coverage for employees, a plan for individuals, and federally contracted coverage for the poor and elderly.	No estimates available.	Benefits phased in over 5 year period. Initially would cover same benefits as Medicare, plus catastrophic illness expense which would commence after certain noncovered expenses reach a specified limit according to income and age. Parts A and B of Medicare merged and the Part B premium eliminated. Medicare deductibles and co-payments would not be applicable to low-income groups. After five years the following Comprehensive Health Care Benefits would be required of all employer-employee plans and the Federal program for the elderly and low-income: periodic health evaluations; physicians services and ancillary care; inpatient services; outpatient services; and catastrophic expense benefits. A detailed and specific list of benefits and coverage is provided for each of the preceding categories.	Federal program for aged financed through payroll taxes and general revenues. Program with some cost-sharing for services. Program for poor and medically indigent financed through general revenues with some cost-sharing and premium contributions by the medically indigent. Employers would pay at least 75% of employee premiums, with employee paying 25%. A 10% premium subsidy would be provided from federal general revenues for anyone registering with a Health Care Corporation (HCC).	Creates a new Federal Department of Health to manage all Federal health programs. The Department would administer the insurance program for the aged and poor and would contract directly with carriers or HCC's to provide covered benefits. HCC's -- community-based, nonprofit organizations capable of providing comprehensive health services -- would be established in every geographic area of the country. Newly created State Health Commissions would be established in each state and would authorize incorporation of HCC's, enforce regulations pertaining to providers, control premium rates charged, and approve expansion of health services and facilities. If a state failed to establish a SHC, the new Department of Health would assume the functions. Private insurance carriers would operate within the context of state and federal guidelines.	State Health Commissions responsible for rate determination for private carriers and/or HCC's; SHC's also would approve charges for covered services. Methods for determining reasonable operating costs and sufficient capital payments for institutional providers would be established by federal regulations, including also reasonable fees, salaries, or other compensation. Non-HCC providers would be reimbursed by private carriers underwriting the health care benefits plan. HCC's would be paid directly by enrollees, or by contracting carriers on a prior-budgeted basis. After the phasing-in period, HCC's would be required to provide a capitation option to enrollees.	Creates new Federal Department of Health, HCC's and SHC's. Medicare initially expanded to cover low-income, after 2 years broader benefits would become effective Medicaid limited to supplementation of comprehensive benefit plan. Federally approved state health plans required. Creates National Health Services Advisory Council. Bill stresses individual's responsibility for health maintenance and promotion. Ownership of HCC's, organizational form, operational procedures, modes of clinical practice, choice of participating providers, etc. based on community preference.

TITLE	SPONSOR	GENERAL APPROACH	SCOPE OF BENEFITS	COST ESTIMATES	FINANCING	ADMINISTRATION	PAYMENTS TO PROVIDERS	EFFECTS ON HEALTH CARE DELIVERY SYSTEM
National Health Care Act-S.1100/H.R.5200 Introduced:3-6-73 Earlier Versions:91st Congress-H.R.19935 (12-10-70) 92nd Congress-H.R.4349 (2-17-71)/S.1490 (4-5-71).	Senator Thomas J. McIntyre/Representative Omar Barleson. Organizational support for bill: Health Insurance Association of America.	Mixed public and private. Bill proposes 3 voluntary health plans: (1)employee-employer; (2)individual plan; and (3)a plan for the poor and uninsurable. Would use income tax incentives to make comprehensive health insurance available to all Americans. All plans would be administered through private insurance carriers. Overall supervision by state and federal governments.	Two benefit packages. Minimum Standard Health Care Benefits (MSHC) for private groups and individual plans--catastrophic coverage; unlimited visits for outpatient surgery and radiation therapy; laboratory services; specified number of physician services in hospital, office or ambulatory care center; specified number of well baby visits and immunizations and specified number of days in general hospital, psychiatric hospital, skilled nursing home and home health care. Most benefits require copayments. State pool benefit plans for the poor, near poor, and previously uninsurable, initially more comprehensive. All MSHC benefits with more lenient specifications, plus dental care for children under 19 and with 20% coinsurance, physical therapy; family planning services, maternity care and prosthetic aids. Initial MSHC benefits include a catastrophic benefit applicable to individuals covered by qualified private and state plans. By 1980, private group coverage to be expanded to cover initial state pool plan level of coverage. Provision for variation in coinsurance and copayments.	Sponsor estimates cost of program to taxpayers to be $8.1 billion in new taxes for first full year of operation (fiscal year 1976).	Costs for people not insured through a state pool borne by employers, employees, and self-employed through premium payments to private carriers, and indirectly to the federal government through tax deductions for these premiums. State pool would be financed with premium payments from enrollees graduated according to income, and by federal-state contributions.Federal matching payments would be graduated according to state wealth, but would not be less than 70%, or more than 90%. Expenses which experience demonstrates to be over-utilized would be subject to copayment, with an aggregate limit on copayment related to family income.	Each private insurer would administer its own policy for qualified group and individual plans, subject to state insurance department regulations. For the qualified state health care plans, each state would establish a health insurance pool, with private insurers underwriting a portion of the risks. The state plan would be administered by one or more designated private carriers. Premium rates state plans would be determined within each state, subject to HEW review.	Present private insurance carrier reimbursement methods for services rendered would prevail. Under state health care plans, payments would be limited to the 75th percentile of prevailing reasonable charges for professional services and for institutions to rates approved by a state Health Care Institutions Cost Commission.	Medicare and Medicaid supplemented. Medicare Part 3 premium eliminated. Grants, loans and loan guarantees would be used to increase and redistribute health manpower, promote ambulatory care, and strengthen health planning. Establishes in the Office of the President a Council of Health Policy Advisors. Includes provisions which would improve cost and quality controls for health services. Provision made for coverage against catastrophic illness. Generous layoff and termination coverage provided.

TITLE	SPONSOR	GENERAL APPROACH	COST ESTIMATES	SCOPE OF BENEFITS	FINANCING	ADMINISTRATION	PAYMENTS TO PROVIDERS	EFFECTS ON HEALTH CARE DELIVERY SYSTEM
Health Care Insurance Act (Medicredit)- S.444/H.R.2222 Introduced:1-18-73 Earlier Versions: 91st Congress-H.R. 18567 (7-21-70)/ S,4419(9-30-70) 92nd Congress-H.R. 4960 (2-25-71) S.987 (2-25-71)	Senators Clifford P. Hansen and Vance Hartke/Representatives Richard H. Fulton and Joel T. Broyhill. Organizational support for bill: American Medical Association.	Voluntary health insurance program called "medicredit", for total population under age 65. Federal government pays health insurance premiums for the poor; income tax credits allowed for all others toward purchase of private health insurance. Medicare would continue as at present.	$12.1 billion for first full year of operation.	Minimum health care policy benefits necessary to qualify for tax credits: (1) 60 days hospitalization-subject to $50 deductible. (2) Home health services, ambulance, emergency or outpatient hospital services-subject to 20% coinsurance on first $500 of expense. (3) All medical care by physician-subject to 20% coinsurance. (4) Dental care for children 2 to 6 years of age, and emergency dental services and oral surgery for all ages-subject to 20% coinsurance on first $500. (5) Catastrophic coverage-unlimited hospital days, up to 30 additional days in a skilled nursing facility, prosthetic aids, outpatient blood in excess of 3 pints-subject to deductible of 10% of combined taxable income of eligible and dependent beneficiaries, reduced by total of deductibles and coinsurance incurred under basic coverage.	Costs of health insurance for poor would be met by federal general revenue funds and by reductions in federal income tax collections for those receiving tax credits. An employer who maintains a qualified plan could continue to claim premium contributions as a business deduction; one-half contribution could be claimed for nonqualified plans.	Establishes an 11 member Health Insurance "Advisory" Board, appointed by the President with Senate consent, to determine policy and regulations. Private insurance companies would administer their approved policies.	Usual and customary charges for all services, including hospital and extended care. Federal supervision or control over the practice of medicine or dentistry, the service delivery mode, the selection, compensation, or operation of providers of services would be prohibited.	No restructuring of health care delivery system. Medicare continued. Benefits claimed under medicredit could not be duplicated under any other federally funded program; hence, medicredit would largely replace Medicaid. Medicaid could continue to pay for services not covered under medicredit and states participating in Medicaid would be required to pay deductible and coinsurance amounts for cash assistance individuals covered by qualified plans. Catastrophic coverage provided with a deductible provision which would vary according to income.

TITLE	SPONSOR(S)	GENERAL APPROACH	SCOPE OF BENEFITS	COST ESTIMATES	FINANCING	ADMINISTRATION	PAYMENTS TO PROVIDERS	EFFECTS ON HEALTH CARE DELIVERY SYSTEM
National Health Insurance and Health Improvements Act - S.915 Introduced: 2-20-73 Earlier Versions: 91st Congress-S.3711 (4-14-70) 92nd Congress-S.836 (2-18-71)	Senator Jacob K. Javits. Organizational support for bill: None to date.	National health insurance program that extends Medicare to all Americans. Benefits broadened to include certain services not presently covered under Medicare. Medicare Part B premium eliminated. Medicaid would continue. Includes option for alternative coverage under private insurance plans.	Adds to present Medicare benefits, maintenance drugs for chronic conditions, annual physical checkups, dental care for children under 8. Program phased in; covering first the disabled, widows and widowers before being extended to all Americans.	HEW estimate of additional cost to federal taxpayer, fiscal year 1974 - $41.6 billion.	Financed by taxes on employers, employees, and self-employed (3.3% each in 1976 and thereafter). Federal government contributes 1/2 the amount collected through payroll taxes from general revenues. Workers under Social Security and governmental employees would be subject to the tax, but state and local governments would be exempt from the employer tax. Annual taxable wages for workers would be $15,000; for employers, no taxable wage base would apply. Employer pays at least 75% of cost of private plan.	Essentially the same as Medicare. Administered through fiscal intermediaries, If intermediaries' management inefficient and uneconomical, federal government authorized to replace them with quasi-governmental corporations. HEW would establish regulations and standards for the program.	Until July 1, 1976, reasonable cost for hospitals and institutions and reasonable charges for physicians (same as Medicare). Subsequently, new methods may be employed.	Through grant and loan provisions, encourages growth of group practice plans, payment plans, which would benefit from cost-savings for efficient operation. Establishes concept of "appropriate and reasonable charges" rather than "reasonable charges". Authorizes HEW to adopt additional standards for physicians concerning requirements for continuing education, national licensing and qualifications to perform major surgery and specialty services. Special grants would be available for planning of comprehensive health service systems in poverty areas. Individuals can "elect out" of programs and thereby exempt themselves from payroll taxation for federal health insurance by securing coverage from private insurers offering comparable or better protection. As in the case of Medicare, program includes cost sharing provisions.

TITLE	SPONSOR(S)	GENERAL APPROACH	SCOPE OF BENEFITS	COST ESTIMATES	FINANCING	ADMINISTRATION	PAYMENTS TO PROVIDERS	EFFECTS ON HEALTH CARE DELIVERY SYSTEM
Comprehensive Health Insurance Act (Administration Bill)-S.2970/ H.R.12684 Introduced: 2-6-74 Earlier Versions: 92nd Congress-S.1623 (4-22-71)/H.R.7741 (4-27-71)	Senator Bob Packwood Representatives Wilbur Mills and Herman T. Schneebeli.	Mixed public and private. Three-part comprehensive health insurance program: (1)a mandated Employee Health Insurance Plan (EHIP), covering the majority of the working population and offered at place of employment; (2)an Assisted Health Insurance Plan (AHIP), covering low-income persons and others not eligible for EHIP and Medicare; and (3) an expanded Medicare plan for the aged.	Basic benefits under all three plans identical for covered individuals regardless of age, income, or membership in a given plan. Reimbursable services include: (1) Hospital services. (2)Physician services. (3)Outpatient prescription drugs. (4)Mental health services. (5)Special and preventive services for children. (6)Other preventive services, including prenatal, maternity, and family planning. (7)Home health services-100 visits/ year. (8)Post-hospital extended care-100 days/year. (9)Blood and blood products. (10)Other medical services, as in Medicare. -Under EHIP, $150 deductible/person with a maximum of three/family. Separate $50 deductible for outpatient drugs. Coinsurance of 25% applied to covered benefits after deductible satisfied. Maximum liability for cost-sharing limited to $1500/year, providing protection against high-cost or catastrophic illness. -Under AHIP, premiums, deductibles, coinsurance and maximum liability all income-related, with families earning less than $2500/ year (individuals $1850 annually)	Approximately $6.9 billion in added federal-state expenditures needed for AHIP, added state spending would be about $1.0 billion. Federal subsidy to assist low-income employees and their employers would total $0.45 billion, with an additional $1.8 billion for increased benefits to the elderly.	EHIP-employer-employee premium payments with employer contributing 65% and employees 35% (after three years employer's share 75% and employee's share 25%). Federal subsidies would be available for employer whose payroll increases by more than 3% due to contributions for coverage. AHIP-financed by premium payments according to family income and federal and state contributions. Families with less than $5,000 annual (individuals $3,500) would pay no premiums. Plan for Aged-financed through continuation of present Medicare payroll taxes (1.8%) plus small premium contributions from insured persons (about $90/person/year).	Federal government would establish eligibility standards, define reimbursable services, and operate expanded Medicare plan for elderly. States would contract with private carriers to administer AHIP, under federal regulations. States responsible for regulating private carriers offering EHIP.	Healthcard given to all enrollees. Participating providers of services would accept Healthcard and bill carriers for covered services, the carriers then reimbursing provider and billing enrollee. Full-participating providers would accept reimbursement through Healthcard as payment in full (required of all institutions); associate providers similarly for all AHIP and Medicare patients while accepting only as payment of insured amount for EHIP enrollees. EHIP patients billed directly for remainder of fee. Non-participating providers would not be reimbursed from any plan for services provided.	Medicare expanded. Medicaid terminated except for certain services not covered by the comprehensive plan. Encourages growth HMO's and prepaid group practice plans. State regulation of insurance carriers and providers. PSRO's would review medical services provided under the plan and outpatient. Indians would be able to participate in state AHIP plans. VA would continue to operate a separate system for eligible persons. Additional standards established for physician extenders.

paying no premiums or deductibles but subject to 10% coinsurance.
-The Medicare beneficiaries annual deductible per-person on all services would be $100 plus a $50 deductible for outpatient drugs. Beneficiaries would pay 20% coinsurance on expenses above deductible, to a maximum liability of $750/year.

from 60 to 365 days a year. Coinsurance would become more flexible and there would be no deductibles. Catastrophic coverage would commence under the new bill after a family had spent a maximum of $2000 (individual $1500) for coinsurance.

The new version of the Health Security Act raises the amount of employees' wages and unearned income on which a 1% payroll tax would apply from $15,000 to $20,000. Freestanding ambulatory alcoholism and drug abuse centers and freestanding family planning and rehabilitation centers now would be recognized as providers of services. In addition the planning, resource development, and administrative sections of the new bill are coordinated with provisions of the recently enacted National Health Planning and Resources Development Act of 1974.

While the National Health Care Services Reorganization and Financing Act contained several new features, the major revision pertained to the provision of expanded home health and nursing home care. Extra benefits would also be added for inpatient and ambulatory treatment of mental illness. The phasing-in by 1985 of an expanded benefits package in two rather than three stages was the major change made in the reintroduced National Health Care Act.

NEWARK COMPREHENSIVE HEALTH SERVICES PLAN[45]

Newark, the largest city in New Jersey, presently has one of the worst health records in the country. Health manpower is well below the national average and continuing to decline. Over 25% of the people lack third-party coverage and are too poor to pay for health services. Consequently they rely for free medical care on the six Newark hospitals, which are increasingly in financial difficulties.

The Newark Comprehensive Health Services Plan (Medicaid Waiver), a bold move to change this crisis situation into a model citywide health system, developed from the proposals of a task force composed of community representatives and providers of care working with New Jersey state officials and the College of Medicine and Dentistry of New Jersey. The task force had originally met to consider how to lower the annual deficit of the state subsidized Martland Hospital, incurred because 50% of the patients cannot afford to pay their bills. However the task force broadened the scope of its study and drafted the citywide project proposals which developed into the Newark Comprehensive Health Services Plan.

At the end of 1974 HEW granted provisional approval for the Newark plan. It was approved under Section 1115 of the Social Security Act, providing for the extension of Medicaid for demonstration projects. This three-year demonstration plan would be the largest single federal health project, operating on an estimated $36 to $54 million budget, half of which is to be provided by the federal govern-

[45]Newark Comprehensive Health Services Board of Trustees and New Jersey Department of Institutions and Agencies, *A Proposal for Newark Comprehensive Health Services Plan*, submitted to Social and Rehabilitative Service, HEW, December 1973.

ment. Provision was made to funnel the federal money through the State's Department of Institutions and Agencies, to be matched there with state money before sending to the Newark Comprehensive Health Plan for the monthly premiums called capitations.

Essentially the plan tends toward the implementation of a citywide HMO, which encompasses the combined strengths of the College of Medicine and Dentistry of New Jersey, the Newark City Health Department, six state departments, the Governor's Office, all six hospitals, five neighborhood health centers, and all private practitioners in Newark. Implementation involved the major restructuring of the city's fragmented health care system into a national model for health care delivery.

One of the Newark plan's main objectives is to improve the health of its members. Operationally one of the indicators will be a planned 20% reduction in the city's excessively high infant mortality rate. The plan calls for the development of an efficient, coordinated medical system that considerably expands the number of primary care providers. The emphasis is on comprehensive, preventative care through increased utilization of nonemergency ambulatory visits.

The plan involves a centrally administered, prepaid health system rather than the usual fee-for-service Medicaid system. The criterion of eligibility includes approximately 60 to 90,000 Newark citizens, present Medicaid recipients, and those who have a net income less than one and one-half times the average New Jersey eligibility level. The estimated final enrollment will be 66,000 people, although additional children will be reached through supplemental school health programs, for which funds have been designated.

Members will be enrolled and thereby sign a contractual agreement to receive all care from one provider, although there is provision for subcontracting with other providers. Each member will be presented with a set of minimum benefits to which he is entitled that encompasses at least medical, dental, and pharmaceutical benefits. There will be standardized treatment programs for hypertension, diabetes, and tuberculosis.

An important aspect of the plan is the integration of levels of care (See Table 5.5). Primary physicians refer patients to secondary and tertiary levels of care. The provider group enrolling members, through power of authorization of Medicaid payment, has fiscal control of cases. There are also built-in incentives to make physicians responsible for integrating health services. Physicians are required to join Foundations for Medical Care, formed by the local medical association, to compete for contracts in the Newark Medical Waiver Plan. Peer review committees and audits of quality of care both for treatment and intervention are part of the plan.

The health care team providing primary care is an integral part of the project, either as the entire staff of a center or as one of multiple teams in the hospitals. The team members include an internist, a family practitioner, a pediatrician, an obstetrician, a registered nurse, a licensed practical nurse, family health workers, a part-time nutrition counselor, a medical social worker, a health educator, an

TABLE 5.5. Newark Comprehensive Health Services Plan: How Members Will Use the Plan

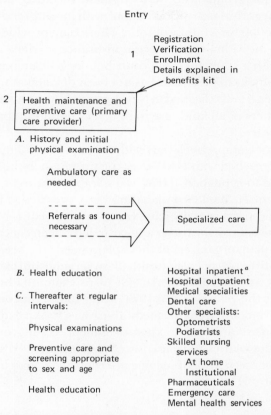

Entry

1 Registration
   Verification
   Enrollment
   Details explained in
     benefits kit

2 Health maintenance and
   preventive care (primary
   care provider)

   A. History and initial
      physical examination

      Ambulatory care as
      needed

      Referrals as found
      necessary

   Specialized care

   B. Health education

   C. Thereafter at regular
      intervals:

      Physical examinations

      Preventive care and
      screening appropriate
      to sex and age

      Health education

   Hospital inpatient [a]
   Hospital outpatient
   Medical specialities
   Dental care
   Other specialists:
     Optometrists
     Podiatrists
   Skilled nursing
     services
       At home
       Institutional
   Pharmaceuticals
   Emergency care
   Mental health services

Source. Newark Comprehensive Health Services Board of Trustees and New Jersey Department of Institutions and Agencies, *A Proposal for Newark Comprehensive Health Services Plan,* submitted to Social and Rehabilitative Services, HEW, December 1973, p. 37.

[a] Not included in primary care contract; not capitated in first six months.

administrative manager, and supporting personnel. Subcontracting arrangements for the participation of pharmacists are envisaged.

It is anticipated that there will be a 20% reduction in the rate of increase of health care costs through the prepayment system which puts the providers at risk, and through the emphasis on high quality preventative care as the alternative to expensive hospitalization. (Separate cost centers will be established for each institutional ambulatory care provider.) The Newark plan provides final dollar coverage in that it considers only those medical costs above any amounts paid by other health insurance.

The plan has been designed to encourage consumer participation in the health care system; consumers are included on the plan's board of directors.

Nevertheless the plan is not without its problems. The plan accepted by HEW does not include some groups who were originally included, that is, the group classified as "noncategorical needy population" with incomes above the eligibility level stipulated as $6000 for a family of four. There is no provision as yet for part payment, although individuals, commercial insurance carriers, and groups can buy into the plan with a 100% financial contribution; $40 a month per person.

The role of the physician's assistant has not been detailed as the PA's practice status has not yet been legally clarified in New Jersey. Despite this uncertainty, PAs and nurse practitioners of all kinds are to be a very important part of the teams providing primary care.

Before the Newark Comprehensive Health Services Plan is implemented, final agreement must be reached with HEW over the transition in the first six months from fee-for-service to capitation. HEW wants capitation to be the method of payment from the outset. While the plan is now incorporated, questions relating to the marketing and fiscal systems have yet to be resolved.

While appropriate control measures appear to have been conceptualized carefully in the Newark plan, organizers of these plans need take heed of the California experience with fifty-two prepaid health plans serving approximately 240,000 Medicaid recipients. In fifteen of the largest plans examined by the California Auditor General for the years 1971 to 1973, it was found that only 48% of state expenditures ($56.5 million) went for medical services.[46] "An extraordinary high 52% went for various administrative expenses (data processing, enrollment, rent, and overhead, and the salaries and expenses of plan officials)."[47] Situations where administrative costs exceed 15% of income are reportedly very unusual, even in the startup phase of a HMO.[48]

[46]"HMO's: Are They the Answer to Your Medical Needs," *Consumer Reports*, **39** (October 1974), pp. 756–762.
[47]*Ibid.*, p. 760.
[48]*Ibid.*

CHAPTER SIX

THE EVOLVING ROLE
OF PHARMACISTS AS
HEALTH CARE SPECIALISTS

A discussion of the evolving roles of the pharmacist involves problems associated with the definition of the pharmacist as one of the providers of health care. Mankind's history from antiquity to the Middle Ages and on into the twentieth century provides much evidence to prove that man perceives drugs as they pertain to health care as a basic need.[1] Individuals with a variety of backgrounds have stepped forward to be the purveyors of active medicinal agents; priests, Greek gods, monks, physicians, and finally chemists. Each added in some measure to the improvement of health care delivery and in some cases to the amenities of life which are usually associated with health care, such as cosmetics, cordials, colas, and cocktails at five o'clock.

The profession of pharmacy has been defined as "that profession which is concerned with the art and science of preparing from natural and synthetic sources, suitable and convenient materials for distribution and use in the treatment and prevention of disease."[2] Just as in other fields of human endeavor, over the past one hundred years there has been a proliferation of specialists within the field of pharmacy. However the community pharmacist is still the most prevalent type in our society today, although the number of pharmacists now serving society as practitioners in institutional settings, as manufacturing pharmacists, medical service representatives, scientists, educators, and administrators is growing rapidly. Obviously the role of the pharmacist has changed dramatically with the growth of the pharmaceutical industry over the last thirty years. Moreover,

---

[1]Glenn A. Sonnedecker, "Evolution of Pharmacy," *Pharmaceutical Sciences,* 14th edition, edited by Joseph P. Remington (Easton, Pennsylvania: Mack Publishing Company, 1970), pp. 8–19. Richard A. Deno, Thomas D. Rowe, and Donald C. Brodie, *The Profession of Pharmacy,* 2nd edition (Philadelphia: Lippincott, 1966), p. 1.

modern technology, coupled with changes in health care delivery systems, will create an acceleration of the rate of change in the role of the pharmacist as a health care provider during the last quarter of the twentieth century.

CURRENT ROLES OF THE PHARMACIST

In addition to the rather simple definition of pharmacy referred to above there are some relatively recent characterizations of pharmacy that tend to expand the role of the pharmacist. Brodie, for example, focuses his definition on drug use control, thus casting the pharmacist into the role of assuring the public "optimal safety in the distribution and use of medications."[3] There is evidence that society has taken this definition seriously. For example, a pharmacist had action brought against him for failure to inform a prescribing physician of the fibrotic side effects caused by the drug methylsergide maleate.[4] The drug manufacturer, physician, and pharmacist all contributed to the $350,000 settlement for the plaintiff.

A report from the Department of Health, Education, and Welfare in 1972 broadens the role and scope of the pharmacist as a health care provider by describing pharmacy as "the health profession that assures safety and efficacy in the procuring, storing, *prescribing,* compounding, dispensing, delivery, *administering,* and the use of drugs and related articles."[5] Some pharmacists today, practicing mainly in an institutional setting, prescribe medications and either administer or supervise the administration of medication. However 80% of today's pharmacists practice in a community setting. It is fair to state that these pharmacists do not perceive themselves in a health provider role of prescribing and administering medications.

The role of the pharmacist in drug product selection is implied but not specified in the definitions presented. In 1970 the American Pharmaceutical Association started a campaign to overturn state laws that forbid the substitution of a chemically equivalent product for a product specified by a proprietary name on a practitioner's prescription. Antisubstitution laws had been adopted by most states' legislatures in response to a problem of counterfeit drugs appearing on the market in the late 1940s and early 1950s. Pharmacists have always played a role in drug product selection, especially among those sold without prescription as over-the-counter products. At issue is the role of the pharmacist and the consumer in selecting products assumed to be equivalent in quality but lower in price than brand name products. The brand name versus generic equivalent issue will be expanded on as a cost savings plan in the discussion of National Health Insurance and drugs.

[3] Joint Committee of the American Nursing Home Association, the American Pharmaceutical Association, and the American Society of Hospital Pharmacists, *Pharmaceutical Services in the Nursing Homes,* 6th edition (Washington, D.C.: American Nursing Home Association, American Pharmaceutical Association, and American Society of Hospital Pharmacists, 1972), p. 8.
[4] *Mahaffey vs. Sandoz, Inc.,* Kansas Sedgwick City District Court, Case No. C-20275, *Clin-Alert,* No. 219–221, November 12, 1974.
[5] U. S. Department of Health, Education, and Welfare, *Health Resources Statistics* (Washington, D.C.: U. S. Department of Health, Education, and Welfare, 1972), p. 209.

Presently, as noted above, the majority of all pharmacists (80%) are community practitioners who are involved in the procurement, compounding, and dispensing of medications. For the future, however, Darley and Somers have suggested that the key factor in determining the role of the pharmacist "quantitatively as well as qualitatively—may depend on his willingness and initiative in assuming larger challenges and responsibilities and on his willingness and ability to become a meaningful member of the comprehensive medical care team."[6]

THE CHANGING WORLD OF DRUG DELIVERY SYSTEMS

The changing world of drug delivery will have a multifaceted effect on the activities of pharmacists as health care delivery specialists. There are also certain overall assumptions that have been made by many planners in the health care field that will have impact on the pharmacist. These are: (1) a health care system is developing in the place of a socalled nonsystem that will cause greater quantities of drugs to be utilized in the future simply because more people will have access to health care delivery services; (2) the potency of drugs and the complexity of therapy and devices for drug delivery will continue to increase, thus creating a need for improved control procedures for the utilization of therapeutic agents; and (3) pharmacists will of necessity assume more responsibility for patient-related care and services.

National Health Insurance and Pharmaceutical Services

There is little question but that the provision of pharmaceutical services will be covered in a national health insurance plan. For example, the *National Health Care Services Reorganization and Financing Act* introduced on January 14, 1975, by Chairman Ullman of the House Ways and Means Committee (H.R. 1) calls for a full range of services, including outpatient drugs. The benefits, however, require copayment by non–low income individuals, except when care is provided by health care corporations operating on a predetermined capitation charge basis, or, when certain catastrophic expense benefits are in effect.

The *Health Security Act* introduced by Senator Kennedy and Representative Corman on January 14, 1975 (S.B. 3, H.R. 21) also provides for coverage of prescription drugs. But, in addition, a list of chronic diseases and a list of drugs to be utilized in treating the diseases would be included in the act. Under the act the pharmacist would be paid a dispensing fee and would be reimbursed for the drugs used on the basis of a price established by a full-time, five-member Health Security Board appointed by the President and placed within the Department of Health, Education, and Welfare. The Health Security Board would be given extensive authority if this act were passed by the Congress and implemented by HEW. For example, the Board would have the authority first, to establish qualifications to be

---

[6] Ward Darley and Anne R. Somers, "Medicine, Money, and Manpower: The Challenge to Professional Education," *The New England Journal of Medicine,* **276** (June 1967), p. 1421.

met by a provider before the provider could be eligible to participate in the program; second, to direct providers, as a condition for eligibility, either to initiate or to discontinue certain services; and third, to establish reasonable continuing education requirements in order to maintain and enhance the competency of the professionals who are providing services under the guidelines of the act.

There are three major issues currently being debated that have direct impact on pharmaceutical services being provided under a national health insurance program. Two of these have been alluded to in the outline of the proposed acts: (1) Maximum Allowable Costs, as they apply to charges for prescribed medications; and (2) the professional or dispensing fee to be paid to the provider, in this case, the pharmacist. The third issue is directly related to Maximum Allowable Costs-—the issue of bioequivalency among products that contain the same active ingredient.

On June 20, 1975, the Food and Drug Administration released the long awaited proposed bioavailability/bioequivalence regulations.[7] These regulations require that 193 problem drugs and dosage forms meet appropriate bioavailability/bioequivalence requirements as a condition of marketing. For certain drugs, human or *in vivo* testing would be required. Drugs such as procainamide HCl, warfarin, and aminophylline are among some forty-seven drugs in this category. Seventy drugs would require only *in vitro* testing. Some examples of drugs in this category are chlorothiazide, sulfadiazine, and diethylstibestrol. Sixty-two products would require special regulatory handling because of special dosage forms, for example, aerosols for inhalation, enteric-coated tablets, radiopharmaceuticals; and fourteen would require special regulatory handling because of manufacturing problems, for example, extracts of biological preparations, intrathecal or intraventricular injection preparations. The proposed bioavailability/bioequivalence regulations are a key element in the Department of Health, Education, and Welfare's proposal to reimburse for drugs available from a variety of manufacturers on the basis of maximum allowable costs (MAC).

The MAC program is a plan to contain costs in a federally funded drug program. As proposed, MAC regulations will place government price controls on reimbursement to the pharmacist for the drug product dispensed under federally supported drug programs. Assurance that products available from several sources are therapeutically equivalent is essential to this price regulation plan.

The MAC proposals are not the only means envisaged to keep the costs of drugs at a minimum and change the pattern of delivery of pharmacy services. The final report of the Task Force on Prescription Drugs did consider the possibility of providing for central procurement of drugs as the most desirable means of controlling drug costs. The State of California has established a central procurement program for drugs dispensed in their welfare program, leading some to predict that a similar federal plan will be promoted and have far-reaching effects on the character of pharmacy practice in the future, reducing the practitioner to

---

[7]"FDA Compresses All the Talk about Bioequivalence and Bioavailability," *FDE Reports–The Pink Sheet,* **37** (June 23, 1975), pp. 3–8. See also, "Human Drugs," *Federal Register,* **40** (June 20, 1975), pp. 26142–26171.

negotiating for fees based on distributional services rendered and eliminating the role of product selection for the patient or client.[8] This issue will be discussed further in the section devoted to changes in community pharmacy.

National health insurance, according to Representative Corman, is still several years away, but he predicts it will be part of our health care system.[9] The effects of national health insurance on pharmacy practice are not totally predictable at this time: some of the proposals tend to negate the role of the pharmacist as a health care specialist (elimination of drug product selection); while others tend to promote new roles (fee-for-services rendered).

The Pharmaceutical Industry

The pharmacist has been involved in the manufacturing of drugs and drug dosage forms for centuries. But it was the scientific discoveries of the 19th century and the rapid introduction of specific and rational chemotherapeutic agents in the first half of the twentieth century that created a new and highly technical industry known today as the pharmaceutical industry. As with all new adventures, it should have been expected that this industry would grow and change in character along with societal and economic changes.

At issue today is the relationship of this industry to society's needs. By every measure imaginable, the U. S. pharmaceutical industry has been the most productive in the world; it has produced the majority of the life-saving and life quality improving drugs available to the people of the world today. The industry's record in responding to increased governmental regulation in the areas of quality control and assurances of therapeutic effectiveness and safety should be recognized as positive and responsible. However the industry is not without its critics. Pricing has and will continue to be a key issue. The public, as represented by consumer groups, governmental agencies such as the Federal Trade Commission, and Congress, is expressing concern that the entire spectrum of the drug distribution system, manufacturing through retailing, has created an uncompetitive atmosphere not in the public's best interest.

That the industry views this as a serious problem is evident. Mr. C. Joseph Stetler, president of the Pharmaceutical Manufacturers Association, in his address to an advertising club, entitled, "Are Drug Prices and Profits Without Honor?," concluded his talk by asking the question, "How can we (pharmaceutical manufacturers) most effectively document our stewardship and accelerate that wisp of a promising trend toward public approval of our work?"[10] The practicing pharmacist has a stake in this controversy and indeed in the past has been subject to pricing differentials that were to the retail pharmacists' distinct disadvantage. For example, a HEW report lists a price range from $13.90 for one thousand tablets of a well known drug Orinase, when purchased by the Federal Government through its central procurement procedures, to $41.14 when purchased by a

[8]J. Leo McMahon, "Central Procurement—Fact or Fancy," *The Apothecary,* **5** (Number 6, 1975), p. 20.
[9]"National Health Insurance: Reassurance from the Left," *Medical Economics,* **52** (June 1975), p. 137.
[10]C. Joseph Stetler, "Are Drug Prices and Profits Without Honor?," *Medical Marketing and Media,* **10** (July 1975), p. 11.

retail pharmacist through a wholesale distributor.[11] Of course changing these price differentials has had and will have a significant effect on the pharmaceutical industry's pricing structure, for it is well known to all that community pharmacy has, according to the statistics gathered by the Social Security Administration, filled the majority of all the prescription medications dispensed at the beginning of the decade—1,070,000,000 of the 2,008,000,000 prescriptions filled in the year 1970.

One more fact about the industry should be noted at this point. The pharmaceutical industry has been a growth industry in every sense of the word since its inception in the 19th century, but a startling change of direction occurred in 1974 that was not appreciated until mid-1975. For the first time in its history the U. S. prescription market declined, by 1%, in the following manner:

1974   new prescriptions   + 3%
1974   refill prescriptions   − 4%

One market analyst, David Labson, speculates that there were several factors contributing to this decline: the economic recession; consumerism; the rise in malpractice insurance rates; the decline in promotion of products by the industry; an increase in prescription size; and finally, growth in non–drugstore prescription activity that was not reflected in the prescription audit for 1974.[12]

There are two major points to be considered under the general topics of the changing world of drug delivery systems and the changing role of the pharmacist as it relates to the pharmaceutical industry. The first is the role of the graduate pharmacist in the industry. For example, one large firm estimates they have 1400 pharmacists employed.[13] To put this figure into perspective, this one company employs more pharmacists than twenty-six of our fifty states: fifteen out of the twenty-four states west of the Mississippi River have fewer pharmacists employed than does this one company.[14] For the entire industry the 1973 figures indicate that over 5000 registered pharmacists were employed. The Pharmaceutical Manufacturers Association reported that in 1973–74 a total of 260,000 were employed in the industry, with 106,560 overseas. As the manpower pool of graduate pharmacists increases, the industry will undoubtedly increase the number of pharmacists employed.

The second point concerning pharmacists and the industry is that the entire industry has clearly begun to change its attitude concerning the pharmacist's ability to influence the market through drug product selection. For example, an article which appeared in the April 1975 issue of *Chain Store Age* makes this quite explicit. The article indicates that the signs are clear that the large companies in the pharmacy industry, while not having given up pursuing the physician, have certainly started to romance the pharmacist. They have invested in new phar-

[11]Social Security Administration, *Medical Care, Costs and Prices: Background Book* (Washington, D.C.: U. S. Department of Health, Education, and Welfare, January 1972).
[12]David Labson, "Let's Talk Marketing," *Medical Marketing and Media*, **10** (June 1975), p. 4.
[13]Robert Manning, Director, Professional Services, Eli Lilly and Company (personal letter to authors).
[14]National Association of Boards of Pharmacy, *Licensure Statistics Census* (Chicago: National Association of Boards of Pharmacy, 1973).

macist oriented newsletters, high quality continuing education programs, tele-
phone information services, and one firm has even given away bumper stickers
reading "Pharmacy is a Life-Saving Profession."[15]

In summary, two events will continue to shape the pharmacist's role in the
future: increased numbers will undoubtedly be employed by the industry, and
drug product selection by the practicing pharmacist will cause the industry to
promote its products to the pharmacists as well as the physicians who are the
prescribers of the industry's product.

Community Pharmacy Practice

By the second decade of the 19th century the distribution of drugs was described
by the Smith Kline Corporation as follows:

Drugs . . . were crude at best, and deadly at worst . . . . Substitution, adulteration, and
misbranding were commonplace. Lack of concern for sanitation in preparing, packaging
and collecting drugs served often to aggravate rather than alleviate disease. Either by
accident or design, tradesmen took over the dispensing of drugs. Standards for drugs were
nonexistent, and no agencies, public or private, functioned to provide them.[16]

In 1821 a group of Philadelphia apothecaries met the challenge and formed the
Philadelphia College of Apothecaries. In 1822 the Pennsylvania Legislature passed an Act of Incorporation and changed the name to the Philadelphia College of
Pharmacy, the first institution of its type in the Western Hemisphere. Thus the
American system of pharmacy began its development, with the American pharmacists being trained in a profession to dispense drugs but continuing to be pulled
by a commercial world to purvey a wide variety of articles which in many instances
had little relationship to health care needs.

The community pharmacist has been characterized as a marginal professional
or as an incomplete professional, primarily because American pharmacy to this
day has not outgrown the character of the general pine board store basically
inherited from the British system. However it is of interest to note that this
character of American pharmacy has not created a low opinion of pharmacy in the
eyes of the average American consumer. Melvin R. Gibson sums this up rather
well in his comments about pharmacists:

The pharmacist is still the professional on Main Street most accessible to the public whose
image remains as that of a reliable person with whom the public can talk in confidence on a
variety of subjects and who does not send a bill for his counsel.[17]

Since the advent of prepackaged medications by the pharmaceutical industry,
the pharmacist has in many instances withdrawn from the view of the American

[15]"The Pharmaceutical Houses: Romancing the Pharmacist," Editorial, *Chain Store Age,* **51** (April
1975), pp. 51, 55, 59.
[16]Smith Kline Corporation, *Philadelphia Medica* (Harrisburg, Pennsylvania: Stackpole Books, 1975), p.
107.
[17]Melvin R. Gibson, "Pharmacists in Practice," *Pharmaceutical Sciences,* 15th edition, edited by Joseph R.
Remington (Easton, Pennsylvania: Mack Publishing Company, 1975), p. 28.

public. This practice of removing the pharmacist from the public view prompted the American Pharmaceutical Association to commission the Dichter Institute for Motivational Research to analyze the public's regard for the pharmacist and for comprehensive pharmaceutical services.[18] Perhaps the most significant finding of the study indicated that the pharmacist has indeed lost contact with the public. The public expressed interest in having contact with a pharmacist but expressed a feeling of being pushed toward the mass merchandisers and discount houses where they were assured of depersonalized service, but at a bargain price. In the words of the report:

The single most important recommendation of our study is that communication has to be reestablished between the public and the pharmacist. It is necessary to explain to the public in considerable detail exactly what the pharmacist does. To achieve this, all modern available channels of communication should be utilized.[19]

There is some indication that the Dichter Report was taken seriously in some quarters. In a feature article in the December 1975 issue of *Chain Store Age,* Mr. Michael Barnd, an executive with one of America's largest chain drug operations, was asked the question, "What is the most dramatic change you've seen in the last few years in pharmacy?" Barnd answered:

The trend to service in the prescription department. With the growth of third party coverage, price is not the factor it once was. Even cash and carry stores don't stress price as much as they did once."[20]

Over the past decade there have been introduced into the arena of community pharmacy activities that could be the forerunners of a wide variety of services to be performed. We examine three:

A.   Patient medication profiles
B.   Drug product selection
C.   Miscellaneous services

Patient Medication Profiles.   By the decade of the 1960s the American drug industry was producing 13,500 tons of aspirin, 400 tons of barbiturates, and 660 tons of tranquilizers per year. All of this tonnage caused Robert P. Hudson to write an amusing article entitled, "Polypharmacy in Twentieth Century America." The first sentence gives the reader a clue to the text: "One of the more vexing problems facing the medical historian of 2067 is the persistence of polypharmacy throughout most of the last century."[21] The fact remains that polypharmacy, which many have defined as the excessive and/or inappropriate use of drugs,

---

[18]American Pharmaceutical Association, *Final Report of the Dichter Institute for Motivational Research, Inc.* (Washington, D.C.: American Pharmaceutical Association, 1973).
[19]*Ibid.,* p. 14.
[20]Michael Barnd, "Barnd-On Pharmacy at Walgreen," *Chain Store Age,* **51** (December 1975), p. 88.
[21]Robert P. Hudson, "Polypharmacy in Twentieth Century America," *Clinical Pharmacology and Therapeutics,* **9** (January–February, 1968), p. 2.

continues to exist in the decade of the mid-1970s. This condition in our drug distribution system has created the need for some protection of the public's welfare. The introduction of family and individual medication profiles was community pharmacy's answer to this vexing problem of drugs being obtained by the public from a variety of sources. The public welfare intent of such action was to reduce drug interactions and overdosages. The profiles also were used to maintain patient records for other matters such as income tax purposes and the like. The State of New Jersey enacted legislation to require the maintenance of medication profiles, and a survey indicated that 82% of 125 pharmacists in Idaho had such records and that more pharmacies claimed to be using them than was suspected at the time, 3174 of 4599 surveyed, or 69%.[22] By 1975 much had been written on the effectiveness or lack of effectiveness of this system.

The use of medication profiles is one factor that will accelerate the introduction of computer terminals in community pharmacies. A 1975 advertisement for such a system by Profile, a division of Health Application Systems, Inc., of Burlingame, California, announced that a pharmacist, "just dispensed 83 prescriptions, checked and updated 83 patient profiles, detected three potential drug interactions, completed 36 third party claims, and printed a label in Spanish for Mrs. Diaz." A graph in the advertisement suggested that it required three and one-half hours less time to accomplish this than if it had been performed without the benefit of the computer and its associated printout/readout system; and that when 200 prescriptions are filled in an eight-hour day, the device will replace one pharmacist (provided the pharmacist's services in patient care do not increase)!

Drug Product Selection.   Our system of patents and licensing agreements allows the inventor of a product to sell or license the product and be rewarded for its invention as well as to recover developmental costs. After seventeen years of such protection, the basic product becomes part of the public domain and others may produce the product. In the pharmaceutical world this means that a single source "brand name product" can be produced by others seventeen years after patent issue with the multisource product then becoming a generic one in the market place. If a physician chooses to prescribe the product using a generic name, the pharmacist has the right to choose the generic product that will be dispensed.

As noted earlier, drug counterfeiting had caused every state in the union to adopt antisubstitution laws by the 1950s forbidding the substitution of one brand name generic product for another. By 1970 the American Pharmaceutical Association had begun a campaign to repeal state laws that prohibited substitution. The bases for this stand by the Association were: (1) it would result in the lowering of the cost of medication; and (2) it would increase the professional status of the pharmacist. The pharmacist, on the basis of education and experience, is considered to be the best qualified person to select the source of a multisource drug product to be dispensed.

By mid-1975 six states had modified their antisubstitution laws.[23] They were

[22]"How Many Use Patient Medication Profiles?," *Academy of General Practice,* **10** (June 1975), p. 1.
[23]John Carlson, "A New Law Allowing Patients to Pick Rx Products," *Medical Economics,* **52** (May 1975), pp. 81–87.

Kentucky, Maryland, Massachusetts, Florida, Arkansas, and Michigan. It is reported that an additional 30 or more states are moving to effect similar changes in their antisubstitution laws. While the trend to repeal antisubstitution laws will undoubtedly continue, in mid-1975 it was reported that 10% of all new prescriptions were being written generically, thus giving the pharmacist the clear choice of product, regardless of the status of antisubstitution laws in effect.[24] This trend in prescribing habits of the physician also will probably continue. The 1975 survey conducted by the *American Druggist* indicated that in a one-year period a noticeable shift had occurred in the source of generic products.[25] Although survey data indicate a continuing preference on the part of pharmacists for brand name products, generic items are increasing in usage. Of course the Department of Health, Education, and Welfare's Maximum Allowable Cost Program, discussed earlier in this chapter, will have the effect of eliminating the pharmacist from the decision process in the area of drug product selection. Nevertheless the pharmacist has clearly stepped forward in recent years in the area of drug product selection and his involvement in this area of professional practice should continue to accelerate over the next decade.

Miscellaneous Services.   Since its inception in America, the community pharmacy has served as a source of health information as well as a source of both prescription and nonprescription drugs. The concept of providing health information without charge is neither new nor highly organized, but numerous examples can be cited across the length and breadth of America where pharmacists have become involved in the public health matters of their communities and find rewards of a personal rather than a financial nature.

In recent years pharmacists have joined others in drug abuse information programs, in programs to increase the awareness of the public of the fact that venereal disease has taken a dramatic upturn, and in activities helping newcomers to a community to secure the services of a physician. Most recently, with and sometimes without the blessings of the local medical societies, pharmacists have become involved in screening for hypertension.

In conclusion, service has been a concept that has remained as part of community pharmacy. There is evidence that this concept will remain a part of the American pharmacy scene and at present there is much evidence to prove that this practice is increasing.

Third Party Payment for Prescriptions

During the decade of the 1960s, community pharmacy began to feel the impact of doing business with a third party. The Medicaid programs implemented in the early 1960s allowed states to reimburse out-of-hospital costs for those covered by various social welfare programs. In addition, labor groups, such as the United Auto Workers, began to include drug benefits as part of their labor contracts with

[24]"How Pharmacists' Generic Preferences Have Changed," Editorial, *American Druggist,* **172** (July 1975), pp. 23–36.
[25]*Ibid.*

business and industry. By 1969, 15% of the total costs of outpatient prescriptions were paid for by third parties; and, in 1970, third-party payment for prescription medication increased by 27.5% over 1969.[26]

All of this activity caused T. Donald Rucker, then with the U. S. Social Security Administration, to predict in a 1970 speech delivered to the California Pharmaceutical Association that by the mid-1970s about 70% of all prescribed medications would be covered by the combined enrollments under private and public drug insurance plans. This percentage has not been realized. In fact, a 1975 HEW publication on medical care expenditures indicates that the total percentage of third-party payments by 1974 was only 13.9%, up from 10.1% in 1970.[27] The best guess is that the total in 1975 was no more than 15%, obviously very short of the 70% mark predicted at the beginning of the decade.

There are probably several factors that contributed to this slower than predicted third-party payment for pharmaceutical services. As illustrated in Table 6.1, drugs constitute a relatively small portion of the total annual expenditure for health. (The distribution of payment between third-party and direct payment is very similar for those for dental care.) Political pressure for third party payment has not been as compelling as for physician and hospital services. Also, proposed programs for preventing cost overruns, such as MAC, generally have not been accepted. And perhaps just as important, pharmacists have been less than enthusiastic when they view the past history of third-party programs. For example, in the State of Michigan the pharmacist was paid a $2.00 fee in 1967 for filling a Medicaid-sponsored prescription. By 1975 the fee had risen to $2.15, an increase of less than 10%. In this same period of time state legislators had an increase in salary from $10,000 in 1967 to $18,000 in 1975.

Third-party payments will increase, but not at the earlier rate predicted for the decade of the 1970s. As they increase, price competition in the community pharmacy will be reduced and, as previously reported, it will lead to competition directed at service and convenience.

TABLE 6.1. Health Expenditures: 1974[a]

Item	Total ($)	Direct ($)	Third Party ($)
Hospital care	40,900	4,274	36,626
Physicians' services	19,000	7,381	11,619
Dentists' services	6,200	5,326	874
Drugs	9,695	8,345	1,350

[a] Amount in millions.
Source.   Adapted from U. S. Department of Health, Education, and Welfare, *Medical Care Expenditures, Prices and Costs: Background Book* (Washington, D.C.: U. S. Department of Health, Education, and Welfare, 1975), p. 13.

[26]U. S. Department of Health, Education, and Welfare, *Medical Care Expenditures, Prices and Costs: Background Book* (Washington, D.C.: U. S. Department of Health, Education, and Welfare, 1975).
[27]*Ibid.*

The Growing Problem of Malpractice

In the introductory paragraphs the judgment against a pharmacist because of injury to one of his patients while receiving methylsergide maleate was cited. This case and several others appear not to be a dynamic force in shaping the behavior of pharmacists, particularly community pharmacists as they are engaged in their practice. In the case of methylsergide maleate it was the pharmacist's and physician's ignoring of the warning statements in the drug package insert that led to their being held liable for their acts. In the August 1973 issue of the *Journal of Legal Medicine,* F. J. Barnett had an excellent article on the role of the package insert as it applies to the health professionals' liability for adverse drug reactions. As noted by Barnett:

In response to an apparent need for accurate, authoritative information on the use of modern drugs, the FDA in 1961 acted to bring into being the pharmaceutical package insert, listing indications, contraindications, side effects, and precautions.

In time, the package inserts were introduced into evidence in trials involving liability for adverse drug reactions. No court has yet held that the package insert, alone, can establish the standards of care required of a physician. But various decisions indicate that where the manufacturer provides adequate warning, via package inserts and detailmen, the physician may be left solely liable for adverse drug reactions.[29]

Others have come to similar conclusions. Michael X. Morrell in an article on the same subject stated: "The package insert has achieved an increasingly important role not only as a device to communicate prescribing information to physicians, but also as a key element in the standard to determine the liability of physicians for adverse drug reactions."[30]

Pharmacy has become more involved in the area of malpractice. Charlotte L. Rosenberg, in a January 1976 issue of *Medical Economics* on the subject of malpractice and drug delivery, states: "The rules for assessing blame in prescription mishaps touch the professionals on both ends of the prescribing process. Now, higher standards imposed on both physicians and pharmacists make mistakes more costly than ever."[31] A physician-attorney, Marden G. Dixon, is quoted in the same article as follows: "The pharmacist of the future may be faced with a high liability potential if he fails either to call the physician and advise him of the contraindications to the use of a given drug, or to intervene in the doctor-patient relationship and advise the patient of the inherent dangers."[32] There is little question that the latter advice concerning intervention in the physician-patient relationship is threatening to the physician and can have economic consequences to the pharmacist if handled improperly.

In addition to drug sensitivity and drug interaction hazards the article referred

[29]Frederic J. Barnett, "Liability for Adverse Drug Reactions: The Role of the Package Insert," *Journal of Legal Medicine,* **1** (August 1973), p. 46.
[30]Michael X. Morrell, "Package Inserts, Adverse Drug Reactions and the Physician's Liability," *Rational Drug Therapy,* **9** (August 1975), p. 6.
[31]Charlotte L. Rosenberg, "Who's Liable—You or the Druggist?," *Medical Economics,* **53** (January 1976), p. 69.
[32]*Ibid.,* p. 71.

to increased liability when drugs are prescribed by generic instead of brand name. Finally the article reports that a case is pending in Minnesota naming the doctor and pharmacist for the practice described by Hudson as polypharmacy.[33] The family of a man being treated for depression claims his suicide was caused by a variety of drugs prescribed in inordinate amounts. The pharmacist is charged with filling prescriptions he knew, or should have known, contained excessive amounts of drugs.

One can conclude that the courts are going to play a major part in shaping the role of the pharmacist in the delivery of quality health care services.

The Health Maintenance Organization Concept[34]

While the federal legislation to help establish HMOs does not list pharmaceutical services as a requirement, they have been built into most systems. How this will affect drug delivery in the future cannot be completely predicted at this time. The systems vary from one plan to another.[35] For example, the Kaiser Foundation Health Plan in northern California offers prescription services to nine San Francisco Bay area counties through nineteen Kaiser Foundation Pharmacies. The Health Insurance Plan of Greater New York has pharmacies in the plan that provide prescription on a mail-order basis. The Physician Association of Clackamas County, Oregon, has signed up participating community pharmacies. In this case the pharmacies assume some of the risk if the service is overutilized. The San Joaquin Foundation for Medical Care, Stockton, California, has a subcontract with Paid Prescriptions. Paid Prescriptions in turn pays pharmacists a professional fee plus acquisition cost for dispensing medications for participating members. Finally, some state pharmaceutical organizations have set up foundations for pharmaceutical services for the purpose of negotiating contracts with any HMO that may organize in the future.

It would appear that the pattern, or perhaps it would be better to call it a nonpattern, has been set for the future. The one important aspect of all the plans for pharmaceutical services within HMOs is that each has provisions for cost controls built into the system: drug utilization review committees, co-pay features, and restrictive formularies.

Institutional Practice

The first division of labor between medicine and pharmacy took place in governmental and religious institutions where economic interests were not of primary concern. In American pharmacy the recognition of hospital practice as an important segment of the profession of pharmacy was very late in developing. The first signs of an "awakening" to the fact that pharmacists had an important role to fill in

[33]Robert P. Hudson, *op. cit.*
[34]Chapter 5 contains a more extensive discussion of HMOs.
[35]Samuel W. Kidder and Arthur G. Isack, "Health Maintenance Organizations and Pharmaceutical Services," *Journal of the American Pharmaceutical Association* **12** (January 1972), pp. 8–12, 14–15.

institutional practice did not surface until the 1920s.[36] During the next twenty years, interest and leadership continued to the point that in 1942 pharmacists associated with institutional practice organized The American Society of Hospital Pharmacists.

The last twenty-five years have witnessed a dramatic increase in institutional practice. The majority of the practitioners in this area of pharmacy are classified as hospital pharmacists; however, a number of pharmacists have emerged as specialists within the institutional setting. Those that are more involved with patient care as opposed to the more traditional drug distribution functions in the institutional setting describe themselves as "clinical pharmacists." Those who have become active in the handling and on the spot preparation of radioactive pharmaceuticals for diagnosis and treatment are now labeled radiopharmacists. Through the advent of federal payment for nursing home costs of the elderly, pharmacists engaged in community practice have become institutional practitioners on a part-time basis serving as consultants for a fee and/or by contracting with a nursing home for the prescription services their patients require. There are examples of pharmacists who have contracted with several small hospitals and nursing homes in an area and practice the consulting role on a full-time basis. Some institutional settings are providing organized drug information services and pharmacists are now acting as full-time specialists in this type of service function. As the knowledge base improves in the area of analytical techniques, a few pharmacists are serving hospitals as pharmacokinetic specialists, providing the drug blood level studies and other similar studies on hospitalized patients to assure establishment and maintenance of optimal drug therapy for individual patients.

The growth of pharmacy service has been documented by Ben Teplitsky, the editor of *Pharmacy Times*.[37] Mr. Teplitsky describes the recent growth of pharmacy personnel services in hospitals. Four hundred hospitals were included in the twenty-year study, with the following increases in personnel observed:

Year	Pharmacist to Hospital Bed	Technicians and Other Non-Pharmacist Personnel to Hospital Bed
1955	1:315	1:448
1960	1:320	1:333
1965	1:231	1:203
1970	1:180	1:154
1975	1:100	1:73

The increase in technical and nonpharmacist personnel gives some insight into the reason why the issue of proper utilization of technicians in the institutional setting has been a major area of concern to this segment of pharmacy.

[36]Gloria Niemeyer, "Ten Years of the American Society of Hospital Pharmacists—1942 to 1952," *Bulletin of the American Society of Hospital Pharmacists* 9 (April 1952), pp. 287–394.
[37]Ben Teplitsky, "A 20-Year Trend: What Chief Pharmacists Think about Detail Men," *Pharmacy Times*, 41 (October 1975), pp. 65–75.

In April and July of 1975 the American Society of Hospital Pharmacists and the American Association of Colleges of Pharmacy approved a seven-point statement concerned with "the competencies required in institutional pharmacy practice."[38] In the preface to the policy statement the organizations agreed that "the practice of pharmacy in health care institutions continues to undergo evolutionary and even radical changes," and that institutional practice has "changed to a personal health service charged with assuring pharmaceutic and therapeutic appropriateness of all its functions in the care of patients." The seven stated competencies required of institutional practitioners are in the areas of (1) managerial skills, (2) drug information, (3) product formulation and packaging, (4) basic research capabilities, (5) development and conduct of patient-oriented services, (6) conduct of educational activities, and (7) the ability to conduct programs of quality assurance in the area of pharmaceutical services.

It can be noted that the institutional practitioner has turned from being the most regressive to the most aggressive practitioner of pharmacy in the course of three decades. Continuing change of a very radical nature in the character of institutional pharmacy practice is not only possible but very probable.

EDUCATION FOR CHANGE

During 1975 the American Association of Colleges of Pharmacy began debate on the appropriate mechanism for continued development of the professional doctorate degree for pharmacy practitioners. In a recent publication, A. R. Haskell and L. Kirk Benedict, Dean and Associate Dean, University of Nebraska College of Pharmacy, noted that in the twentieth century significant changes have occurred in pharmacy education on a regular twenty-year rhythm.[39]

At the turn of the century the majority of pharmacists were awarded registration as pharmacists by state boards of pharmacy based on their practical training under the sponsorship of another pharmacist. By the end of the first decade of this century the three-year Pharmaceutical Chemist, Ph.C., became popular and almost universal in its acceptance.

Over the next twenty years accreditation standards for the educational process were being adopted by health professionals. Thus by the decade of the 1930s, pharmacy had established the American Council for Pharmaceutical Education, charged with the responsibility of adopting and maintaining standards for the educational programs in pharmacy colleges and schools. In the decade of the 1930s the four-year Bachelor of Science degree became the standard.

The art of compounding prescriptions was fading as prepared dosage forms were becoming the norm in the late 1940s. Expansion of the science components in pharmacy education led to the next step in the progression, the five-year

---

[38]American Society of Hospital Pharmacists, *Statement on the Competencies Required in Institutional Pharmacy Practice* (Washington, D. C.: American Society of Hospital Pharmacists, 1975).

[39]A. R. Haskell and L. Kirk Benedict, "The Universal Doctor of Pharmacy Degree," *American Journal of Pharmaceutical Education*, **39** (November 1975), pp. 425–427.

Bachelor of Science in Pharmacy degree required for accreditation, starting in 1960. Two schools, the University of Southern California and the University of California at San Francisco adopted six-year programs and offered the Doctor of Pharmacy degree in lieu of the five-year BS in Pharmacy degree. Therefore Haskell and Benedict concluded that pharmacy is ready to adopt a six-year degree. Hence the University of Nebraska announced in the fall of 1975 that it would become the third school of pharmacy to have a six-year program with the doctorate as the first and only professional degree offered.

In the decade of the 1950s the increased length in education was based on the need for more science in the curriculum. Over the past twenty years it has been recognized that the pharmacist's active role as the medication compounder has shifted to that of a passive observer of drug use in our society. James Doluisio and Charles Walton, Dean and Assistant Dean at the University of Texas College of Pharmacy, pinpointed this problem as follows:

Traditionally, the pharmacist has been only a passive observer of drug utilization practices. He has responded in a supportive role to consumer, prescriber, and producer demands and has witnessed countless repetitions of inappropriate use, misuse, abuse, and inappropriate exclusion from use of all kinds of drug substances. Thus restricted to the periphery of drug use behavior, he has been a non-participant in an important aspect of health care for which he could be prepared to serve a most valuable role.[40]

At issue is how best to accomplish the transition from a passive role to an active one. On the one hand it is proposed that all programs convert to a program of approximately six years in length and award a professional doctorate degree. On the other hand there are those who propose that such a drastic change is not desirable and that the shift be slower with more extensive training provided those who will be able to find practice settings that will utilize the advanced clinical training.

Some have described the mid-1970s as a time of revolution in pharmacy with the issue being "relevance in health care and a clinical practice contributing directly to patient welfare."[41] There is little question that innovations in practice and pressure for curriculum reforms have come primarily from pharmacists associated with university teaching hospitals who also serve on faculties of pharmacy schools in full-time or part-time capacities. In general the most frequent innovation has been the development of clinical pharmacy. Schools of pharmacy began by adding one to three years of training beyond the bachelor's degree since there was the feeling that not enough time was available to allow the development of a sufficient degree of clinical emphasis in the five-year bachelor's program. The revised accreditation standards for Doctor of Pharmacy degree programs are illustrative of what is expected of a clinical pharmacist. The American Council on Pharmaceutical Education states:

[40]Charles A. Walton and James T. Doluisio, "Commitments for Tomorrow in Pharmacy Education: Two Professional Degree Programs," *American Journal of Pharmaceutical Education,* **39** (November 1975), pp. 418–419.
[41]Don C. McLeod, "Pharmacy Practice in the Year 2000," *Drug Intelligence and Clinical Pharmacy,* **9** (August 1975), p. 406.

A Doctor of Pharmacy program should prepare pharmacists who can cope with the complex problems in the delivery of comprehensive health care; who possess both the knowledge and skill that enable them to function as specialists in the clinical use of drugs; and who can apply pharmaceutical and biomedical sciences to the practical problems of drug therapy; who are motivated to participate in the interdisciplinary delivery of health care; and who can function as an easily accessible health care informant and educator.[42]

In early December of 1975 the American Association of Colleges of Pharmacy produced a set of materials entitled *Abstracts of Selected Innovative Programs in Pharmaceutical Education and Research.*[43] Some of the abstracts give indications of new roles for pharmacists as health care specialists. In the area of clinical pharmacy the following programs were reported: Training Pharmacy Students for Clinical Roles in Ambulatory Care; Enhancement of Role of the Clinical Pharmacist through Computerization of the Unit Dose System; Pharmaceutical Education in Emergency Cardiac Care; and a Training Program in Clinical Drug Investigation—programs initiated at the University of Kentucky. Anti-coagulent Therapy—A Pharmaceutical Service, and Aspects of Introducing Pharmacy Students to the Clinical Environment were programs reported by the University of Southern California. A Role Model for Smaller Colleges of Pharmacy Teaching Clinical Pharmacy—Utilizing an Institution for the Mentally Retarded, was the title of a program at Idaho State University College of Pharmacy. Other programs reported were Computer Assisted Case Studies in Patient Care, the University of Mississippi; Talking with Patients—A First Step in Expanding the Role of the Pharmacist, the University of Florida; and Developing Clinical Research Skills—A Requirement for the Doctor of Pharmacy Degree Curriculum, Wayne State University.

In the area of research and education, three programs reported by the Virginia Commonwealth University School of Pharmacy are typical of the direction pharmacy is taking in the decade of the 1970s.

1. *Clinical Pharmacokinetics Service.* This program provides analytical data and computerized programs to improve dosage schedules for individual patients. Members of the School of Pharmacy faculty have developed a program that will rapidly determine individual schedules for several drugs which are of concern, such as digoxin, warfarin, and theophylline.

2. *Improvement of Drug Therapy Through Clinical Pharmacists' Monitoring of Patient Response.* Clinical pharmacists analyze patient's drug history, review current therapy for improper utilization, and provide medical and nursing practitioners with drug information and consultation services.

3. *Improvement of Patient Compliance Through Patient Education Programs.* At many institutions pharmacists are becoming involved in the production of multimedia

---

[42]American Council on Pharmaceutical Education, *Accreditation Manual,* 7th edition (Chicago: American Council on Pharmaceutical Education, 1975), p. 15.
[43]American Association of Colleges of Pharmacy, *Abstracts of Selected Innovative Programs in Pharmaceutical Education and Research* (Bethesda, Maryland: American Association of Colleges of Pharmacy, 1975).

materials to be used as aids and backup to verbal instructions to patients on the proper use of drugs. Audiovisual materials, programmed texts, brochures, and checklists have been produced for the education of patients in the hope of improving the response to therapy initiated.

It is clear that the nation's colleges of pharmacy, through research and innovations in teaching and service functions, have taken an active role in changing the nation's system of drug delivery.

THE FUTURE

Since the end of World War II there have been two in-depth studies of pharmacy. The first of these was known widely as the Elliott Report.[44] The report recommended a six-year curriculum for schools of pharmacy in order to provide a graduate who was not only well grounded in the basic and pharmaceutical sciences, but had a rounded liberal arts education as well. Pharmacy education responded with a compromise, a five-year bachelor's degree. The major change involved the addition of general elective courses in the social sciences and humanities.

Twenty years later, in September of 1970, a conference was held on the campus of the University of California at San Francisco for the purpose of reviewing the past and looking at "The Challenge to Pharmacy in the 70's." A recurrent theme heard by the participants of this conference was that the curriculum of the decades of the 1950s and 1960s produced "street corner scientists" whose scientific knowledge atrophied from disuse. Pharmacy began to acknowledge that the science instruction in the undergraduate curriculum was not used to its potential in the dispensing of drug products in the average American pharmacy.

The 1970 conference was a forerunner to the second major in-depth study of pharmacy. In 1971 the American Association of Colleges of Pharmacy formed an independent Study Commission on Pharmacy. On December 5, 1975, in Washington, D.C., its chairman, John S. Millis, presented the basic findings of the Commission to a gathering of pharmacy leaders. As he addressed a gathering of pharmacists and media representatives, Commission Chairman Millis reported that the task of the Commission:

> . . .was to acquire data, to gather informed opinion, to think, and to make rational and practical suggestions for . . .improvement in the education of. . . pharmacists. . .all of this to the end that more excellent drug-related services can be provided to the citizens of our nation.

The Study Commission in its summary listed fourteen concepts, findings and recommendations.[45] On the day of the Study Commission's unveiling one theme

[44]Edward C. Elliott, *The Report of the Pharmaceutical Survey* (Washington, D.C.: American Council on Education, 1950).
[45]The American Association of Colleges of Pharmacy, *Pharmacists For the Future: The Report of the Study Commission on Pharmacy* (Ann Arbor: Health Administration Press, 1975).

surfaced in the verbal reports of all Commission members. Specifically, in looking to the immediate future, the members generally agreed that the most cost-effective activity society could embark on to improve health care delivery should center on the improvement of the drug delivery system. The tone of the entire report suggested that the major deficiency in the health care delivery system "is the unavailability of adequate information for those who consume, prescribe, dispense, and administer drugs," and that the "deficiency has resulted in inappropriate drug use and an unacceptable frequency of drug-induced disease."[46]

The recommendations of the report are not revolutionary for pharmacy practice but do point to the direction for the future. The following is a summary of concepts, findings, and recommendations:

1.   The Commission expressed concern for the lack of adequate information for those who are responsible for proper use of drugs as described in the preceding paragraphs. The Commission believes the pharmacist can make a significant contribution to the health care system by providing to consumers and other health professionals information about drugs. In the future the training of pharmacists should include the necessary background to meet this responsibility.

2.   The Study Commission advanced the concept that pharmacy should be very broadly defined as "a *knowledge system* which renders a *health service* by concerning itself with understanding drugs and their effects upon people and animals."[47] Thus, according to the Commission, pharmacy generates and acquires knowledge from the sciences and translates a significant portion of that knowledge into drug products which, in turn, are widely disseminated. Pharmacy knowledge and its products are distributed to physicians, pharmacists, other health professionals, and the public in order to provide for the health of individuals and the general welfare of society.

3.   A pharmacist has been defined as an individual "engaged in *one of the stages of a system called pharmacy.*"[48] A pharmacist is not one who simply practices pharmacy but one who practices a part of one of the subsystems of pharmacy. A general characterization of the pharmacist is that he or she is basically knowledgeable about drugs and has acquired additional knowledge and skills that are required for practice in his or her subsystem of pharmacy.

4.   The Commission found the system which translates knowledge into drug products highly efficient, but of limited success "in delivering its full potential as a health service to the members of society."[49] This is especially true when pharmacy is viewed as a knowledge system charged with the responsibility of developing, organizing, and distributing knowledge and information about drugs to health professionals and consumers.

5.   The Commission recommended that major attention be given to the problem of drug information. Pharmacy was charged with determining, in the most

[46]*Ibid.,* p. 139.
[47]*Ibid.,* pp. 139–140.
[48]*Ibid.,* p. 140.
[49]*Ibid.*

expedient and economical manner, who, what, and how to best address this issue.

The Study Commission heard testimony indicating that friends, relatives, and neighbors were the most frequent sources of drug information, followed by physicians and the news media. Pharmacists were listed last, and they concluded that: "It is no wonder that many Americans are overusers and misusers of drugs."[50]

6.   The Commission found that there is a standard body of knowledge and professional capability all pharmacists must possess, and that the objectives of pharmacy education *"must be stated in terms of both the common knowledge and skill and of the differentiated and/or additional knowledge and skill required for specific roles."*[51]

7.   In keeping with its findings in point six, the Commission recommended the following three objectives for pharmacy education:

a.   The mastery of the knowledge and the acquisition of the skills which are *common* to all of the roles of pharmacy practice.
b.   The mastery of the additional knowledge and the acquisition of the additional skill needed for those differentiated roles which require additional *pharmacy* knowledge and experience.
c.   The mastery of the additional knowledge and the acquisition of the additional skills needed for those differentiated roles which require additional knowledge and skill *other than pharmacy.*[52]

8.   The Commission report found the definition of "Clinical Pharmacy" not yet ready for clear definition. Nonetheless it recommended that schools promptly assist faculty members as they strive to serve as effective role models for their students in clinical settings.

9.   In keeping with current educational thinking the Commission was of the opinion that schools of pharmacy should be basing their curricula on the acquisition of desired competencies, rather than just subject matter sciences.

10.   For future teaching of pharmacists, the Commission was of the opinion that the greatest weakness within schools of pharmacy was the lack of an adequate number of clinical scientists. Chairman Millis used simple terms to explain the problem. Faculties have scientists with specialized knowledge, called "Knowers." On the other hand there are growing numbers of faculty who have practice responsibilities, the "Doers," but only a very few pharmacists would be now identified as those who both know and do. The clinical scientist is one who can relate specialized scientific knowledge to the development of practice skills required to provide the highest level of patient service now required.

The Commission recommended that pharmacy set about the task of producing at least a hundred clinical scientists so that each school of pharmacy could obtain the services of one or two of these specialists.

11.   The Commission explained that in the pharmacy knowledge system, biologically active chemical substances (drugs) and people (patients) interact. It follows

[50]*Ibid.*, p. 56.
[51]*Ibid.*, p. 141.
[52]*Ibid.*

that effective drug therapy can be achieved only when both drugs and those who consume them are understood by the pharmacist. The Commission recommended that each college weigh the relative emphasis given to the physical and biological sciences in their curriculums.

12.   The Commission recommended development of educational programs beyond the first professional degree for more differentiated roles in pharmacy.

13.   The Commission recognized that the optimal setting for educational programs in pharmacy is the university health service center, although the Commission did concede that at the baccalaureate level not all schools need be located at the health service center if alternate clinical arrangements could be made.

14.   Finally the Commission recommended that all aspects of credentialing of pharmacists and pharmacy education would benefit by the foundation of a National Board of Pharmacy Examiners.

A number of forces causing changes in the role of pharmacists as they practice pharmacy have been examined. Looking back at pharmacy and the majority who practiced it during the middle of the twentieth century, it can be characterized as a profession released from its stabilized mooring of extemporaneous compounding and dispensing into a vast sea of high technology. To many in pharmacy today, a new mooring place is in clear view— the dispensing characteristics look familiar but the housing has changed. There are more institutions; some have new names, such as ambulatory care centers, tertiary care centers, HMOs, and health care communities that are outgrowths of what had been known as nursing homes. There are a number of directional signs that point to special areas such a radiopharmacy, pharmacokinetics, drug information service, and clinical pharmacy. In close proximity to every pharmacist stands a computer terminal—now a symbol of responsibility for the pharmacist. Its printout/readout mechanism is marked with signs such as individual drug records/patient histories, drug utilization review, product selection information, and patient counseling information. At this new mooring of active participation in the delivery of drugs the incidental role of dispensing is but a fond memory for those who steadfastly cling to the past.

INDEX